CHURCHES OF THE RESTORATION

A Study in Origins

CHURCHES OF THE RESTORATION

A Study in Origins

George Allen Turner

Mellen University Press
Lewiston/Queenston/Lampeter

Library of Congress Cataloging-in-Publication Data

Turner, George Allen.
   Churches of the restoration : a study in origins / George Allen Turner.
      p.   cm.
   Includes bibliographical references and index.
   ISBN 0-7734-9843-5
   1. Dissenters, Religious. 2. Reformation. 3. Free churches.
4. Perfection--Religious aspects--Christianity. I. Title.
BX4817.T87 1994
280'.4--dc20
                                                                     93-48201
                                                                          CIP

Copyright © 1994 George Allen Turner

All rights reserved. For information contact

The Edwin Mellen Press   The Edwin Mellen Press
Box 450   Box 67
Lewiston, New York   Queenston, Ontario
USA 14092-0450   CANADA L0S 1L0

The Edwin Mellen Press, Ltd.
Lampeter, Dyfed, Wales
UNITED KINGDOM SA48 7DY

Printed in the United States of America

For

Don and Betty Morgan

Friends since 1931

Investors of thousands

For Turners lecturing abroad

and for Margaret Kinthia

ATS student from Kenya

CONTENTS

FORWORD	v
PREFACE	ix
ACKNOWLEDGEMENTS	xi
INTRODUCTION	xiii
I. THE PIETISTS	15
A. FORERUNNERS OF THE RESTORATION-RESTORATION	17
1. John Wycliffe	17
2. John Huss	23
B. THE HUSSITE MOVEMENT	27
1. The Bohemian Brethren	27
2. The Renewed *Unitas Fratrum* (Moravian)	31
C. PIETISM IN ENGLAND	37
D. APPRAISAL	39
II. THE ANABAPTISTS	45
A. SWISS ANABAPTISTS: CONRAD GREBEL	46
B. HUTTERITES	52
C. MILITANT ANABAPTISTS	54
D. DUTCH ANABAPTISTS: MENNO SIMONS	57
E. MENNONITES AND AMISH IN AMERICA	61
F. APPRAISAL	63
III. THE BRETHREN	69
A. DEMAND FOR A FREE CHURCH	70
B. DIVISIONS IN EUROPE	71
C. DIVISIONS IN NORTH AMERICA	74
D. THE RIVER BRETHREN	86
1. Doctrinal Issues: Sanctification	90
2. Other Changes	93

		E. APPRAISAL	96
IV.	THE PURITANS		101
	A.	IN ENGLAND	102
		1. Growth	103
		2. The Congregationalists ("Separatists")	107
	B.	IN NEW ENGLAND	108
		1. The Half-Way Covenant	109
		2. The Covenant Theology	110
	C.	PURITAN PERFECTIONISM	114
	D.	PURITANISM AND METHODISM	115
	E.	APPRAISAL	120
V.	THE METHODISTS		127
	A.	ORIGINS OF THE EVANGELICAL REVIVAL	127
	B.	THE QUEST FOR HOLINESS	130
	C.	PERSONAL ASSURANCE	133
	D.	THE LOVE OF NEIGHBOR	135
	E.	THE SACRAMENTS	138
		1. Wesley on Baptism	138
		2. The Lord's Supper	145
	F.	METHODIST INFLUENCE TODAY	148
	G.	APPRAISAL	152
VI.	DISCIPLES (CHRISTIANS)		159
	A.	WILDERNESS REVIVAL	161
	B.	THE STRUGGLE FOR UNITY	162
		1. Barton Stone and the Christians	163
		2. The Campbells and the Disciples	167
		3. Merger of Christians and the Disciples	171
		4. Walter Scott's Contribution	172
		5. The Church of God (Anderson)	180
	C.	APPRAISAL	185
VII.	THE PENTECOSTALS		191
	A.	ORIGINS	192
		1. Revival in Appalachia (1886 --	193
		2. Revival in Kansas (1900 --	199

3. Revival in Los Angeles (1901 --	201
4. Revival with the Catholics	206
B. CONSISTENCY WITH SCRIPTURE	209
C. APPRAISAL	217
VIII. WHICH CHURCH IS CLOSEST TO THE NEW TESTAMENT?	225
A. THE PRIMITIVE CHURCH IN THE NEW TESTAMENT	225
B. TODAY'S SEEKERS OF THE "RESTORATION"	229
1. The Pietists	229
2. The Anabaptists	229
3. The Brethren	230
4. The Puritans	230
5. The Methodists	231
6. The Christians (Disciples)	232
7. The Pentecostals	232
C. BACK TO THE NEW TESTAMENT	233
APPENDIX A	237
APPENDIX B	239
BIBLIOGRAPHY	241
INDEX	259

Foreword

This project claims to be unique, to some extent, in that it lays out several influential Christian churches, each of which claims to be more like the church portrayed in the New Testament. The contrast of the Roman Catholic Church to the Eastern Orthodox Church, and especially to the Protestant Churches are examined. The Reformation claimed that the Roman Church was a departure from the primitive church of the New Testament. The reformers rebelled against much in the state church and founded churches they were convinced to be more truly Christian. The Reformed churches in Switzerland, France, and England were linked to their respective States. The Lutheran Church was dependent on the German princes, to avoid persecution by the Roman Church. Like the Reformed Churches they were not "free" from their secular magistrates. In England the Anglican Church served under the King or Queen. In each of the three segments of the Reformation (Lutheran, Reformed, Anglican) state churches were dependent on the taxes raised by the State.

Several Christian leaders in western Europe demanded a church that was "free" from the government. They preferred to surrender their lives rather than surrender their convictions in religion. Among those leaders were Wycliffe in England, Huss in Bohemia, Conrad Grebel in Switzerland, Menno Simons in Holland, Wesley in England, and the Campbells in Pennsylvania to name a few.

Seven movements, which became denominations, had in common a demand to go beyond the Protestant Reformation to a *Restoration* of a church like that of the New Testament. The seven denominations, chosen for their influence, are Pietists, Anabaptists, Brethren, Puritans, Methodists, Christian/Disciples, and

Pentecostals. These all have much in common. All are devoted to the Bible and are eager to be "reborn" (that is transformed by the grace of God to become disciples of Jesus their Saviour). They are zealous to win others to Christ. Each of the seven denominations came into existence because of a spiritual awakening, or religious revival, initiated by the Holy Spirit to whom they responded.

Why did I decide to pursue this group of "Free Churches" which demanded a RESTORATION of the "primitive Church?" While studying in The Biblical Seminary in New York my S.T.B. Dissertation dealt with the early church in its theology culminating in the Nicene Creed. My S.T.M. Dissertation was on Jesus' self-contiousness as revealed in his Parables. At Harvard Divinity School to acquire the Ph.D. on the New Testament, my dissertation was advised by Professor Dr. Henry Joel Cadbury. He suggested an examination of John Wesley's doctrine that he called "entire sanctification" and determine to what extent this doctrine was consistent with the Bible. (He noted that Wesley's "Christian Perfection" was widely debated). This review included the theme of sanctity during the Christian Church through the Middle Ages, and in England from the 16th century until today. This focused on the Reformation. Recently I was aware that during this quest I had overlooked the "Radical Reformation" (Williams) or "Free Churches" (Stoeffler); those earnest Christians who were determined to follow the New Testament even at the cost of persecution.

In addition to Restoration, Primitivism, Freedom, and Perfectionism are terms to include those groups who were determined to have a church like that of the New Testament. As Richard T. Hughes put it,

> *"Perfectionism in Christian history has worn many faces. Usually the term signifies emphasis on the sanctification of the individual believer. But another form of perfectionism has been equally persistent: The concern to perfect the church by rejecting*
>
> *Christian history. . . and by restoring instead the primitive church of the apostolic age."*[1]

vii

The Anabaptists were among the first to free themselves from the Reformation by seeking perfection, or primitivism, by adhering to the New Testament regardless of the consequence. Christian perfection was the goal of the Puritans and the Methodists led by the Wesleys. These two perfectionist denominations sought BOTH the sanctity of the individual believer and the righteous community. Unity among believers were centality in the New Testament, as priority for Barton Stone and Christians, as well as Spirit's energy of the Pentecosts.

A sabbatical granted by Asbury Theological Seminary permitted time to pursue this exciting project. The work included travel in the East and South and the investagion of libraries, churches, and interviews.

Why should one read this account? Because of this fascinating facet of Christian history, of the changes made by earnest Christians, their influence on other Churches and even on several nations. Clergy may find it informative and an enhancement to their ministry. My motive was not some "axe to grind," nor to prefer one denomination over another, but rather to gratify my curiosity and pass on some useful insights. The focus is on the Scriptures and the extent that the "Free Churches" discovered and promoted the "primitive church" today. To understand the early Church the Letters of Paul, Peter, John, plus the first Christian history (The Acts of the Apostles), were of course indispensable. Specialists were consulted and their judgment weighed. Objectivity was sought throughout the process. The most important factor, of course, was seeking the truth. I must not claim to have found the truth, but only like Socrates, to be only a seeker of truth.

The review of claimants in being closest to the early church should be of interest to historians and students of Scripture as well as to alert and courious laypersons. Which of these "Restoration" denominations have the most convincing claim to be like the church of New Testament times? What can we learn from their origin and growth? How can the past give guidance to the present and predict the future as the Bible repeatedly emphasizes? All this has relevance today.

1. Richard T. Hughes, *Christian Primitivism as Perfectionism: From Anabaptists to Pentecostals.* In Stanley M. Burgess, Editor, *Reaching Beyond: Chapters in the History of Perfectionism.* (Peabody, Mass.: 1986. p. 313). The Anabaptists were among the first to free themselves from the Reformation and seek perfection, or primitivism, by reading the New Testament and by obedience.

Preface

Why did the Christian Church dig up the corpse of Oxford's most distinguished professor and burn it? Why was Prague's most influential professor burned at the stake for preaching the truths of the Bible? Why did Catholics and Protestants hunt down and kill thousands of believers simply because they refused to have their infants baptized until they were old enough to become believers?

Why were both Catholics and Protestants convinced that they could not work together when both shared the same goal? These are some of the questions that led to research in the origins and message of those who wanted to go beyond the REFORMATION of the Church to the RESTORATION of the church of the New Testament?

Among those who claimed to be closer to the primitive church than any other group are the Pietists, the Anabaptists, the Brethren, the Puritans, the Methodists, the Christians/Disciples, and the Pentecostals. It is significant that each of these major denominations began as a spiritial awakening, a religious revival or renewal. Initially they were in a unity brought about by the work of the Holy Spirit, like that of the believers after the historical Pentecost (Acts 4:32-34).

Why did the unity not continue? Which of these "Restoration" denominations have the most convincing claim to be like the church of New Testament times? What can we learn from their origin and growth? How can the past give guidance to the present and predict the future as the Bible repeatedly emphasizes? All this has relevance today. Will the reader find the story as fascinating as the author found it to be? We seek now to find the answers of some of these important questions.

Acknowledgements

A Sabbatical given by Asbury Theological Seminary was the beginning of this project which extended over a decade. The B. L. Fisher Library and its staff were more than adequate, even to pursue books published in the 1760 area. Dr. William Faupel shared research in holiness and Pentecostal areas; Don Butterworth opened areas closed to normal use. John Serry was at my side when there were problems.

The Reformed Theological Seminary at Jackson, Mississippi, was generous with resources, especially with the Anabaptists in the sixteen century, including photos of their leaders.

Mrs. Denese Southgate computerized and printed the entire Dissertation with patience and skill.

My wife Lucile was indispensable. She helped research during the months of travel in libraries from New Orleans, to Cambridge-Boston and areas between. I frequently marvel at her criticism with proofreading, invariably finding mistakes which escaped my scrutiny.

Dr. Robert Mulholland, Provost, found funds to assist the project.

Harold W. Burgess, Professor of Christian Education, and with an editor's experience, read the Dissertation and gave his assessment of the project.

Dr. Kenneth C. Kinghorn, Professor of Church History, and author, read and evaluated the Dissertation.

Dr. Robert West, after reading the product, determined that it should be printed and supplied expert guidance.

Mr. John Rupnow, Acquisitions Director, welcomed this project at first, and now finishes the publication.

Mrs. Joanna Zeiner, missionary and teacher, helped finalize this project.

Introduction

This study examines the churches in the Protestant Reformation which claim that they go beyond a REFORMATION of the existing Roman Catholic Church to the RESTORATION of the primitive church of the New Testament. They also claim to be the Free Church, free from the state church. Those who seek this goal are examined in a group of seven major movements or denominations: the Pietists, Anabaptists, Brethren, Puritans, Methodists, Christians (Disciples), and Pentecostals. These seven are measured against Scripture as to the merit of their claim. All of these denominations began as a spiritual renewal or revival. The extent to which this goal continues now is noted in passing. This research can be helpful to those interested both in Church History and in New Testament history. The research seeks primary sources and secondary sources recognized as definitive. The study claims no "axe to grind." It does claim to seek truth.

Chapter I
THE PIETISTS

"The resources of knowledge were few and unsatisfactory: museums and libraries which are now at the service of all were then beyond the wildest dreams. Wycliffe and his fellow clerks pored over the faded characters of worn manuscripts in chambers deprived of the sun by day, and in a nightly darkness faintly relieved by flickering oil lamps or rush lights. The nature and extent of their learning were amazing; their industry probably surpassed that of any later scholars. They lived a separated life, . . . Yet its tasks were illuminated by the ambitions which burned within them more steadily because of their privations."

Three Religious Leaders of Oxford, S. Parkes Cadman, (Macmillan, 1916), p. 38.

The nature of the church is the keynote in the movements for church renewal which dominates the pages of church history for the past five centuries. Four views of the church are in tension even today.

(1) The Orthodox Churches base their claim to this title on the four great ecumenical Councils: Nicene (325), Constantinople, (381), Ephesus (431), and Chalcedon (451). Their location in the eastern portion of the Empire, closest to Christian origins, lends credence to this claim.

(2) The Roman Catholic view, which was unchallenged during the Middle Ages (500-1500) in the west, held that the church consists of the "hierarchy based in the Roman pontiff, ruling over the communicants."

In the mind of the Fathers ... the hierarchical order is a ministry commissioned by Christ to serve the communion of Christian faith, to ward off the problem of heresy by authoritatively handling the message of faith ..., and above all to serve the community of sacrificial life ... by admitting to or denying Eucharistic Communion and by administering the penitential procedures ... [1]

In addition:

> *The local church finds in its bishop, as the representative of Christ, the qualified center and criterion of its communion, competent to teach, to rule, and to sanctify . . . with its Roman center the criterion of total communion.*[2]

(3) The Protestant view, as defined by the Church of England, is "a congregation of faithful men in which the pure word of God is preached and the sacraments duly ministered."[3] In short, the church is a congregation where biblical preaching and two sacraments (served by the clergy) are essential.

(4) The Radical Reformers, or those of the Restoration, believed they went further in the direction of the New Testament than the Reformers of the sixteenth century dared to go. They defined the church as consisting of a gathering of at least two believers gathered in Jesus' name. (It is with this group -- those who were convinced that reformation of the Roman Church was not enough -- that this study is concerned). The main elements in this Restoration, as distinct from Reformation, include (1) Pietists, (2) Anabaptists, (3) Brethren, (4) Puritans, (5) Methodists, (6) Disciples, and (7) Pentecostals.

The term "Pietism" has many connotations. It is often a term of opprobrium, and often implies hypocrisy. To some it signifies an emotional subjectivism, deficient in objectivity, altruism, and practicality. To others it denotes the movement, within seventeenth century Lutheran communities, away from creeds and formal liturgy, towards an emphasis on life in the Spirit.

As used in this study it includes, not only the renewal within Lutheranism and Anglicanism, but also a concern with vital Christianity, modeling itself on the New Testament and finding expression in many segments of the Christian church. Because its emphasis is on new life in Christ it tends to be irenic and ecumenical.

Pietism stresses discipline as well as doctrine. It is a religion "of the heart." The focus is on love for God -- hence devotion is stressed. Its focus is one's love of neighbor -- hence social action is stressed. It preserves the "experiential element in Protestantism,"[4]

Which of these four major segments of the Church of Christ is most compatible with the primitive churches as reflected in the New Testament. Let us review those who claim to be in the Restoration. First in historical sequence are the Pietists, those who trace their origins back for five centuries to the Bohemia of John Huss (1375-1415). But before Huss came Wycliffe (ca. 1324-1384) to whom Huss owed so much; it seems appropriate therefore to begin the research with Wycliffe. Space forbids the inclusion in this study of the Brethren of the Common Life, the Waldensians, and similar groups, because those of the "Radical Reformation" do not acknowledge indebtedness to them.

A. FORERUNNERS OF THE RESTORATION

This quest takes one to events prior to the Reformation.

1. John Wycliffe (1324-1384)

John Wycliffe was born and reared in Yorkshire, an area then notably austere and remote, an environment which was reflected in the reformer's austere temperament.[5] A brilliant student at Oxford he received there his Master's degree (1360) and his doctorate (D.D.) in 1372 at the age of forty-eight. He was made Rector at Lutterworth in 1374. In 1375 he represented the claims of the king against the papacy at Bruges, his earliest involvement in politics. Asked to defend Parliament's refusal to send tribute to the Pope, Wycliffe wrote a treatise on *Civil Dominion* which urged the financial independence of the Church of England. Later Wycliffe argued in *De Domino Divino* that dominion (authority) comes direct from God and is invalidated if the human authority lives in mortal sin. By appealing to the simplicity of the Gospels he became increasingly critical of the priests who exploited the poor and enriched themselves ("liberation theology"?). He contrasted the meekness of Christ with the arrogance of the Pope who demanded that leaders kiss his feet.

If the church is in sin it is unworthy to administer the sacraments and should be reduced to "evangelical poverty" with its wealth reverting to the state.

Although denounced by Pope Gregory XI the Oxford authorities refused to arrest their most distinguished scholar.

In 1378 Wyclife spoke against the Right of Sanctuary for criminals, thus strengthening secular authorities against the church. He then turned against the power of the priests to withhold the sacrament. Anticipating Luther and Calvin he argued that only God can forgive sin, that good laymen can absolve a sinner more effectively than wicked priests.[6]

Secluded in Lutterworth he continued his attack in writings against evils in the Church. He attacked the doctrine of trans-substantiation, arguing that the "Real Presence" exists only in a non-corporal manner. In *On the Eucharist* (ca. 1379) he rejected the idea of transubstantiation which was rooted in Ambrose, Augustine, and Anselm.[7] The elements, Wycliffe argued, are "efficacious signs and symbols ... but are not physically present."[8]

Lanfranc, a Realist, insisted that "by the act of consecration the substance of the elements was changed while the sensible properties remained the same." This is based on the alleged distinction between the universal substance held to be present in any particular thing included under it and those accidents or sensible properties which appeared only when the pure form clothed itself in matter.

In 1215 the Fourth Lateran Council confirmed this theory. Christ is really and truly present in the Holy Eucharist under the appearance of bread and wine, so that His real Body and Blood, His soul and His Divinity are present .... The change that takes place at the moment of and by the act of consecration is transubstantiation. It is a change whereby the substance of the bread and wine passes over into the substance of Christ, who under the form of bread and wine becomes and remains present so long as the accidents remain uncorrupted (pp. 118-119). In theory Christ made this change at the Last Supper, so when the priest repeats Jesus' words of consecration the miracle occurs, made such by the *repetition* of Jesus' words, not the words of the priest.[9]

This view was not "consubstantiation" because the bread and wine are not the equivalent of body and blood. Rather it is sacramental, "namely, as a material substance symbolizes a spiritual content", or as Augustine phrased it, "an outward symbol of an inner grace."[10]

Wycliffe's contemporaries were not prepared to go this far in the rejection of the Mass. But his views were based on the New Testament and, on this basis, he dared to stand virtually alone. For him the Scriptures were his "primary and constant authority" in the tradition of Grossteste and Ockham, but unlike them, he called attention to the divergence between the Bible and church dogma. Against the claims of both Church and State, Wycliffe placed the Bible as the supreme authority. In this he anticipated Luther, declaring boldly that every person, layman or clergyman, has the right to direct examination and interpretation of Scripture.[11]

This conviction called for a translation of Scripture from Latin to the language of the people, hence his insistence upon making the Bible in the vernacular available to the people. Portions of the Bible were translated by his secretary, William Purvey, who revised an earlier work by Nicholas of Hereford. Purvey supported the Lollard movement, an association of laymen, who preached and sang the gospel in the streets and in private homes. Copies of Purvey's version were eagerly sought and read by all classes high and low. "Today ... he holds an established niche in the temple of fame as the translator of the first readable English Bible."[12]

Archbishop Arundel complained to Pope John XVIII concerning Wycliffe's influence:

> *That wretched and petulant fellow, the son of the serpent, the herald and child of the antichrist, John Wycliffe, . . . [is] filling up the measure of his malice by devising the expedient of a new translation of Scripture into the mother tongue.[13]*

Wycliffe wrote that "friars, bishops and their abettors are shocked that the gospel should be known in English."[14] But by making the Bible available to laymen Wycliffe anticipated the Reformation.

In response to papal bulls against him, Wycliffe, in 1378, wrote *De Ecclesia*. He challenged the prevailing view that the Church is essentially the hierarchy headed by the Pope. Instructed by Scripture and by Augustine he concluded that the church consists of three parts: (1) the church triumphant (believers in heaven), (2) the church militant (believers on earth), and (3) the church dormient (those now in purgatory). Debate focused on the church militant. The "militant" included both "tares and wheat," that is the "predestinate" and the "reprobate." The "predestinate" are the elect "containing 'only those that shall be saved' and who cannot cease to be such even by mortal sin, for theirs is the grace of final perseverance."[15] No one knows whether he is among the elect; Christ's redemption is available only to the "predestinate." The "foreknown" are those destined for eternal damnation including many of the priesthood. These are united with the devil and antichrist as the "elect" are united with Christ. Prayer is effective only if offered by the predestinate. Even the Pope is not of the Church of Christ unless his life conforms to Jesus and the New Testament. All should search the Scriptures and examine themselves in its light. All of the elect are "priests" and hence can serve the Sacraments -- thus, in his "priesthood of all believers," he went even further than did Luther.

Although he adhered to Augustine in this doctrine of predestination, Wycliffe never grasped Augustine's doctrine of grace. Instead, with Duns Scotus, he stressed God's sovereignty and omnipotence (as Calvin did later).[16] In his doctrine of the church he stressed individualism more than unity, placing more emphasis on laymen and less on sacerdotalism than Luther did.

Wycliffe anticipated the Reformation in nearly all of its great tenets: (1) wealth of the clergy, (2) return to the simplicity and morality of early Christianity, (3) authority of the Bible to replace the authority of the Pope, (4) sovereign grace to replace salvation by works, (5) rejection of indulgences, (6) priesthood of all believers, and (7) independence of the national church from the Roman church.

All the major elements of the Reformation were in Wycliffe: . . .
If the Great Revolt had not ended the government's protection of

> *Wycliffe's efforts, the Reformation might have taken form and root in England 130 years before it broke in Germany.*[17]

Wycliffe's ideas were premature in the sense that the country was not ready for them. The influence of the Bible in the vernacular was not widely available for the public to share Wycliffe's critique. There was no historical continuity between his writings, the furor they inspired, the Lollard movement among the people, and later historical developments. Thus the Wycliffe reformation stood as a monolith in a desert "without father or mother," yet a tribute to the insight and courage of this heroic pioneer. He died of a stroke just after the summons to appear before Pope Urban VI in Rome. He was buried in Lutterworth December 31, 1384, only to be exhumed on order of the Council of Constance (May 5, 1415) and his dust scattered in the river Swift to be carried on to the sea, a prophecy of his widening influence.

A few days later (July 6, 1415) the hot ashes of Wycliffe's disciple, John Huss, who had just been burned at the stake, were likewise dumped into the Rhine river and thence into the sea and a world-wide influence. Was Wycliffe the forerunner of the Reformation, or, as Workman concludes, of the Restoration, "father of the Puritans, covenanters, and non-conformists of Great Britain and America"?[18] He was both. But Workman's assessment justifies the inclusion of Wycliffe in this study of the "Radical Reformation" or more, appropriately, the "Restoration."

Like the Wesleys and Whitefield, Wycliffe's insights began with the study of the Bible at Oxford. Like these leaders he attracted to himself bands of dedicated lay leaders who zealously promoted the convictions they shared with their leader. Like them he was concerned with the poor. While Wycliffe anticipated the Reformation, these Oxford "Methodists" sought to extend and revitalize it.

Despite the many affinities between Huss and Luther one can appreciate the astute perception of Wycliffe's chief biographer:

> *In the fearlessness of his courage he is the equal of Luther . . . In the higher moral courage he was the superior of Luther . . . He lacked, however, Luther's warm emotions. His humor is rare and generally acid . . ., Poetry, music, singing, architecture made no appeal to him. But for the downtrodden, the serf, and the poor his sympathies were unbounded, and well out in the midst of arid, scholastic reasoning . . . One secret of the success of Luther lay in his consciousness of the reality of sin, just as one secret of the failure of Wycliffe lay in his doctrine that sin is but a negation -- "that it has no idea." Thus in the earnestness of his life he stood almost alone, for the interest of others in reform was too often that of politics and greed.*[19]

But Wycliffe was not alone, as the Lollard movement testifies. The name "Lollard" (Dutch meaning "mumbler") was given to the evangelical followers of Wycliffe derisively (as with Quakers and Methodists) after 1352, because they were viewed as heretics with pretensions to piety. They stressed, in opposition to church authority, the authority of the Scriptures, the importance of preaching, and the needs of the poor. The movement originated at Oxford among Wycliffe's students, (including Nicholas of Hereford and John Purvey). As in Luther's Germany so here, those with Lollard sympathies were not only the poor but also many of the landed gentry whose interest was more than spiritual. Together, peasant and landlord found common cause in a revolt against an apostate and oppressive clericalism. The Lollards increased in influence among the nobles, merchants, townsmen, peasants, and some of the lower clergy. Persecution by the Church began in 1382 leading to laws proscribing the group and the burning of the first Lollard martyr, William Sawyer, in 1401. A Lollard revival in 1414 and again in 1500 kept the movement alive until the Reformation.

Lollard views were best expressed in the *Twelve Conclusions* presented to Parliament in 1395. Among other things they stressed:

(1) Priestly confession is not essential to salvation.

(2) The present priesthood is not ordained by God.

(3) All should have access to Scripture in their native tongue.

(4) Warfare is inconsistent with the New Testament.

(5) The Catholic Eucharist, as transubstantiation, has no basis in Scripture, and fosters idolatry.

(6) Priests should preach the gospel.[20]

Their most lasting contribution was the Bible in the language of the people and their concern for justice to the poor. In these matters they bore witness to the transforming power of the Scripture when studied and acted upon in the power of the Holy Spirit.

A Bohemian Psalter of 1572 pictures Wycliffe striking a spark, Huss igniting the coals, and Luther lifting high a flaming torch.[21] Wycliffe is correctly seen as the first of the Reformers and the last of the medieval schoolmen. In addition he proved to be "the last outcome of the intellectual vigour of the great medieval university."[22]

2. John Huss (1373-1415)

In 1380 a Bohemian princess became Queen of England and Czech nobles were influenced by Oxford University at a time when the influence of John Wycliffe was at its zenith. From Oxford "heretical" ideas, especially Wycliffe's doctrine of the Church, deeply influenced John Huss in Bohemia.

The Catholic Church was especially vulnerable to criticism during the life of Huss. The pope resided at Avignon in France for seventy years -- the "Babylonian Captivity of the Pope." As if this were not enough, there followed the papal schism in which rival popes, one in Rome and the other in Avignon, hurled anathemas at each other. Meanwhile the sale of indulgences and the sale of church offices (simony) flourished. At the University of Prague, as at the Universities of Paris and of Oxford, the papacy and the Church were subjects of intense debate.

At Prague Huss was given the degrees of B.A. (1393), B.D. (1394) and M.A. (1396) by the University. In 1401 he lectured at the University and was elected Dean of the Faculty of Philosophy. In 1402 he was elected Rector of the University. "Qualities of eloquence, moral elevation and personal magnetism must have been apparent even at this time in his career."[23]

Ordained a priest in 1401 he was appointed as preacher to the Bethlehem Chapel, the most important pulpit in Prague. From this pulpit his influence extended to all segments of society -- from king to beggar.

Wycliffe was the more learned; Huss was the more evangelical of these famed reformers. Both linked spiritual insight and moral courage to an extraordinary degree. It is noteworthy that the Protestant Reformation was pioneered by scholars: Wycliffe, Huss, Erasmus, Luther, and Calvin. (Also from Oxford emerged Methodism and the Keswick Movement.)

On the selling of Church offices and indulgences, Huss (*On Simony*, 1413) exposed the practice of making appointment to church benefices only *after* the appointee laid his money on the table. He accused the Pope of naming appointees who were qualified only to herd swine! He decried the papal decree that preaching could only be done in parish churches and monasteries -- contrary to Christ's command. He boldly declared that a Christian community should not obey a command of a Pope which was contrary to the teaching of Christ. "Otherwise by following a blind man they would both fall into the pit of eternal damnation."[24] In conclusion, he explained, "I have spoken plainly and simply that I may ... uproot simony. May the merciful Saviour aid me therein ...."[25]

The most important writings of Huss focused on the Church. He wrote *De Ecclesia* in exile and read it at Bethlehem Chapel on June 8, 1413. The immediate occasion, as with Luther's revolt, was the call from Pope John XVIII for the sale of indulgences to raise money for his war against the Prince of Naples. Among other things he attacked the infallibility of the Pope, citing as evidence the choice of a wicked woman named Agnes who reigned as "pope" for two years. He noted also the rivalry between the two "popes" during the papal schism. To *fail* to rebel against an erring pope, he declared, "is to sin against God .... Only God can forgive sin."[26] The Scriptures, not the Pope nor the Church, are the only rule of faith and conduct. He rejected the idea of Augustine and others that heretics should be killed.

In his definition of the church he was influenced, not only by the Bible, but also by Augustine and Wycliffe. The church, in his view, consisted of the house of God, the priest(s) that ministered therein, and especially the *congregation under Christ*. Like Augustine he stressed predestination and divine sovereignty. With Augustine and Wycliffe he divided the church into the church triumphant (in heaven), the church dormient (in purgatory), and the church militant (on earth). The latter consists of the "predestinate" (those foreordained to eternal life) and the "reprobate" (those foreordained to eternal damnation, who are in the church but not of it).[27] While Wycliffe, like Augustine, believed the predestinate would not fall from grace, Huss believed even the predestinate must persevere (like Paul) to be saved, otherwise (like Judas) they would be lost.[28]

By appealing to Scripture over and against church tradition, he argued that "Christ is the true Pontiff upon whom salvation depends." On the basis of Matthew 18:20 Huss argued that "two righteous persons, congregated together in Christ's name, constitute, with Christ at the head, a particular holy church."[29] In the light of Matthew 25 he taught the co-existence of two churches: the sheep and the goats, the latter being the reprobate (*praesciti*). The parable of the tares was invoked to defend the position that the church militant includes both saints and sinners.

But inconsistently, Huss quotes with approval statements by Jerome and other fathers that there is only one universal church and that it consists only of the saints with "no spot or wrinkle or anything of that sort, but he who is a sinner or is soiled with any filth cannot be said to be of Christ's church."[30]

Because his appeal was to Roman Catholics, Huss based his arguments on Scripture, the church fathers (especially Augustine) and on common sense. He exhibited a wide and accurate acquaintance with patristics and also with the religious and political situation in his own generation. He failed to see, or at least to solve, the contradiction between grace and free will, or explain how the reprobate are responsible for their own fate.

26

After explaining the unity of the church he encountered the objection that if the church is of the saved and is united, then the "reprobate" are not a part of the church. Huss sought to refute this objection by arguing that the good and the bad coexist in the same congregation as in some of the parables (Matt. 13:30,41 -- the tares; 13:47 -- the net; 22:2 -- the wedding feast; Luke 3:17 -- the threshing floor). Also, as waste is separated from the body, so in the body of Christ the unsaved are finally separated.[31] This paradox originated in Augustine's dogma of double predestination (at the expense of free will and human responsibility), as well as in mistaken exegesis. In the passages cited above the parables speak of a separation at the *final judgment* of the totality of mankind -- this Huss assumed to be the equivalent of the church militant. Huss was both a creature of his age and also one who transcended and lived in advance of his age. In agreement with his age he concluded that society consists of clergy, nobility, and common people, the ascension and intercession of the Virgin Mary, purgatory, and transubstantiation (objecting only to the *abuse* of all seven sacraments).[32]

On the other hand he *transcended* his age in his view of the *church*, the importance of *Scripture* and in his recognition of Christ as the *only* Head of the church. Contrary to the prevailing view that the church consists of all the baptized, Huss insisted that the church consists only of the "predestined." Against the view that the Church of Rome is the only true church he taught that Christ's church includes the true believers ("the predestinate") in all nations and communions -- a truly holy catholic or universal church of saints. The unity of the church, he believed, is spiritual -- those who possess the Spirit of Christ.[33] Also he demanded the New Testament principle of the Lord's Supper in *both kinds*, thus anticipating the Reformation. He also insisted that only God can forgive sins.

In all this Huss was more than a dogmatician, more than a polemist. He was a sincere, informed, courageous disciple of Christ to whom the world is deeply indebted -- chiefly for his definition of the authentic Church of Christ, notwithstanding some accretions from church tradition of the elders.

Huss was declared a heretic and summoned to the Council of Constance (May 1415). He was guaranteed safe conduct by Emperor Sigismund; later this guarantee was ignored. He was imprisoned. The Council first condemned the teachings of Wycliffe (May 5, 1415) and ordered his body exhumed, burned, and the ashes thrown in the river Swift (as noted earlier). The enemies of Huss made false accusations which he denied. He was willing to submit to examination, to be convicted if in error, but he refused to accept the decree of the Council as being superior to Pope and Scripture.

On July, 6, 1415, Huss was burned at the stake and his ashes thrown into the Rhine, an end remarkably like that of his mentor Wycliffe. Later, Luther approved the position of Huss and declared that the Council had erred in their treatment of him. Both Luther and Huss believed Scripture to be more authoritative than either Pope or Council. But Luther escaped the fate of his predecessors because he enjoyed the support of the German princes. The Church had met its match at last; truth could not be ultimately frustrated or thwarted.

Wycliffe and Huss were primarily interested in the *reformation* of the Roman Catholic Church. Later the "radical reformers" would demand a *restoration* of the church to its New Testament pattern. The Reformation itself stands historically between these martyrs and Restoration movements which demanded more than reformation.[34] This study focuses on the "radicals" who boldly sought what they called a "restoration" of the primitive church.

B. THE HUSSITE MOVEMENT

1. Bohemian Brethren

The martyrdom of Huss produced a reaction of sorrow, frustration, and anger throughout Bohemia. The Archbishop of Prague was forced to flee for his life. Over four hundred members of the Bohemian Diet signed a letter of protest over the action of the Council of Constance which had made Huss a martyr. The Hussite League was organized on September 5, 1415.[35]

Originally the Bohemians worshipped in Greek Orthodox Churches, in which communion was served with both bread and wine. When Eastern Orthodoxy waned and Roman Catholicism became dominant in Bohemia, the priests served only the wafer to the laymen -- a change the laymen resented.[36] In addition to condemning Huss, the Council of Constance forbade the giving of the cup to laymen. The chalice, therefore, became the symbol of the Hussite movement in Bohemia.

Some 40,000 Hussites met on a hill called Mt. Tabor on July 22, 1419, to celebrate Holy Communion -- serving *both* wine and bread. Sixteen years of warfare followed in which the Hussites, led by John Ziska, successfully defied and defeated the armies of King Sigismund. Then the Hussites began fighting among themselves. The moderates, who favored reconciliation with the Roman Catholics, were called Utraquists (communion in both kinds). These were mostly from the upper classes and were in the majority. The more radical group, including the peasants and lower classes, were called Taborites because, in 1428, they had gathered on Mt. Tabor to await the Second Coming of Christ. Intensely chiliastic, they became militant and communal. They sought to extend their influence by force of arms, and demanded a complete separation from the Church of Rome. While the Utraquists believed Christ was in the Eucharist essentially and naturally, the Taborites spoke of Christ being present symbolically.[37]

Eventually the moderate Utraquists entered into an agreement, called the Compacta of Basel, with the Catholics who consented to the cup for laymen. The radical Taborites were nearly annihilated by the Utraquists, aided by the Catholics, at the Battle of Lipan (May 30, 1434). The leader of the Utraquists, John Pokitsauna, became Archbishop of Prague. Soon afterwards he preached against the abuses of the Catholic Church, after the manner of John Huss. But he was unwilling to go all the way. Instead, he recommended that his nephew Gregory follow the leadership of a layman named Peter Chelchicky (1379-1467) who had written a book called *The Net of Faith*.

Under Peter's leadership were those Hussites who demanded more than the Utraquists were willing to give and yet were less fanatical than the militant Taborites. This moderate faction believed in non-violence and a return to the simple but stern principles of the Gospels. This group, calling themselves the Unity of the Brethren, attracted others like-minded and settled on an estate near the castle of Lititz. Here Gregory was recognized as their leader. They adopted the name *Unitas Fratrum* (United Brethren) and in 1457 formally organized the "first international Protestant Church in history" sixty years before Luther discovered justification by faith.[38]

Persecution by the king for political reasons led to their being scattered from their community at Lititz. In the mountains of Bohemia, in 1464, they reaffirmed the establishment of an independent Church. They issued a statement of faith, and by lot selected three Elders.[39] With the help of a Waldensian bishop, who had been ordained a bishop by Catholic bishops, the Brethren ordained Michael Bradacius as their first bishop. Thus the Brethren claim an order of bishops intact to this day.

After the death of Gregory leadership passed to Luke, a graduate of the University of Prague. Consecrated a bishop in 1500, Luke wrote the influential "Catechism for Children" and helped in the publication of the first Brethren hymnal. On the basis of the above the *Unitas Fratrum*, or Moravian Church, can claim five centuries of continuous growth.

This period of peace was not to last. King Ferdinand tried to force Bohemians to become Roman Catholics by demanding that all had either to become Catholics or leave the realm. Since they were pacifists and unwilling to become Catholics, the Brethren were forced to flee from Bohemia. Many settled in Poland where they multiplied; others remained in Bohemia under severe repression. Relief came in 1575 and soon the majority of nobility and peasants of Bohemia were adherents of the Brethren. Their *Kralitz Bible* (1593), an excellent translation from Hebrew and Greek, is still in print.

Although Bohemia was now nine-tenths Protestant, the Jesuits did not give up. They resolved to liquidate all "heretics." The Thirty Years War, led by Catholic Emperor Ferdinand II, led to the defeat of the Protestants in Bohemia. In one day (June 21, 1621) twenty-seven Protestants were beheaded in Prague under the blessing of the Jesuits. Protestant Bohemia never recovered. The remains of Ziska were disinterred and burned; bibles and churches were destroyed. Believers fled and the population of Bohemia was reduced from three million to less than one million.[40]

Meanwhile an orphan son of Brethren parents was growing up in nearby Moravia. John Commenius (1592-1670) was to become a world-famous educator as well as bishop of the Brethren. In 1628, after the burning of his books (*Orbis Pictus* and *Labyrinth*), the loss of his wife and child, plus the burning of his school, Commenius led a band of refugees from Moravia into Poland. A later persecution led to his flight to a refuge in Amsterdam. During these years his teaching and writings kept alive a spark of hope among the scattered Brethren. This "hidden seed," as Commenius characterized it, survived to emerge as the renewed *Unitas Fratrum* in Saxony. The line of continuity survived in (1) the hearts and minds of the believers, (2) in the Bohemian Bible, and (3) in the line of bishops (including Bishop Jablonsky, grandson of Comenius)

Few churches in history have suffered more than the Bohemian Brethren. From the earliest days, five hundred years back to Huss, the United Brethren have been a free church. By having the Bible in their native language, serving Holy Communion with both bread and wine, often meeting in conventicles, often sharing their goods, and renouncing the use of force, they anticipated the Anabaptist movements of post-Reformation times. They retained infant baptism and thereby avoided some of the persecution experienced by the early Anabaptists.[41]

In many ways the Brethren represent a "restoration" of the church of the New Testament. They differed from the Reformers chiefly in the idea of a free church not dependant upon the magistrates or the state. They insisted only on a free association of believers. Both Catholics and Protestants believed that church and state must be united. Catholics believed the church should be over the state; Protestants believed the state should be over the church. Both were intolerant of these "heretics" whom they feared would destroy the fabric of society. They believed the state church should determine the religion of the citizens. The free church concept did not become viable until Roger Williams's Rhode Island Colony came into existence in New England. Free Churches, not supported by the state and consisting of a group of believers with shared convictions, represent more than a reformation of existing churches. They represent a return to the pattern of groups of believers as pictured in the New Testament -- hence a Restoration.

2. The Renewed *Unitas Fratrum* (Moravians)

The survival of the "Hidden Seed" in eastern Europe was due to the influence (under God) of Bishop Comenius and a carpenter named Christian David. In 1715 a religious awakening among the scattered Brethren occurred in Fulneck in Moravia and also in Lititz in Bohemia, independent of each other.[42] In 1722 Christian David led little bands of Brethren in Bohemia, Moravia, and Poland to a haven in Saxony on the estate of a nobleman named Count Nicholas Van Zinzendorf. During the next five years some three hundred families settled at Herrnhut (The "Lord's House").

The Count, born in Saxony in 1700, was educated at Halle, the school founded by the Lutheran Pastor, Augustus Franke. Here Zinzendorf helped found the "Order of the Grain of Mustard Seed," a group pledged to be loyal to Christ and to lead righteous lives. After graduation from Wittenburg University he traveled in western Europe. At the museum at Dusseldorf he saw a portrait of Christ with a crown of thorns. This emotional experience became his "new birth" and he resolved to devote his life to winning others to Christ.

The Count was not a systematic theologian. His doctrine combined Lutheranism and some mysticism. He insisted on a "religion of the heart." He matured when Lutheran orthodoxy was on the defensive against the intellectual ferment in western Europe.[43] His concern was not in theological definition, but in the study of Scripture in the light of Christ's suffering and death and with the resultant emotional response in the believer. For him faith was not based on feeling, but on fact, as revealed in a pre-critical examination of the Bible.

Importance was placed on the believer's identification with Christ's suffering and death (cf. Phil 3:10; Gal. 2:20). Unlike Franke, he did not stress the *busskampf* ("penitential struggle") in conversion (as in Methodism) but rather the link with Christ's sufferings (cf. the Roman Catholic "sacred heart"). Like Luther he paid less stress on ethical claims and "legalism" (cf. Puritans and Methodists). This led to the primacy of faith over works and the charge of "antinominianism" by the early Methodists (cf. Fletcher's "Checks to Antinomianism"). The will of God was sought by the use of lots as in Acts 1:26. In his zeal for inter-faith cooperation Zinzindorf was ahead of his time, as his futile attempts in Pennsylvania proved. In his zeal for missionary endeavor he set a pattern widely followed for two centuries. In public worship the Moravians are joyous, hence the use of many hymns and songs.

The Herrnhut Community, five years after its founding, included three groups: those who favored the Lutheran Church, those who preferred a society within the Lutheran Church, and those who wanted a free church in the New Testament pattern. Tensions among these groups increased. Zinzendorf summoned all three factions to a meeting and read the Rules, formulated by Commenius, which called for a disciplined, holy lifestyle. All accepted this "Brotherly Agreement" of the Discipline of May 12, 1727. On August 13, 1727, the congregation experienced a corporate "baptism of the Holy Spirit" which dissolved tensions and united them in Christian love. This "birthday" of the renewed United Brethren, similar to the Apostolic Pentecost, had far-reaching effects and was a *rebirth* of the Moravian Church.

As in apostolic days, "love feasts" in private homes followed (Acts 4:46), a practice continued to this day among Moravians and some Methodist gatherings. A prayer vigil was started then which continued, twenty-four hours a day, without interruption, for one hundred years! Here also was born the modern missionary movement, before the days of William Carey.

Two of the brethren felt led to labor among the slaves in Danish-held islands in the West Indies (cf. Acts 13:1-4). Their involvement in missions resulted from their attendance in 1731 at the coronation of Christian VI as king of Denmark. Here Zinzendorf met a slave named Anthony whose master had brought from the West Indies. Two members of the Moravian delegation to the coronation could not sleep the night after meeting Anthony. One of the two, Leonard Doer, then decided he must bring the gospel to the West Indies. When he confided his conviction to his friend Tibias Lapeled, his friend exclaimed, "I could not sleep either; I heard the Voice also."[44]

When Anthony spoke at Herrnhut about slavery in the Islands he told them, missionaries would have to become slaves themselves in order to reach slaves, since the slave holders did not permit teaching slaves. This only encouraged their dedication to their task. Refused by the Danish West India Company, Doer and Lapeled appealed to the Queen and soon the royal household was busy assisting in preparations. Soon they were on a Dutch ship bound for St. Thomas Island where the slaves could understand Dutch and where these pioneer missionaries could communicate in a common tongue. By 1736 two hundred slaves had become Christens; and Bishop Spangenberg baptized three of them.

Missionary activity soon spread, among other places, to Georgia, where the Wesleys labored, and to South Africa where their mission school for Hottentots served as a example to those who came later. In the 1780's Moravians successfully evangelized among the Delaware Indians to an extent unparalleled in missions to native Americans.

The *Unitas Fratrum*, or Moravians, as they came to be known, represent a return to New Testament Christianity in several ways. (1) In exalting Christ as the object of faith, they were "on target." (2) Their emphasis on intercessory prayer was exemplary. (3) They pioneered in Protestant faith missionary work. (4) Their emphasis on the "love-feast" and joyous Christian fellowship was in tune with primitive Christianity (cf. Acts 2:42-47). (5) They exemplified the dual concern with *devotion* to Christ and *service* to neighbor.

Some reflections of a negative nature seem appropriate. Why have these pietists not been more numerous? Influenced by Zinzendorf they preferred to infuse spiritual life into existing denominations rather than founding a new one. This is a Christian motive and strategy, but it was counter productive, because sectarianism rather than ecumenicity was dominant then. Zinzendorf's efforts to bring together diverse Christian entities in the English Colonies were futile; he was a leader ahead of the his time (like Wycliffe). These Brethren did not seek new members. Spangenburg, in Georgia, refused to accept John Wesley as a member, because he was not convinced that Wesley was a Christian.[45] (Wesley was not sure himself).

Zinzendorf encouraged evangelism but refused permission for local congregations to organize and become rooted in a community. He was an innovative visionary, ecumenical but impractical. Because he refused to permit "societies," or preaching places, to become organized congregations, the number of societies in England became smaller each year. He did not believe in "planting churches."[46]

Because of early persecution they retained a "fortress mentality," on the defensive against "the world." Like the Anabaptists, they were not "success oriented," not aggressive in evangelism. They transferred to the New World the Herrnhut mentality of a community of exiles rather than aggressive evangelists such as the Baptists and Methodists. Communal living was their lifestyle, like the earliest believers in Jerusalem before being scattered because of persecution. In North Carolina, for instance, they remained in well-organized enclaves instead of scattering with the "good news." Hence, the Moravians, in spite of "an immensely rich and ancient history," remain "a small, little-known body."[47]

Still, their influence is far in excess of their numerical strength. It is seen in modern *missionary enterprise*. For example, in South Africa their mission school and farm, in the early eighteenth century, was a shining example to other missions. Their enthusiastic congregational singing was innovative. Their *hymnody* has entered every major hymnal. They are admired as giving expression of the synthesis of faith and work. Their influence of early Methodism is pronounced: it is seen in the class meeting, on holy living, on the love feast, and of a life of faith, as Wesley was glad to acknowledge. In addition their emphasis on ecumenicity and Christian unity set a worthy example at a time then dogmatism was dominant. To them Christianity, and Methodism in particular, owes much.

If John Huss and Peter Chelchicky were the spiritual fathers of the *Unitas Fratrum*, then Johannes Arndt (1555-1721) and Philip Jakob Spener (1633-1705) were the spiritual fathers of German Pietism.[48] Influenced by Arndt (*True Christianity*), as well as by Scripture, Spener, the Lutheran pastor at Frankfort-on-Main. began to preach "awakening sermons" to his congregation of Lutherans. This led to a spiritual awakening among his parishioners; several were "born again." They began gathering for mid-week Bible study. They even gathered again on Sunday evenings to share testimonies and to worship in sermon and song.

Spener published his classic *Pia Desideria* ("Desired Piety") about 1665 which affirmed:

(1) Exposition of Scripture by the preacher in classes.

(2) Laymen constitute a "spiritual priesthood."

(3) Theology is of the heart as well as of the head.

(4) In essentials unity, in non-essentials liberty, in all things charity.

(5) Sermons are not to display learning, or defend doctrines, but to edify the hearers.

(6) Prayer is needed to heal schisms and increase love.

(7) Purity of life is more important than purity of creed.[49]

Among evangelical Christians today these would evoke no surprise, but among third generation Lutherans this could be feared as "enthusiasm" (i.e., fanaticism).

As defined by Spener's successor, Bishop Spangenberg, "Sanctification" consists in our being freed and cleansed from such things as are not according to

His mind and being formed into His image."[50] This, he continues, "involves 'perfection' (Matt. 5:44-48; 1
Cor. 14:20; Eph. 4:15; 1 Thess. 4:1) yet we need to pray, 'forgive us as we forgive others.'"[51]

In his view infant baptism is neither commanded or forbidden in Scripture. In baptism all sins are removed not by the water, but by the blood of Jesus Christ as "faith lays hold." Since the Brethren were "orthodox," with reference to baptism, they were not subjected to the persecution experienced by the Anabaptists.

One result of the "Moravian" movement was the founding of the University of Halle by Augustus Franke. Endorsed by Frederick the Great, it had a world-wide influence. Here such leaders as Zinzendorf, Spangenberg, Bengel, and Schliermacher were trained. Franke introduced the "Buzekampf" (penitential struggle), by which he meant true faith requires a conviction of sin and its renunciation. This tradition continues in Methodism, in contrast to those who believe only a confession of faith is necessary. It was a corrective of the "dead orthodoxy" of Lutheran "scholasticism" which placed a higher premium on "purity of doctrine" than "purity of life." Earlier, Luther had placed emphasis on the "heart"; later Lutheran dogmatists put the emphasis on the intellect.[52] Halle's emphasis on grace alone later led a separation from the Methodists who insisted on discipline (works) as well as faith. The Moravians were accused of antinomianism and even of quietism, of neglecting the "means of grace."

As a movement Continental Pietism exerted a vast influence which is now being recognized and appreciated despite some detractors. Its influence continues in hymnody, philanthropy, missions, evangelism, and publications. In churches who consider themselves evangelical, regeneration, sanctification, devotional services, intercessory prayer, personal evangelism, home Bible studies, small group fellowship, and stewardship of time and treasure -- follow the pioneers who called themselves *Unitas Fratrum*. We continue in their debt.

37

C. PIETISM IN ENGLAND

Evangelical Pietism in England may be defined as a movement within established churches in the direction of personal transformation of church members into earnest disciples of Christ. In this survey only a few leaders and their influence may be traced.

William Perkins (1558-1602) studied at Cambridge, England, and became a very effective preacher. In addition to this, his writings made his influence second only to that of Hooker and Calvin among English readers. In his *Golden Chain*, like Calvin, he stressed the covenant of works, the covenant of grace, and the Holy Spirit. Unlike Calvin, he emphasized the salvation of mankind more than the glorification of God. In spite of his avowal of predestination, he stressed mankind's responsibility for repentance and adherence to the covenant relationship. He urged believers to go on to "perfection" without expecting to reach that goal "in this life." Like Wesley, he stressed *assurance* as something "felt" yet "religion doth not stand in feeling but in faith."[53]

The influence of Perkins and other English pietists extended to Holland and William Teellinck (1579-1629), the "Father of Reformed Pietism." In his many books and tracts he sought to edify readers amid acrimonious theological contentions. Although insisting that sound doctrine must be matched with holy living, he was suspect by both Calvinist and Armenian theologians. He called for repentance and reformation of life rather than merely a reformation in doctrine and polity.[54] He insisted that faith calls for commitment as well as trust, actively expressed in loving deeds, including missions. The new life in Christ, by way of the Holy Spirit, calls for a disciplined lifestyle. Luxury in dress and gluttony, for example, should be replaced by a concern for one's neighbor.

If Teellinck was the "father" of Reformed Pietism, William Ames (1576-1633) was its theologian. He studied under Perkins, fled to Holland, and served as Professor at the University of Franeker. His *Medulla Sacrae Theologie* (The Marrow of Theology), published in 1629, became "the standard textbook of theology" in England, Holland, and New England (at Harvard). For him "theology is the doctrine of the loving God."[55] Bypassing contemporary Calvinists, he went back to John Calvin himself saying "Faith is the resting of the heart in God."[56]

For Ames, as with Wesley, sanctification begins at conversion and continues until death. In distinction from justification (a changed relationship), "Sanctification is a real change in man from the sordidness of sin to the purity of God's image (Eph. 4:22-24)."[57] He continued:

> *If sanctification relates only to calling or that first rebirth in which faith is communicated as a principle of new life, a common confusion of regeneration and sanctification hereby arises . . . . Just as in justification a believer is . . . freed from the guilt of sin and has life given him . . . so in sanctification the same believer is freed from the sordidness and stain of sin, and the purity of God's image is restored in him.*[58]

As with Wesley, Ames believed that "an inner difference arises between the sin remaining in believers and the sin remaining in others. In the others sin reigns, prevails and dominates; in believers it is broken, subdued, and mortified."[59]

But Ames admitted that "perfect sanctification is not found in this life . . . yet all that are truly sanctified tend to perfection (Matt. 5:48; 1Cor 13:11; 2 Pet. 3:18."[60] In these statements Ames comes close to Wesley's distinction between initial sanctification (regeneration) and entire sanctification. For example, he cites Romans 6:22, 1 Thessalonians 5:23, Ephesians 4:24, and 1 Peter 1:4 in support of the latter.

The doctrine of the *Church* for Ames was different from that of Wycliffe and Calvin in that predestination was less prominent. For Ames the church is "a company of believers, a company of those who are in Christ, and a company of those who have communion with him ... it exists by faith ... through Christ to God."[61] With Ames the church is essentially "union and communion."[62] The influence of Ames is seen, not only in the tradition of pietism, but no less in that of Puritanism, especially in New England. At Harvard College his work on theology was *the* textbook for nearly all students.

APPRAISAL

"Pietism", like "church", is not easy to define. To some extent it is discernable in all communions, depending on how narrowly defined. It is widely acknowledged that a "changed heart" is central in the genius of Pietism. Basic to all facets of Pietism is the emphasis on the new spiritual "birth from above" as the condition for entrance into the "kingdom of God" (cf. John 3:5-8). Also basic is Christian perfection or sanctification, a holistic view of life. Christian maturity involves love of God and, equally important, love of neighbor (Matt. 22:37-40).

The many critics of "pietism" list individualism (self-centeredness), a "mini-ethics" or an ascetic tendency which forbids tobacco, alcohol, gambling, dancing, and a legalism which insists on church attendance, tithing, and other "good works."[63] It is also accused of fostering a "holier than thou" attitude.

Among the positives in this legacy are times of spiritual renewal which initiated, or accelerated, a return to the authentic New Testament Christianity. This involves conformity to Christ, the Spirit illuminating the written Word. The Pietist strategy from changed individuals to a changed church and then to a changed society, is a sound one. It calls for a gradual leavening of society rather than change through legislation alone, or even force, as with some in the Puritan heritage. Pietists are relatively tolerant of other's views, believing in ecumenicity (in the "unity of the Spirit") rather than forced union of uniformity, a diversity within unity.[64] Consistent with this, Pietists tend to work for spiritual renewal within existing churches (as Spener with Lutherans and the Wesleys with Anglicans).

The five major thrusts of Pietism, (a) renewed church, (b) unique authority of Scripture, (c) regeneration and *sanctification*, (d) Spirit-filled life, and (e) concern for one's neighbor (far or near), have had an influence far wider than is commonly realized, as Stoeffler and others have demonstrated.

In some measure Pietism permeates each segment of the "radical reformation" including the Anabaptists, Puritans, Brethren, Pentcostals, and Disciples of Christ. These five major thrusts, as indicated above, are all derived

40

from the New Testament, as distinct from church tradition. Are these characteristics of Pietism more akin to the New Testament teaching than most of the major Protestant denominations? This concern with regeneration and sanctification is more in line with the New Testament than the Lutheran focus on sound doctrine, the Angelical insistence on Apostolic succession, or the Roman Catholic monarchical structure, often at the expense of ecumenicity.

Pietism has leavened contemporary Calvinism to the extent that the five points of the Synod of Dort have been, in practice, reduced to retain only "effectual calling" ("once in grace, always in grace").

Pietists like Andrea (1586-1640) "who hoped to make religion a matter of life rather than merely doctrine" should be widely appreciated today.[65]

Chapter I Endnotes

1. F. X. Lawler, "Theology of the Church," *New Catholic Theology*, (Washington, D.C., 1967), III, p. 689.
2. Lawler, III, p. 691.
3. E. J. Bicknell, *Introduction to the Thirty-nine Articles*, (New York: Longmans, 1919, 1981), p. 229.
4. F. E. Stoeffler, *Rise of Evangelical Pietism*, (Lieden, E.J. Brill, 1965), p. 13.
5. Herbert B. Workman, *John Wyclif*, (Oxford: 1926), I, p. 26.
6. cf. Workman, II, p. 42.
7. The Roman Catholic doctrine of the Mass developed over several centuries.
8. Matthew Spinka, *Advocates of Reform From Wyclif to Erasmus*, (Phila.: Westminster, 1953), p. 30.
9. This summary is gleaned from S. P. Cadman, *Three Religious Leaders of Oxford*, (New York: Macmillan, 1916), pp. 118-120.
10. Spinka, p. 30.
11. Workman, II, pp. 149-151.
12. Workman, II, p. 170.
13. Workman, II, p. 186.
14. Workman, II, p. 197.
15. Workman, II, p. 8.
16. Workman, II, p. 8.
17. Will Durant, *The Story of Civilization: The Reformation*, (New York: Simon and Shuster, 1917), p. 37.
18. Workman, II, p. 321.
19. Workman, II, p. 322.
20. "Lollards," *Encyclopedia Brittanica; Micropedia* (1974), VI, p. 306.
21. Buddensieg, *Ver Script* 1. p. xliii, cited in Workman, I, p. 8.
22. Workman, II, p. 375.
23. David, S. Schaff, *John Huss*, (New York: Scribners, 1915), p. 21.
24. John Huss, *On Simony (Library of Christian Classics)* tr. by M. Spinka, p. 218.
25. Spinka, p. 278.

26. Schaff, p. xviii.
27. Matthew Spinka, *John Huss's Concept of the Church*, (Princeton: University Press, 1966), p. 257.
28. Spinka, *Church*, p. 259.
29. Huss, *The Church*, (tr. by D. Schaff), p. 2.
30. Huss, p. 3.
31. Huss. p. 21.
32. Spinka, p, 386.
33. Spinka, p. 389.
34. F. E. Stoeffler, *Rise of Evangelical Pietism*, (Lieden, E. J. Brill, 1965), p. 13.
35. A. W. Shattschneider, *Through Five Hundred Years*, (Winston-Salem: Comenius Press, 1956), p. 24.
36. C. S. Davis, *Hidden Seed and Harvest*, (Winston-Salem: Wachovia Historical Society, 1973), p. 1.
37. G. A. Williams, *The Radical Reformation*, (Westminster Press, 1962), p. 209.
38. This claim may be challenged by the Waldensians of the twelfth century who lived in Italy, France, and Switzerland.
39. Schattschneider, p. 31.
40. Schattschneider, p. 42.
41. Gunnar Westin, *The Free Church Through the Ages*, tr. by V.A. Olson, (Nashville: Broadman Press, 1954, '58), p. 38.
42. Edward Langton, *History of the Moravian Church*, (London: Allen and Unwin, Ltd, 1950), p. 56.
43. F. E. Stoeffler, *German Pietism During the Eighteenth Century*, (Leiden: E. J. Brill, 1973), pp. 142ff.
44. Schattschneider, p. 60.
45. C. S. Davis, *Hidden Seed* p. 15.
46. Shattschneider, p. 114.
47. Davis, p. 16.
48. F. E. Stoeffler, *The Rise of Evangelical Pietism*, (Brill, 1965), p. 203.
49. F. F. Walford, *Philip Jacob Spener*, (London: S.P.C.K., 1893), p. 37.

50. August Gottlieb Spangenburg, *Exposition of Christian Doctrine*, (Bath: S. Nazard, 1796) p. 259.
51. Spangenberg, pp. 286-287.
52. E. S. Waterhouse, "Pietism," *Hasting's Encyclopedia of Religion and Ethics*, X, p. 6.
53. F. E. Stoeffler, *The Rise of Evangelical Pietism*, p. 58.
54. Stoeffler, p. 129.
55. Stoeffler, p. 134.
56. Stoeffler, p. 137.
57. Wm. Ames, *The Marrow of Theology*, xxix.4; tr. by J. D. Eusen, (Boston: Pilgrim Press), p. 168.
58. Ames, p. 168.
59. Ames, *Marrow*, xxix.24; cf. Wesley's Sermon "Sin in Believers."
60. Ames, *Marrow*, xxix.29, cited in Eusen, pp. 170,171.
61. Ames, *Marrow*, xxxi.7,8, in Eusen, p. 176.
62. *William Ames*, tr. by Douglas Horton, (Cambridge: Harvard Divinity School Library, 1965), p. 217.
63. Dale Brown, *Understanding Pietism*, (Grand Rapids: Eerdmans, 1948), p. 140.
64. Brown, p. 148.
65. F. E. Stoeffler, *German Pietism*, p. 90.

Chapter II

THE ANABAPTISTS

"I have written . . . knowing well that I shall receive for it neither praise, favor, or material profit . . . If I receive denunciation and persecution, I have decided that it is better to suffer death for the truth than to receive material reward for flattery . . . I have spoken plainly and simply that I may in some way destroy and uproot simony, may the merciful Saviour aid me therein."

John Huss (1372--1415), Bohemia: follower of Wycliffe, forerunner of Luther.

One of the most "radical" of the several groups of Protestants who rebelled against the Church are known as Anabaptists. Their spiritual descendants are now honored world wide. They wanted more than Reformation; they wanted it extended to a RESTORATION of the primitive church.

The Roman Catholic Church in Europe was unchallenged for eleven centuries, or from the time of Constantine to Martin Luther. After the fall of Rome (410) the Church took over most of the prerogatives of the Roman Empire and become under Charlemagne the "Holy Roman Empire." The "Age of Faith" prevailed from the fourth to the sixteenth centuries (400-1500 A.D.). Efforts to reform the Church by Wycliffe in England, Ximenes in Spain, and Huss in Bohemia were frustrated because the times were not yet right; the church was too strong.

Reformation was frustrated until Martin Luther, in 1517, lit the torch which ignited the Protestant Revolt or Reformation. The protest against the Pope and Church came as a result of reading the Bible and applying its truths to contemporary Church doctrines and practices. Luther's bold words and deeds were so effective because of the truth he articulated so effectively, and also because the German princes and people supported his position. Church and state were united, whether Protestant or Catholic.

No one believed in a church independent of the state. Before the Reformation the Church controlled the State; after the Reformation in northern Europe the state controlled the Church.

The demand for a church free from secular control, a church consisting of believers who were determined to the follow only the Bible, emerged in Switzerland. In Geneva John Calvin led the movement which led to the Presbyterians (rule by Elders). In Zurich pastor Ulrich Zwingli led the movement called Reformed. They went further than Luther in attention to Scripture. Rather than follow the lectionary (portions of Scripture), Zwingli in 1519 preached a series of sermons going through Matthew verse by verse. But, like Luther, Zwingli dared not push Reformation further than the Magistrates were willing to go. Also, Zwingli alienated some of his followers by taking up arms against the Catholics (in self defence) in a battle in which he was killed.

A. SWISS ANABAPTISTS: CONRAD GREBEL

In Zurich these "radical" reformers came to be called Anabaptists because they insisted on believer's baptism. They were abhorred and feared by both Catholics and Protestants.

This label given to a segment of the Protestant Reformation is a misnomer like several other names given by "the world." The term means "re-baptism" and was applied to those believers in the state church who insisted that infant baptism is inadequate. Hence, they were baptized the second time as a confession of repentance, faith, and the new life in Christ. It is a misnomer in that it focuses attention on the rite of baptism instead of considering the factors which led to an insistence on baptism for believers only. Basically, it was their view of the church which distinguished them from both Catholics and Reformers: Anabaptists believed the church was a community of those "in Christ" free from state control.

Reformation had taken seven forms: Zwinglians, Lutherans, Calvinists, Anglicans, Spiritualists, Socinians, Pietists, and Anabaptists. The latter became divided into four main branches: Swiss Brethren, Hutterites, Melchiorites (militants), and Dutch Mennonites.

Zurich was the "cradle of the new world-wide Anabaptist-Mennonite-Baptist tradition."[1] In Zurich, under Zwingli, the Reformation comprised three groups: (1) those who hated the Roman Catholics, (2) the "libertinistic Protestants, " and (3) "those who work in the Word of God." The latter were evangelical Christians who became convinced that Zwingli was compromising with "the world" by refusing to go all the way back to the New Testament pattern of the church of Christ. Zwingli was in a tight spot: if he had gone all the way with the Anabaptists, the city would have reverted to Catholicism, and the Protestant cause would have been lost in this important stronghold. Zwingli therefore decided to go slowly enough to carry the magistrates with him. Like Luther he relied on "the State" to protect the church. After a public debate in 1523 and again in 1525 between Anabaptist leaders and Zwingli, the City Council decided in favor of Zwingli. The Brethren broke with Zwingli for these reasons: (1) Zwingli believed in a *volkskirche* (peoples' church), that is all those baptized in infancy, rather than a church of believers only. (2) They insisted on a free church of membership by choice. (3) Conrad Grebel and his associates refused service in the state, civil or military. (4) They refused to baptize their children.

Zwingli accused the Brethren (whom he dubbed the "re-baptizers", or Anabaptists) of rejecting Scriptures used against them by appealing to the Spirit and denying Scripture "as if indeed the heavenly Spirit were ignorant of the sense of Scripture which was written under its guidance . . . the sign of audacity and impious confidence."[2]

Zwingli also accused them of lawlessness or antinomianism: if accused of sin (such as adultery) they replied they were not in the flesh, but in the Spirit -- hence, no sin.

Zwingli and the magistrates refused to permit the Anabaptsts to form a free church independent of the city government. Instead, they were forbidden to separate or to refuse baptism of their infants.

Confronted with this decision of the Council the Brethren gathered in the home of Felix Manz on January 21, 1528, near Zwingli's church. In the earliest extant document of Anabaptist history we learn that

> *after prayer George Cajacob [Blaurock] stood up and begged Conrad Grebel for God's sake to baptize him with true Christian baptism upon*

> *his faith and confession . . . Conrad baptized him because there was no minister ordained to take such action.*[3]

Soon fifteen of them were re-baptized in defiance of the ban and were persecuted as outlaws, rebels, and heretics. Thus began the second free church movement six decades after but independent of the Hussite Movement in Bohemia. This movement, in turn, led to the establishment of the *Unitas Fratrum* (United Brethren).

These "rebels" did not see *baptism* in itself as the major issue. For them the issue was the *Church*, patterned after the New Testament and independent of secular authority. Zwingli and the Council made re-baptism the issue, hence the name Anabaptists. As with the names "Christians" and "Methodists," their enemies furnished the name for their movement. The name they chose for themselves was "Brethren."

As with the early church, persecution did not crush the movement. Instead it spread the more rapidly with ten thousand joining the movement in one decade.

The position of the Reformers, whether in Europe or in Britain, is a bit difficult for us to understand. Neither Catholics nor the Reformers believed in the principle of separation of church and state. All agreed that the union of church and state is indispensable to the fabric of society. All believed that their "truth" could not co-exist with another's "falsehood." The Church, whether Catholic or Protestant, believed that heresy was a threat to orthodoxy and must be eliminated by persuasion, if possible, by force if necessary. The idea of the separation of church and state as a viable option was pioneered by Roger Williams in Rhode Island and was first made official policy by Thomas Jefferson and the defiant Colonists in their Declaration of Independence. Historians agree with Zwingli that if the free church movement had then prevailed in Zurich the city would have returned to Catholicism.[4]

The "outlaws" gathered in Zollikon, a rural community near Zurich. On Sunday, January 22 or 23, 1525, Conrad Grebel conducted a communion service in the home of Jacob Hottinger. Unlike Zwingli who still retained the Catholic mass, the Brethren partook of *both* bread and wine. A few days later, during group Bible study, Hans Bruggbock confessed his sins, repented, believed, and requested re-baptism. A revival followed characterized by a deep conviction of sin by respected church members, repentance, and the new birth by the Holy Spirit. Thus the free church movement was accompanied by a Spirit-sent revival. The result was changed lives. Blanke asks, "Where else was revival present in Reformation circles?"[5]

Penalties for refusal to baptize infants increased, including banishment, imprisonment, torture, and drowning. [Felix Manz and three others condemned by the city council were drowned in the Limmat (lake) in Zurich.] The Brethren fled in all directions, many to Austria and south Germany. Persecution intensified as did their evangelistic zeal. The movement spread rapidly. The (Catholic) Diet of Spires in 1659 decreed death without trial. It became a capital crime to be an Anabaptist. It is estimated that 4,500 in central Europe met martyrdom by fire, water, and sword during the next decade.

In what way did the Anabaptists differ from the Reformers? Grebel's letter to Thomas Müntzer provides the first clue. Four points stand out: (1) While both Catholics and the Reformers believed in infant baptism (hence every citizen was a church member) they limited church membership to *believers only*. (2) They demanded a church *free* from governmental control. (3) The Brethren refused to serve in the armed forces or in any governmental office. (4) They refused to baptize their infants.

Michael Sattler's confession of faith also expressed their convictions. (1) Anabaptism originated not in medieval movements, such as the Waldensian, but rather in the Reformation. (2) Anabaptism is not a class struggle of the poor against the rich but rather a religious struggle for freedom. (3) Anabaptists are not anarchists but biblicists.

Balthasar Hübmaier (1485-1528) was an exception among Anabaptist leaders in that he had formal theological training and did not rule out the use of force. He was a doctor of theology and a cathedral preacher in Regensburg. In Zurich he had been influenced by Grebel and others of the brotherhood. Summoned to a trial in Waldshud, Austria in 1524 before Catholic theologian John Eck, Hübmaier was an eloquent and articulate witness. He affirmed eighteen "dissertations" or theses. Among them (1) Faith alone makes one "pious" before God; (2) The mass is not a sacrifice offered to God, but a memorial of Jesus' death; (3) We should be judged by Scripture alone; (4) Christ alone died for our sins -- no other intercessors are needed. (5) It is better to read one Psalm in one's own native tongue than many matins in a foreign language; (6)

True priests *teach* the word of God; and (7) He who misrepresents the word of God for temporal gain will be denied by Christ.[6]

During his trial he voiced an eloquent appeal for truth and justice. Said he,

> *Let me give an account of myself whether true or untrue. If I have taught errors expose them, help me back to the right path through the word of God. If it is one's duty to bring a wandering ass or ox . . . far more does one owe that to me, either in writing or orally . . . let the truth prevail.*[7]

His plea was refused. John Eck forbade an examination, and Hümaier was burned at the stake at Vienna in 1528.

In the perspective of time both were wrong: the Reformers in refusing to return all the way to the New Testament, the Brethren by refusing responsibility in civil service. But most of the positions taken by these "radicals" (who were viewed as a threat to society) are now accepted by most Christians.

Another difference between the Reformers and the Brethren was the commitment of the latter to Christian perfection or spiritual maturity. From the beginning Anabaptists were accused of hypocrisy.

> *There is . . . a major difference in emphasis between state-church Protestantism, with its tolerance of almost all degrees of sin in the church, both of omission and commission, and Anabaptist with its insistence on a high level of personal and group performance in character, life, and service.*[8]

In the articulation of their doctrine the Brethren were no match with theologians of the Reformation. With the exception of Balthasar Hübmaier, the Brethren lacked formal training in theology. Rather than a formal creed they had convictions which they believed were from the Bible and for which they were determined to live and die. Theirs was not an explicit theology, but rather an implicit or existential theology.[9] The word "existentialist" seems appropriate because it connotes living the gospel and discipleship. The term "discipleship," as Bender correctly affirms, is appropriate to describe Anabaptism. Yet as Friedman points out it can hardly be called a theology. *Existentialism*, however, serves to designate the Anabaptist insistence that Christian doctrine involves living the Christ-Way; the term helpfully indicates its difference from "explicit" (or "propositional") theology. Existentialist theology involves both a statement of faith and the actual living out of that faith -- a personal involvement in one's belief.

The classical Reformers concentrated on the more explicit theology of the Pauline Epistles. The radicals focused on the more implicit theology of the Gospels. The Epistle to the Romans (with Galatians) may be called the earliest "Institutes of the Christian Religion," antedating both Augustine and Calvin. Paul, like other Pharisees, had an articulate system of doctrine. Jesus put the emphasis on *living* the doctrine, going beyond "the righteousness of the scribes and Pharisees" (Matt. 5:20) as did Paul later when he declared that he longed to "know Christ" (Phil. 3:10).

The early Anabaptists mistrusted learned expounders of doctrine, fearing that it would distract from the central importance of obedience. For them it was more important to *obey* than to *know*. Later, in the similar tradition of Pietism, the early Methodists produced a "Discipline" rather than a creedal statement. By contrast the classical Reformers produced confessions, concordats, and catechisms. They emphasized systematic doctrine as having primacy over discipline or discipleship.

The early Anabaptists had a theology "of the heart." It involved the renewal by the Holy Spirit as well as intellectual assent to theological formulas. In this way they were like the Pietists in the Lutheran-Calvinistic tradition. They differed from the Pietists in placing emphasis on obedience (in lifestyle) more than on personal experience or the new birth.

In Anabaptism, as with St. Paul, the motif of suffering played a major role. Like the Pietists the Anabaptists stressed the suffering of Christ. Unlike Pietism they were alienated from the main-stream of Protestantism. Persecution by other Christians provided their theology of martyrdom. "It was this martyr-mindedness which gave Anabaptism its particular quality and character."[10]

Later, as they settled in free societies where persecution was not experienced, the Anabaptists experienced a crisis of identity. How could they remain authentic Anabaptists unless the state appeared to them as demonic? How could they be disciples of Jesus unless suffering the overt hostility of "the world?"

Persecution during the mid-sixteenth century tended to dampen the enthusiasm of the Anabaptists for evangelism. Instead it fostered a defense-mentality in which the main concern was survival. Theological interest focused on the Second-Coming more than upon mission and evangelism.

They tended to despair of salvation for "the world" and felt obliged to content themselves to subsist as little "colonies of heaven" amid a hostile environment. Self-perpetuation by procreation and discipline rather than aggressive evangelism became the norm.

B. THE HUTTERITES

While Catholics sought God indirectly by way of the priesthood, the Protestants sought God directly, assisted by the Word and the Holy Spirit. The Anabaptists sought God in communities of other believers. Those among them who placed greatest emphasis on the communal concept were the Hutterites.

Jacob Hutter (d. 1536) was born in the Tyrolean Alps, learned the trade of hatter in Prague, and then worked in Klagenhurt. There he met the Anabaptists and accepted the covenant of grace of a good conscience in Christian baptism with true resignation to lead a godly life. God's gifts were richly felt in him and he was chosen and confirmed in the service of the Gospel.[11]

When persecution arose in Tyrol, the Anabaptist congregations fled to Moravia and settled in and near Austerlitz. In spite of rival leaders, Jacob Hutter was recognized by the adherents as "our bishop and shepherd." As their history book records, "He put the true church in pretty good order by the help and grace of God, hence we are still called Hutterites."[12]

In Moravia King Ferdinand now demanded that all Anabaptists be expelled. Hutter returned to Tyrol in 1535 and wrote an eloquent letter to the governor of Moravia emphasizing the peaceful attitudes of his followers. King Ferdinand was likened to the "dragon" pursuing the church into the wilderness (Rev. 12:1). Hutter, the "apostle" of the brotherhood, was captured, tortured in Innsbruck and publicly burned on February 25, 1536, after only seven years involvement in the Anabaptist movement. He left a literary legacy of only eight letters. Leadership then passed to John Amon.[13]

Another leader, Peter Riedemann, because of his missionary zeal and doctrinal writings, was called the second founder (conserver) of the Hutterites. During his three-year prison term he wrote a spiritual treatise ("Rechenscheft") and during a second imprisonment he penned *The Account* (1540). In his writings he dealt with faith, the Lord's Supper, baptism, community of goals, warfare, government, taxation, the ban, dress, and the ministry. Unlike the Reformers, justification by faith was stressed less than "the Spirit of Christ working in the regenerate." He stressed "sanctification of life as the proof of inner rebirth and obedience."

For Riedmann the church is a congregation of believers only with "a regenerative assignment in the world."[14] The Christian commune is more than a sharing of goods; it is also "a communion of love and production." Suffering (*Gelassenheit*) is expected until vindicated by God. Brotherly love and unity are stressed together with full surrender and obedience. As another leader (Ulrich Stadler) expressed it, if a believer refuses the community of the Saints, he is "outside of Christ."[15] Each is to help the others and contribute to the welfare of the whole community. Since conditions are worse now than in the apostolic age, communal living is even more important now than then. It is important to seek abandonment to the group, cease from self-concern, trust the deacons to manage the affairs and thus live in contentment among the elect.[16]

This pattern of disciplined communal living continues to the present time. As of 1960 there were about 10,000 Hutterites world-wide; of these 8,500 lived in North America. Canadian Hutterites numbered 6,472 and lodged in 77 communities. In the U.S.A. there were 2,028 Hutterites located in 26 communities.[17]

During the "golden period" (1565-1590) the Hutterites were the most aggressive missionaries in Europe. Men were sent annually into countries of North Europe and were supported by prayer, money, and letters of encouragement. Since then, however, their survival has depended on natural increase rather than evangelism. They may be said to preserve to a unique degree the New Testament pattern of a church with "all things in common." Persecution has followed them from Europe to America and thence to Canada.

During World War I the Hutterites of South Dakota wrote to President Woodrow Wilson requesting exclusion from the draft. "Please do not ask us to violate our covenant with God", they implored.[18] In common with other Bruderhof (communal Mennonites) they stressed communal living, obedience to God, community deacons, disciplined lives, and non-resistance. They continue to survive and thrive in their North

American colonies. Their agricultural communities are less mechanized and, therefore, more viable today than many individual "family farms."

C. MILITANT ANABAPTISTS

The Brethren in Holland fell on hard times. It is interesting to see how their critics viewed Anabaptism in northern Europe. An English author likened them to the worm in Jonah's gourd, an evil influence in the Reformation.

According to Melanchton, the founder of the militant Anabaptists was Nicholas Stock. His disciple was Thomas Müncer whom Luther urged the magistrates not to harbor.[19] Stock claimed God spoke to him "by an Angel."[20] He said the Saints must reign and kill off "all the kings and princes of the world and repurge the church."

In order to promote the kingdom of Christ all the ungodly must be killed. Said an anonymous author, "This doctrine filleth the simple people with a furious and unnatural zeal."[21]

When Anabaptism crossed the English Channel it found points of similarity with Puritanism. However the connection has yet to be clarified.[22] Anabaptists were viewed by most English with horror.

A seventeenth century publication purports to give the Anabaptist position, but quotes an unsympathetic questioner. Some of the questions and answers are as follows:

> Q. Why are not called Anabaptist?
> A. "Because we . . . were dipped in the holy streames where we cleansed our bodies . . . in the presence . . . of the congregation."
>
> Q. What are the opinions of the Anabaptists?
> A. ". . . they may do what they will if conscience moves them to it, . . . infants are not to be baptized . . . . till they be of bigness fit to accompany with."
>
> Q. How are they different from the Independents?
> A. "We differ very much . . . . They do not allow of laws and orders and blacke-coats, and prophane learning, and superstitious preaching in the pulpits, and many such things."
>
> Q. By what Discipline do you walk?
> A. "By what Discipline he think in his own conscience is best . . . We are a free-borne people."[23]

This hostile account does not do justice to most Anabaptists, but it does reflect the prevailing attitude in the mid-seventeenth century. They were feared because of the precedent of anarchy at Munster and also because of their divergence from contemporary Christian groups. Much of this fear was ungrounded, because it was based upon prejudice (ignorance) of Anabaptism in its total impact.

Among the other characterizations as seen from England are as follows: (1) regenerate men cannot sin, (2) the Lord's prayer was never intended to be said, (3) there is no distinction between clergy and laity, (4) one with a spiritual gift needs no ordination, (5) prophecy must be permitted, (6) all human laws must be abolished. The writer concludes that

> *the preaching of cobblers, feltmakers, tailors, groomies, and women, the choosing of any place for God's service but the church . . . will bring us in time to a community of wives, goods, and the destruction of all.*[24]

Some of this criticism was justified. But this antinomian "lunatic fringe" caused the entire Anabaptist movement to be viewed with fear and contempt. Luther called them fanatics (*Scharmer*).

In a similar vein an anonymous tract entitled "A Warning for England," charged

> *some Turbulent Ministers especially Thomas Muncer . . . began to preach against Luther . . . He [Müncer] pretends to some divine revelations . . . that he had received a command from god to kill & root up all wicked Princes & Magistrates, and to chuse better in their places.*[25]

A peasants' attack on the nobility followed. This Anabaptist war coincided with the Peasants' Revolt which began in 1525 and terminated in the fall of Münster in 1535. During this turbulent decade in Holland and Germany some five thousand men, beside women and children, were killed.[26]

According to Melanchton these Anabaptists believed that sin is not in infants, hence, they need not be baptized. All infants, including Turks, Jews, and pagans, enter heaven without baptism.[27]

Because of their insistence on believers' baptism, both Catholics and Lutherans declared a war of extermination on all Anabaptists.[28]

The extremists among these Anabaptists derived inspiration from Melchior Hoffman (b. 1495). An influential preacher and writer in North Europe, Hoffman was a furrier by trade. He was influenced by the *Deutsche Theologie* and gained Luther's approbation in 1525. Unlike most Lutherans he emphasized the "sanctification of life ... shown in all the fruits of the Spirit" in addition to justification by faith.[29]

Lutheran clergy rejected him because "he insisted on the necessity of holy living."[30] The lack of the fruits of faith among Lutherans led Hoffman to the conclusion that they were not Christians. He differed from Luther regarding the Eucharist. Yet like Luther, at a public disputation he exclaimed, "I stand alone in the word of God, let each do likewise." In Strassburg Hoffman joined the Anabaptists. He stressed the imminence of the Second Advent declaring that "if with steadfast hearts we believe this about him, we are washed and cleansed from all our sins."[31]

Despite lack of theological training he wrote extensively, preached effectively, and became both influential and controversial. He interpreted Scriptures allegorically and became increasingly involved in prophecies of the end times. He came to the conviction that he was the Elijah destined to lead Anabaptism to victory throughout the world as head of the 144,000 witnesses (Rev. 11:5,6; 14:3). He predicted that Christ would appear in July 1533; he later postponed the date until 1534. His zeal and writings had a wide influence on the radical wing of Anabaptism, but he was a pacifist by conviction and was no more responsible for the fanaticism in Münster than Luther was responsible for the Peasants' Revolt.[32]

Thomas Müntzer held ideas similar to those of Melchior Hoffman. He preached before princes at Allstedt on July 13, 1524, saying among other things, "The devilish holding of the mass is the abomination of desolation (Matt. 24:15). We need daily fresh revelations of God."[33] "Daniel's prophecy is being fulfilled. Soon the fifth monarchy (iron and clay feet) will destroy the vipers (priests) and eels (princes). The peasants see this more clearly than you" princes.[34]

> *For the godless have no right to live except as the elect wish to grant it to them as it is written in Exodus 23:29- 33: "Godless rulers must be killed especially the priests and monks who revile the gospel as heresy for us and wish to be considered at the same time as the best Christians."*[35]

Repeatedly, Müntzer exhorted the protectors of Luther to destroy "enemies" of the truth. He appealed to biblical texts of judgment and imagined that he and his adherents were the chosen instruments of divine judgment.

The delusion of grandeur led eventually to the radicals' take-over of the episcopality of Münster in Westphalia in 1532. Here the bishops had rejected the Reformation. Jan Matthys, a baker from Haarlem and a disciple of Melchior Hoffmann, took charge of Münster and made it a theocracy. Catholics and Lutherans fled. John of Leyden later assumed leadership; lawlessness and immorality prevailed. The city fell after a siege led by an army of bishops and the princes. Torture and massacre followed.

This militant fanaticism stigmatized the entire Anabaptist movement all over Europe. Catholic rulers were convinced that anarchy was the logical consequence of Anabaptism. Some of the radicals went to England and probably had some influence on Independents and Puritans under Cromwell.[36]

D. DUTCH ANABAPTISTS: MENNO SIMONS

Apart from this decade of violence in Westphalia, Anabaptism was steadfastly non-violent. Unlike Catholics and Reformers they stressed illumination by the Holy Spirit, a church of believers only, the state a necessary evil. They believed the New Testament to be more relevant than the Old Testament, that baptism was for believers only, and that church and state should be separated. Sanctification was stressed more than justification. They refused to bear arms, looked for the Second Coming of Christ, and stressed brotherhood.

Anabaptists in the Netherlands and Northwestern Germany, who did not expect the millennium immediately and who rejected militarism, rallied to the leadership of Abbe Philips (a surgeon) and to his brother Dirk (a Franciscan). These, together with the disillusioned survivors of Münster, found a leader in Menno Simon (1496-1561).

Like Luther, Simon's parents were peasants. At the age of twenty-eight and with little formal education, he became a village priest in his native Friesland near the North Sea. Like most priests of the area he took his parish duties rather lightly and found ample time for "playing, drinking and frivolous diversions."[37]

He covertly read some of Luther's writings with an open mind. Simon gradually came to the conclusion that the bread and wine he served could not be the actual body and blood of Christ. His troubled mind and conscience found light and relief by reading the New Testament. After failing to find infant baptism in Scripture, and after learning that a tailor had been beheaded for being re-baptised, he began to question this subject as well. Soon fanatical Anabaptists from Münster appeared, and Simon spoke out strongly against them, thus gaining recognition as a Catholic leader opposed to re-baptism. Simon became troubled, for he was not comfortable in the ambiguous role of defender of an unscriptural church. After nearly three hundred Anabaptist laymen were assassinated in a nearby community, he felt constrained to identify himself with their "cause." In 1536 he resigned the priesthood, left the Catholic Church, and became a fugitive like others in the Anabaptist persuasion.

The non-violent Anabaptists found in Menno the courageous yet moderate leader they needed. He was re-baptized by Abbe Philips, married, and was ordained an elder by the Anabaptists. For the rest of his life, after leaving a comfortable and respectable "living," he became an itinerant teacher, and writer, without visible support for himself or his loyal wife Gertrude. He endured much more suffering and hardship than leaders like Luther and Calvin. He was an outlaw. A decree of Emperor Charles forbade anyone to provide him food, shelter, or funds, or to read his writings or converse with him.[38]

Meanwhile Simon continued to formulate his theological position. Influenced perhaps by Melchior Hoffman, he concluded that the Incarnation was "a new creation of the human flesh of Christ in Mary so that Christ took being *in* Mary but was not born of Mary's flesh."[39] This theory proved to be difficult for Menno to defend and he mentioned it only when questioned. It had little influence among Mennonites.

From the perspective of history, it is generally agreed that this turbulent time of persecution, defection, and fanaticism would have completely annihilated Anabaptism in Northwestern Europe had it not been for the heroic labors of Menno Simon.[40]

From 1536 until the time of his death Menno Simon was a fugitive, and lived "underground" as an outlaw. Many who provided him shelter were later exposed and martyred. Placards offering rewards for information about his whereabouts proved ineffective. Despite this he continued to travel, minister to believers, and write tracts. Among his literary contributions is a book of 250 pages entitled *Foundation of Christian*

Doctrine and *The True Christian Faith* (1541). By his preaching, teaching, counselling, and writing Menno Simon was the human instrument by which the cause of Anabaptism survived. He was not the founder, but his labors justify giving his name to the entire movement.

After penning a tract which warned against "The Blasphemy of John of Leiden" (1535), an essay on "Spiritual Resurrection" (1536), and a personal "Meditation on the Twenty-fifth Psalm" (addressed to God), he exploded with a sermon on *The New Birth* (1537). Like John Wesley in a sermon at Oxford,[41] Menno blasted the pseudo-Christianity of his day and explained the necessity of becoming new creations in Christ via spiritual regeneration. Basing his pronouncements on the New Testament, he warned that repentance, then birth from above and "received in the heart through the Holy Ghost" is the sole condition of spiritual life now and eternal life after.[42] He described the twice-born as manifesting the Spirit of Christ in all of their interpersonal relationships and manner of living. These have one supreme spiritual king, the Lord Jesus Christ. They are "children of peace" who renounce war, and wield only "the sword of the Spirit." He challenged all church leaders, including princes, bishops, and popes, to prove from the Scripture how masses and confessions, without regeneration, can save someone. He closed his sermon by exhorting the readers to follow the word of God and the example of Christ. It is a powerful and direct challenge as relevant today as then.

Simon's most influential book was the *Foundation of Christian Doctrine*, the chief means by which he became the acknowledged leader of nearly all Anabaptists. In this essay twenty pages are devoted to baptism. The Scriptual arguments for and against infant baptism are thoroughly dealt with. Not surprisingly, he finds biblical evidence for believers' baptism only. Another section deals with the issues which first led him to leave Catholicism and embrace Anabaptism -- the Lord's Supper. He compares the mass to the worship of the Golden Calf by the ancient Israelites and castigates it as idolatry fostered by the antichrist. He sees the Eucharist as the memorial of Jesus' vicarious death and as an indispensable means of grace -- much like Zwingli. Its efficacy depends upon the communicant's faith.[43]

As with the Swiss Anabaptists, much attention (thirty pages) is given to the contrast between true and false ministers of the Gospel. An eloquent appeal is made to the magistrates for tolerance of Anabaptists. He asks civic leaders to be as tolerant of these evangelicals as Cyrus was of the Jews. He appeals to their sense of fairness, to their conscience, and also warns them of God's judgment if they judge unjustly.

He does not spare intellectual leaders, whether Catholic, Calvinist or Zwinglian, but charges them with compromise with the world, with sin, and with selfishness. Yet his appeal is compassionate and permeated with references to Scripture. The Church of Christ does not need rebuke, it needs only encouragement. As the "bride of Christ" the church is urged to walk worthily of her vocation and let her light boldly illuminate a darkened world.

There is little systematic theology in this doctrinal treatise; it is a tract for the times and addresses the major contemporary issues. It is dogmatic, apologetic, hortatorical, and pervaded with prophetic, evangelistic fervor. Its note of assurance arises from the author's foundation in biblical truths. He is made bold by the Scriptures.

In an essay of nearly forty pages Menno deals with the thorny problem of church discipline. He tried to mediate between those leaders who administer the ban too severely and others who were lenient. Based on Matthew 18 and 1 Corinthians 5 he tried to outline the New Testament principles and procedures. Reluctantly he concludes that the ban (rejection of the careless) should apply even in conjugal relationships.[44]

Probably the greatest contribution made by Menno Simons was his writings. Like Paul he wrote as he traveled, fled, prayed, and preached. He labored under conditions even more hazardous than Paul since he lived under the sentence of death and his presence exposed his protectors to the death penalty. Fifteen hundred were martyred in this area before the victory of William of Orange (1553-1584) provided relative freedom of worship after the "Pacification of Ghent" in 1576 and the "uneasy peace" which followed.[45] The total number of Anabaptist martyrs from 1525 to 1576 in all of Europe must have been about ten thousand.[44]

After the period of intolerance and martyrdom the "Golden Age" for Dutch Mennonites followed. Many of them engaged in professions and trades; some became wealthy and respectable. A century after the last martyr's death (1574) Dutch

Mennonites had lost much of the zeal and dedication of the forefathers. Some held offices in the government and the older tensions between church and state subsided. Decades of "gradual but continuing decline" followed.[45] While there were 160,000 in the Netherlands in 1700 there were only 26,953 in 1808. One hundred congregations had vanished during this eighteenth century.[46] Since then, however, a modest resurgence has occured, and by 1964 there were 40,000 members.

When persecuted by the Catholics in Holland the Anabaptists and Calvinists had much in common. However, when Calvinism triumphed and became orthodox, the Mennonites were viewed by the majority as a menace. A public debate in 1578 at Eimnden, between Mennonite and Reformed leaders, dealt with the points at issue. These included (1) the oath, (2) baptism, (3) the ban, (4) pacifism, and (5) free will. The majority view prevailed and Mennonites endured a series of rules restricting their freedom of worship.

Mennonites shared with unorthodox Socinians-Unitarians opposition to war, the oath, and an effort to restore Apostolic Christianity as they saw it.

The Mennonites also found congenial many doctrines of the Arminians (Remonstrants). These included (1) free will, (2) opposition to the five points of Calvinism (Synod of Dort) and (3) separation of church and state.[47]

E. THE MENNONITES AND AMISH IN AMERICA

As noted before when the Mennonites in Holland were less persecuted they were more relaxed and more prone to lose their "first love" (Revelation 2:4). When persecuted they knew "the faithful meant to suffer."[48] When not suffering they wondered on what basis their unique characteristics needed to continue, to witness and to win converts. They were less certain of their mission.

This led to a cleavage among the Mennonites. Some grew more "worldly." Others were more strict like the "older" Mennonites. A Swiss minister by the name Jacob Amain demanded a more strict discipline among the Mennonites. He felt that they should continue the older attire, continue the "shunning" (the less strict), and continue the "ban" of the careless. Those who shared his convictions became the "Amish."[49]

By 1730 many Amish settled in "Pennswood" (Pennsylvania) where tolerance was demanded by its owner (William Penn). Many of them gathered on farms in the area of Lancaster. Today this area remains their focus, although they scattered westward, especially to Eastern Ohio. They avoid "modernism," preferring the lifestyle of the "real" Mennonites in the "good old days" of the eighteenth century. Hence, many or most of them, still use horses rather than tractors, trucks rather than autos (thus avoiding luxury), clothing of an earlier time, and often avoid attending public schools. Public road signs in this area urge care when passing the horse-drawn buggies used by the Amish.

The Amish are friendly. My wife Lucile and daughter Carol cherish our cordial welcome to a farmer's house in central Pennsylvania. The wife invited us "strangers" to dine with them; she gave us a pie; and her husband took us to visit their school. The Amish welcome the visitors who enter their shops to invest in their unique "Dutch" wares.

Some avoid portraits because of the warning against forbidden images in Exodus 20:4. In Ohio, while a friend of mine was visiting with his Amish friend, I joined the conversation and asked permission to take a picture. Explaining that he never had his picture taken, our host declined, being unaware that I had taken his picture a few minutes before I had joined the group. In many Amish homes it is difficult for teenagers to embrace the austere lifestyle of their parents.

But the Amish have some advantages. Rather than own costly machines using costly oil, they use horses which eat the fodder grown on the farms. Their honesty is welcomed by neighbors as well as by visitors seeking their produce. Their diligence and discipline often result productive farms, even when other farms in the area are abandoned.

The Amish live near, and sometimes with, the Mennonites in the New World. Their basic beliefs are similar: refusal to use arms, avoidance of any involvement with magistrates, desire for peace among nations as well as with neighbors, and service where ever there is need. They believe in the importance of the Bible, of regeneration by faith, in the death and resurrection of Christ. The major belief of evangelical Christians today are the same as today's Mennonites. They were, and remain, conservative. During the eighteenth century they avoided Sunday Schools, Bible schools, midweek Bible studies, church camps, Sunday evening worship, missionary organizations, and ecumenical cooperatives.[50] One of the major changes for the Mennonites was the introduction of Sunday Schools in 1840.[51]

In their effort to live according to the Bible, many Mennonites, and more of the Amish, erect a "fence around the Torah." In other words, they make a careful effort to obey the Bible by adding cautions which go beyond the written Law (a "second fence" to protect the first). This same tendency is illustrated by the Pharisees before and during the days of Jesus. In order to ensure keeping the Sabbath holy they, refrained from plucking corn when hungry (Mark 2:23-28). They thought it sacrilegious to heal on the Sabbath (Mark 3:1-6). Eating with Gentiles was a betrayal of their sanctity (Acts 10 and 11). On the Sabbath they walked no more than three miles, or "a Sabbath Day journey,"[52] This is a rule in some places in Israel today. They would not carry food from one house to another on the Sabbath, unless a rope was drawn around both houses thus making one house.[53] In Jerusalem today touring visitors may be pelted with stones by the Hasidim (holy ones) to avoid sacrilege on the Sabbath.

In early days, the sincere Pharisees and strict Mennonites were sincere and had good intentions. Their "fence" to defend the Law is like that of Free Methodists who once forbade the use of wedding rings (no exterior adornments, I Peter 3:3), and one segment of Disciples who ban instruments during public worship, to maximize the human voice.

E. APPRAISAL

The early Anabaptist movement and consequent struggle in Europe evoke admiration when seen in historical perspective. That the movement endured at all is remarkable considering the persecution encountered.

On the negative side, their individualism often fostered intolerance and divisiveness. Their refusal to baptize infants seems irrelevant to a commitment to apostolic Christianity. Their biblical literalism tended to major on minors, such as observing the Lord's Supper only in the evening. Their negative attitude toward the state led to a position of irresponsibility for civic affairs, which only evoked hostility from the public. Their emphasis on community and separation from "the world" left them no option for urban life or participation in a society which became increasingly interdependent. In addition their "martyr complex" led to an identity crisis when persecution ceased. It is not good when the hostility of neighbors is a major reason for one's existence.

On the positive side, they seem vindicated by history in their preference for believers' baptism, freedom of conscience, separation of church and state, non-resistance, church discipline, holy living, sensitivity to the Holy Spirit's leading, social concern and the recognition that love demands obedience to Christ (John 15:10). Their adherence to the principles of the Sermon on the Mount, obedience, discipline, and love of neighbor demands respect and often admiration. Their renunciation of war and use of force challenges all other believers.

Chapter II Endnotes

1. Fritz Blanke, "Anabaptism and the Reformation" in Hershberger, ed. *Recovery of the Anabaptist Vision*, p. 58.
2. Ulrich Zwingli, *Select Works*, (Phila., 1901, 1972), p. 126.
3. Cited in H. S. Bender, *Life and Letters of Conrad Grebel*, (Goshen, Ind.: Mennonite Historical Society, 1950), p. 139.
4. Fritz Blanke, *op. cit.*, p. 64.
5. Fritz Blanke, "The Anabaptist Congregation at Zollicon," *M.Q.R.*, XXVII (1953), p. 24.
6. Balthasar Hübmaier, writings collected and photocopied by W. O. Lewis, at Wm. Jewell College, Liberty, Mo. 1939, pp. 10-20 passim.
7. *Ibid.*, p. 21.
8. H. S. Bender, "Perfectionism," *Mennonite Encyclopedia IV*, p. 1115.
9. See R. Friedman, *Theology of Anabaptism*, (Herald Press, 1973), pp. 18-23.
10. Friedman, *Theology of Anabaptism*, p. 56.
11. Loserth, "Jacob Hutter," M. E., II, p. 851.
12. *Ibid.*, p. 852.
13. G. H. Williams, *The Radical Reformation*, p. 418.
14. *Ibid*, p. 428.
15. Williams, G. N. Mergal, *Spiritual and Anabaptist Writers*, p. 178.
16. *Ibid.*, p. 283.
17. R. Friedmann, "Hutterite Brethren," M. E., II, pp. 857-862.
18. "A Petition to the Honorable Woodrow Wilson," n.d., now in the library at Goshen, Indiana.
19. *Ibid*, p. 6.
20. Robert Austin, *A Short History of the Anabaptists of High and Low Germany*, (London: 1647), p. 3.
21. *Ibid.*, p. 54.

22. Littell, *Free Church*, p. 40.
23. *Anabaptists Catechism*, (printed for R. A. 1645), p. 2-5.
22. *Ibid.*, p. 56.
23. Anonymous, *A Warning for England*, (London, 1642), p. 2.
24. Alexandre Weill, *Histoire de la Guerre des Anabaptists*, (Paris, 1874), p. 3.
25. Weill, p. 61.
26. Weill, p. 7.
27. Christian Neff, "Melchior Hoffman," M. E. II, p. 779.
28. *Ibid.*, p. 779.
29. Mark H. Noll, "Melchior Hoffman and the Lutherans." p. 61. Deerfield, IL. M. A. Thesis at Trinity Evangelical Divinity School.
30. Neff, M. E. II, p. 785.
31. Williams and Mergal, editors, *Spiritual and Anabaptist Writers*, p. 58.
32. *Ibid*, p. 63.
33. *Ibid*, p. 69.
34. W. J. M'Glothlin, "Anabaptism." H.E.R.E. I, pp. 409, 410.
35. C. H. Smith, *The Story of the Mennonites*, (Newton, Kansas, 1957), p. 85.
36. C. J. Dyke, *Introduction to Mennonite History*, (Scottsdale, Pa., 1967), p. 81.
37. H. S. Bender, "Brief Biography," *Complete Writings of Menno Simons*, J. C. Wenger, ed., (Herald Press, 1956), p. 14.
38. Bender, *op. cit.*, p. 16.
39. J. Wesley, "Circumcision of the Heart," *Works*, IV, p. 24.
40. *Writings*, p. 92.
41. *Writings*, p. 92.
42. Menno Simons, "Final Instruction on Marital Avoidance," *Writings*, p. 1064.
43. A. L. E. Verheyden, *Anabaptism in Flanders* (1530-1660), (Scottsdale, Pa.: Herald Press, 1961), p. 76.
44. Cf. Alexandre Weill, *Historie de la Guerre des Anabaptistes*, (Paris: Dentu, librare-èdition 1874), pp. 4-7.
45. Wm. Keeney, "Anabaptism in the Netherlands," in C. J. Dych, ed., *op. cit.*, p. 102.
46. Keeney, *op. cit.*, p. 118.

47. C. H. Smith, *Story of the Mennonites*, (Newton, Kansas, 1957), pp. 184-187.
50. Theron F. Schlabach, Peace, Faith, Nation. (Scottdale, PA 1966) p. 20.
51. Ibid., p. 21.
52. J. C. Wenger, The Messonite Church in American. (Scottdale, PA 1966), p. 81.
53. Harold E. Bender, "New Life Through the Sunday Achool," in Wender, pp. 144 181.
54. George Foot Moore, Judaism. Volume 11. (Cambridge, Mass., Harvard University Press) p. 32.
55. Ibid. p. 31.

Chapter III
THE BRETHREN

"Sanctification embodies both the entire consecration or setting apart of the believer (Romans 12:1,2 and 6:19), as well as the cleansing of the heart from carnality (James 4:8; Ephesians 5:26; Hebrews 9:13,14) accompanied by the baptism of the Holy Spirit (Matthew 3:11; Acts 2:1-10)."

Brethren In Christ Affirmation

In what ways are those called "Brethren" similar or diverse from other branches of the Radical Reformation (or Restoration)? The answer lies primarily in their historic origins. The Movement known as the German Baptist Brethren, as distinct from the Bohemian *Unitas Fratrum*, originated in central Europe. They emerged from three main streams: mysticism, Anabaptism, and Pietism. Of these the major influence was Pietism, a term used first by Joachim Feller of Leipzig in 1699. He defined a Pietist as "one who studies God's Word and leads a holy life in accord with it."[1]

In general Pietism embraced five facets of Christian living: regeneration, separation from sin, sanctification, Bible study illuminated by the Holy Spirit, and a protest against "conformity to the world" in many churches.[2] These mainstream Pietists wanted to remain within, and revitalize established churches.

In contrast to this Evangelical Pietism, as represented by Arndt (1555-1621), Spener (1635-1705), and Franke (1663-1727), there emerged a group of radical Pietists. These looked to Jakob Bohme (1574-1624), a mystic whose views were so anathema to John Wesley (*Journal*, March 5, 1764). From the writings of Bohme: *Aurora* (1612) and *Der Weg zu Christo* (1624), the radical Pietists concluded that both Catholics and Lutherans were of the anti-Christ. They placed a premium on emotionalism in worship including speaking in tongues. Their chief spokesman and intellectual leader was G. Arnold who wrote *Erste Liebe (First Love)* in 1696 and four years later a church history showing that often "heretics" best preserved basic Christianity. These radical Pietists demanded separation from all existing churches.

The Treaty of Westphalia (1648), which ended the Thirty Years War, specified that the only religions to be tolerated were the Catholic, Lutheran, and Reformed. All others were unlawful heretical sects. The ruler determined which of these three faiths would be practiced within his sphere of influence. Conflicts were inevitable; each citizen was obliged to attend only the church approved by the magistrate.

The relative tolerance of magistrates in the Palatinate (the valley of the Rhine) led to the demand by some for separation from all of these three established churches. In 1702 Matthew Baumann attacked the church and soon after led a group to the tolerant Penn's Woods (Pennsylvania). In 1704 four men from the same area were put in prison when they refused to take the oath of allegiance to one of the established churches.

A. DEMAND FOR A FREE CHURCH

The leading evangelist of these radical Pietists was E. C. Hochmann (1670-1721). He wrote little, but after studying law at several universities he experienced a dynamic conversion at the Pietist school in Halle. He became an eloquent and effective evangelist in several countries of central Europe. After years of travel and several imprisonments he built at Schwarzenau a "hut" which he called Friedensburg (City of Peace) as a place of spiritual retreat.[3] Hochmann became the "pathfinder" of the radical or separatist group of Pietists.

Public anxiety increased as Hochmann began gaining adherents with the assistance of a miller named Alexander Mack. The Reformed churches felt the most threatened, the Lutherans less, and the Catholics least. A request by the Reformed Church to take action to restrain these evangelists and their followers is dated August 7, 1706. It reads in part:

> *For some time the so-called Pietists have been getting the upper hand here in the city as in various places in the country, especially in Schriesheim. They meet from time to time in their homes and hold conventicles. They also preach in the streets, sing, and distribute books in order to attract the inhabitants when the latter return from the fields to their homes. Through this, the congregation might . . . be led astray by these errors. Many souls might be caused to doubt through this hyprocisy.*[4]

This window brings to mind the early church witnesses, the Lollards in England, the early Methodists, and numerous others who experienced spiritual "awakenings" throughout Christian history. Like other "radical reformers," the Brethren Movement began in a revival.

Many dissenters gathered at Schwarzenau toward the end of the seventeenth century because of persecution in the German Palatinate. Alexander Mack conducted Bible studies at his mill, and in 1705 he invited Hochmann to visit the little group. Hochmann's influence extended to what later became three separate groups of Brethren. In addition to the group led by Mack, the Society of True Inspiration was organized at Marienborn in 1714. These Inspirationists later migrated to Buffalo, New York, and then to Iowa where they became the Amana Colonies. The third group migrated to Count Zinzendorf's estate at Berthelsdorf in 1722.[5] Hockman's beliefs had a wide and lasting influence. While a prisoner at Detmold in 1702 he was forced to write his confession of faith. It may be summarized thus:

> *There is "one, eternal, sole, almighty omnipotent God," revealed in the Bible as the source of all life. Baptism is only for adults; if infants were to be baptized, as the successor to circumcision, the New Testament would have said so. The Lord's Supper is only for obedient disciples of Christ. . . On Christian perfection, one may be sanctified not only forensically, but also perfectly, that is, really, so that no more sin will remain in him . . . This perfection must be effected internally, i.e., mystically, within the soul through the living God, and a spiritual image of Christ must be won by us. Where this does not occur in this life, men cannot come unto the immediate vision of God . . . since without holiness no one can see God.[6] . . . Only Christ, though the Holy spirit, can appoint preachers and teachers . . . Government is a divine ordinance and should be obeyed in all civic matters . . . The Bible teaches, and Christ's power assures, the final "restoration" (redemption) of damned men.[7]*

This statement expressed "more clearly than any other" the views of the Brethren.

B. DIVISIONS IN EUROPE

Alexander Mack differed from Hochmann and the radical Pietists in three areas. He found that the Pietists lacked precision in doctrine; they needed better church organization; and they slighted the sacraments. Mack turned in the direction of the Anabaptist influence and away from the mysticism of Jakob Bohme. After being questioned by Gruber, Mack issued two printed treatises explaining his position: *The*

Ground Searching Questions and *Plain View of the Rites and Ordinances of the House of God.* Both appeared in 1713.[8]

Mack's *Questions* concerned the importance and mode of baptism held by the German Baptists, or Tunkers. Of the forty *Questions* asked, twenty-five focused on baptism. In response to several questions Mack affirmed his conviction that for centuries no real church existed except with the very few whom he assumed practiced baptism by a three-fold immersion.[9]

Mack was uncertain whether even devout Christian martyrs were eventually saved unless they were baptized by immersion! Asked whether making any outward rite so indispensable makes salvation dependent on works, Mack answered that faith must be validated by obedience. Children should be baptized only after a confession of faith. Mack agreed that one could be regenerated before baptism, but the work of grace would be forfeit unless it was followed by baptism (by immersion).[10] These Baptists stressed immersion even more emphatically than Anabaptists whom these New Baptists (Tunkers) considered lukewarm, having lost their "first love."

In 1708, within two years after hearing Hochmann and Mack, the Church of the Brethren came into existence by the triple immersion of eight charter members -- five men and three women. The one who initiated the procedure was chosen by lot and his identity kept secret in order to avoid the cult of personality. Filled with joy and zeal, they spread the word. By 1728 they numbered about one thousand. Although they preferred the term "Brethren," they lacked any official name. Outsiders called them "Tunkers" (Dunkers) because of triple immersion. Despite their emphasis they disavowed "baptismal regeneration."[11]

For the first seven years they practiced communal life and celibacy. In this they followed Jakob Bohme at a distance; they also emulated Hochmann and Guber who were near.[12]

Mack warned of the dangers of a "non-biblical mysticism" and of those who believed that the law written in the heart is superior to the Scriptures. He also warned against the misuse of the ban, another departure from the Mennonites. He insisted that brotherly love limits the ban to persons of gross immorality (cf. 1 Cor. 5:11). Mack followed Zwingli in defining the Lord's Supper as a memorial. They observed the sacrament in four phases: foot washing, the love feast, the Eucharist, and the "holy kiss."

Schism developed at Schwarzenau over such issues as celibacy, the community of goods, and the ban. Judging was so highhanded that by 1720 only forty families (200 persons) remained.[13] Several families, loyal to Mack, migrated to Germantown, Pennsylvania, from 1719 to 1729. Those from Krefeld came to the Philadelphia area in 1719. Mack brought 126 people, while in 1733 John Naas brought the third and last group. The total numbered less than 500.

In Germany their antecedents were a matrix of Waldensianism, Mysticism, and Pietism, to which was added the lifestyle of the Anabaptists. In America, however, as in the Palatinates, they emerged from and were shaped by "a series of awakenings, or revival movements not unlike, but earlier than, those described in the religious history of ... the English-speaking communions."[14]

Not far from Germantown, Theodore J. Frelinghuysen, a Dutch Reformed preacher trained under the influence of Pietism, preached "awakening sermons" and evangelized in 1720-1730. This was the "first fruits" of the Great Awakening which began in the Middle Colonies and spread to both New England and the Southern Colonies.[15]

In 1708, in Europe and again in Germantown, the Brethren as well as many others experienced a spiritual awakening characterized by a conviction of sin, criticism of unregenerate ministers, unwillingness to commune with the unregenerate, rejection of formal liturgy, and meetings for prayer and fellowship outside of established churches.[16]

In 1723, four years after they landed, seventeen Dunkers gathered in the home of Peter Decker who had arrived earlier in 1722. This was the beginning of the first Dunker church in America, and Decker was chosen as leader. On December 20, 1723, six new converts were baptized in Wissanicken Creek near Germantown. Afterwards they gathered at a table for singing, Scripture, prayer, footwashing, a love-feast, the Eucharist and the "holy kiss."[17] This event is regarded as the rebirth of the Tunker, Dunker, or German Brethren Church (the first "birth" was in 1708). However, as Durnbaugh observes,

These "first fruits" should more accurately be considered to be the beginning of a period of renewal, akin to the Great Awakening of colonial America spearheaded by Frelinghuysen, Whitefield and Edwards.[18]

It is significant that the Anabaptist origin in Switzerland was initiated by the activity of the Holy Spirit and was characterized by conviction of sin, repentance, regeneration, and transformed lives. It then was spread by enthusiastic witnesses. Likewise the renewed *Unitas Fratrum* (Moravians) date their rebirth in August 1727 to the moving of the Spirit as at Pentecost.

In England John Wesley, along with the other Oxford Methodists, began the quest for holiness of heart and life. Simultaneously in Colonial America, the Great Awakening (and the Dunkers's rebirth) occurred in 1723-1740.

God's Spirit moved simultaneously in Europe, England, and in Eastern North America during that decade of spiritual awakening (1730-1740). The results of that profound and extensive renewal are still with us. Many are now praying, "Lord, do it again!"

C. DIVISIONS IN AMERICA

Sometimes the Brethren were less than brotherly. The Dunkers split soon after their spiritual rebirth. Conrad Bissel, a charismatic leader, was baptized and ordained by Becker in 1724. Bissel later accused Becker of arrogance and of breaking the faith. Bissel then led a large group of Dunkers to an ascetic community at Ephrata where they kept the Sabbath on Saturday and continued to proselyte members associated with Elder Becker.[19]

Bissel's Sabbatarians at Ephrata attracted much attention, favorable at first, because of their enthusiasm, asceticism, and music. As seen by Moravian neighbors Wiegner and Bohnisch,

> *The Sabbatarians believe they succeed most in sanctification. They practice voluntary poverty, and chastity ... Whoever lives a life of celibacy among them is allowed to wear a long gown ... At the dedication of this large house for single people they had a great love feast to which they invited all God-fearing people around the country.*[20]

The Moravian Bishop Spangenberg saw the Brethren at Germantown as divided, diminished, and undisciplined, in contrast with the flourishing Sabbatarians who were seen as "more spiritual".

The Brethren (Dunkers) split again. Those who had emigrated with Elder John Nass quarreled over the matter of discipline. They refused communion to the daughter of Nass at Amwell, because she sat for an hour in the lap of her boyfriend. Her father defended the girl and separated. He then held meetings which were attended by many sympathizers.[21]

The zeal of the Ephrata community was so strict that dedicated Moravians were not acceptable because they had been baptized in infancy (Bissel had been baptized four times). By March 7,1 1739, Spangenberg had seen enough of the Sabbatarians at Ephrata, because "false powers and not the Spirit of Christ are ruling the congregation.[22]

Brethren at Ephrata were widely admired for their skill in music and for their zeal. But fanaticism intruded, as did misguided zeal. The Sabbatarians placed priority on the spirit; they considered all others as lacking in spiritual power and zeal. The Brethren who followed Becker put the written Word above the presumed leading of the Spirit.

The Dunkers recovered slowly from Bissel's defection and maledictions. The Moravians were hopeful of cooperation among all other German speaking churches, but were forced to give up because of provincialism, suspicion of the Moravian motives, and because the Moravians baptized infants.

In Pennsylvania there were several independent groups or sects. Each considered its own group nearest to the church of the New Testament. As listed by spangenberg in 1742, they included:

1. *Quakers*
2. *Mennonites*
3. *Dunkers (Taufer)*
4. *Sabbatarians*
5. *Schwenkfelders*
6. *Inspirationists*
7. *Separatists*
8. *Hermits*
9. *The self-styled "New Born" (antinomians).*

Each of these sects scorned Lutherans, the Reformed, and Episcopalians because they were seen to be only nominal Christians.[23]

(It was Spangenberg who in Georgia refused to accept John Wesley because Wesley could not affirm his spiritual rebirth).

The Lutheran pastor, Muhlenberg (1711-1787) complained that the appeal of these sects lay in their belief in baptism by immersion only (scorning infant baptism) and in their appeal to the book of Revelation. The Brethren won converts from the Mennonites, because they were similar to them although more zealous. Most

Mennonites developed a martyr complex and became more concerned with survival than with winning the world for Christ.

Also influential among German Baptists was Alexander Mack, Jr. (1712-1803), son of the founder. He served as elder many years and did much writing, mostly polemic and apologetic in nature. Influential among Quakers, Brethren and Mennonites were J.C. Sauer (1695-1758) and his descendants. They were pacifists and printers. Christopher Sauer II (1712-1784) published the Bible (1743, 1763, 1776), and the first religious magazine in North America. The Germans in Pennsylvania made major contributions in music, poetry and printing.[24]

As with the early Methodists, the German Baptists in Colonial America placed more emphasis on lifestyle and spiritual vitality than upon doctrinal statements. Their conservativism, German origins, and German language kept them relatively isolated for decades.

Since they adopted no official doctrinal statement, it is difficult to ascertain their theological positions. Their distinction lay in how they applied their understanding of the New Testament. In this area history is more specific.

In our faith we do not differ from any evangelical body of Christian . . . The only difference is in matter of application. We believe that faith, repentance, and baptism are inseparably joined together. We believe in thrice immersion, face forward. We believe [the] Lord's Supper consists of a full meal, to be taken in the evening . . . Directly after the meal is eaten, bread and wine are partaken of as the Communion, representing the body and blood of Christ; foot washing and the kiss of charity follow.[25]

Differences developed with reference to Sunday Schools, protracted meetings (extended evangelistic campaigns), missionary boards, and a salaried ministry. Their problem, like that of the Christians (Disciples), was trying to adhere to the letter of the New Testament and not add anything of human origin to it. They also differed with reference to the "single mode and double mode" in foot washing. The double mode apparently described the procedure in which one person washed and another wiped; it was said to be a departure from earlier practices.[26] Congregations which sprang from Germantown promoted the "single mode." Those influenced by Ephrata (Bissel's group) practiced the "double mode," and were accused of an unjustified innovation by those from Germantown.[27]

Because of their eagerness to be the primitive church in every detail and their excessive fear of departing therefrom, it is not surprising that the Brethren were schismatic-prone from the beginning. In Germany they reflected the mystic, the Mennonite, and the Pietist traditions in order to return to the truly New Testament church. Soon afterwards the tiny group split three ways as noted earlier. In Pennsylvania they split two ways soon after their "rebirth" in Germantown. They refused cooperation with the ecumenically minded Moravians as well as with the despised Lutherans, Calvinists, and Anglicans. One faction, following one of the doctrines held by Hochmann and Mack, became Universalists.[28]

Their conservatism, isolation, and introversion doubtless resulted in a tendency to "major on minors." A perfect example was a nationwide schism over the "double mode" or "single mode" in foot washing. In theory they are united, having no doctrine except the New Testament, like the Quakers earlier and the "Campbellites" later. But this not only failed to avoid schism, it apparently facilitated it.

Zinzindorf, in a series of general gatherings, tried to unify nine diverse groups of German speaking separatists in Pennsylvania. The Tunkers left the third of these general gatherings, or "synods," because three born-again Indians were baptized by sprinkling rather than by triune immersion. Thereafter they held their own annual meetings in 1742 and each year thereafter.[29]

The early Brethren were like the Quakers with respect to simplicity in dress and in their refusal to take oaths or to bear arms. They were unlike Quakers in the importance they placed on baptism and the Lord's Supper. They differed from the Mennonites in their insistence on the trine immersion, and in foot washing. They claimed to be more "spiritual" and more influenced by Pietism.

A Brethren historian and archivist reflects with mingled pride and sorrow on the mentality of the early Brethren. He observes:

> *Their fervor for the sacramental rights (ordinances) seems to have been the main burden of their preaching and teaching. Were they as faithful in preaching about the fruit of the Spirit as taught by Paul? If we Brethren had given more attention to love, joy, peace, long-suffering, kindness, . . . self-control, throughout our two hundred and fifty years, there would have been no divisions among us, and God alone knows what the impact of our ministry to the world would have been.*[30]

One reason for their divisiveness may have been their determination to stress their identity and justification for their existence by enlarging the areas where they were unique. This in turn led to the insistence on what were "major" to them. Legalism has its perils.

The Revolutionary War made things as difficult for the Brethren as for the Anglicans, Quakers, and Methodists. They refused to swear allegiance to the revolutionary colonial governments, and they refused to bear arms in the crisis. Since their grain could not be marketed in Philadelphia, many Brethren began turning grain into alcohol. Annual conferences from 1781 and thereafter condemned the traffic in distilled liquors, [31] but apparently this action was not enforced. Was it because there was no *specific* Bible text to guide them? Did their legalism hinder them from adequately grasping the *principles* of Scripture?

Apparently, from their perspective, more serious than traffic in liquor was the mode of immersion in baptism. Early in the nineteenth century David Sower baptized a candidate by a single backward immersion. This unprecedented procedure "raised a storm of protest and Elders Peter Keeper and John Riese put him out of the Church."[32] For a time (1821-1834) Baptists were taken into membership without being rebaptized by forward action in Trine immersion. The earlier "correct" mode was again made mandatory in 1834.[33] Obviously where the New Testament was silent the Brethren were ready to supply the vacancy!

The period from the American Revolution to the mid-nineteenth century (1775-1850) is seen as a "dark period" in Brethren history.[34] Most of the German Baptist Brethren (Tunkers) were conservative and resisted change.

The main media of communication were church papers. Editors of several periodicals included Kurtz (*Gospel Visitor*, 1851), H. R. Holsinger (*The Christian Family Companion*, 1865), and James Quinter (*The Primitive Christian*, 1878). These papers discussed subjects on which opinions differed: the introduction of Sunday Schools, a salaried ministry, and plainness of attire. Holsinger, in particular, called for a recognition of the changing times. He stressed the need to change from meeting in private homes to worshipping in church buildings.

In 1878 *The Progressive Christian* was started by Holsinger and J. W. Beer. They believed the Brethren were a generation behind in such matters as Sunday Schools, colleges, dress styles, houses of worship, and a democratic church government.

In a protest against the influence of the "Progressives," Samuel Kinsey gave expression to the conservatives by founding *The Vindicator* in 1870. Its stated purpose was to resist the trend toward "innovation" and "to contend for the order of the Brethren as it has been established."[35] This periodical expressed the views of the *Old Order* as distinct from the *Progressives* and also from the middle-of-the-road *Conservatives*. The Conservative faction was the most numerous.

The "Old Order" opposed "higher education" in high schools and colleges, viewed Sunday Schools with suspicion, and was against evangelistic "protracted meetings" because they were "innovations." Sometimes the elders were jealous of the success of visiting evangelists.[36] All this transpired after the First and Second Great Awakenings and the labors of evangelists like Charles Finney!

Other issues were debated for decades during the last half of the nineteenth century. Ultra conservatives opposed a paid ministry, and missions; they insisted on plain clothes and hair style. This illustrates their determination to remain compatible with the primitive early church and their fear of a loss of identity in the "New World" far from European beginnings.

The use of alcohol continued as a problem. Annual meetings consistently advised against its use, but tensions continued to intensity for several decades. It is curious that discipline was effective in modes of baptism, but less effective in this area.

Those of the *Old Order* in southern Ohio demanded the exclusion of the "Fast Element" because they favored high school, Sunday Schools, protracted meetings, revival hymns, "giving instruction to rise or come forward," a salaried ministry, "the single mode of feet washing," fine furniture, "fancy paintings of our houses, costly carriages, etc.[37]

The Old Order group, about 4000 in number, carried out their threat to leave if the "Fast Element" were not excluded. They severed connection with the other Brethren in November 1882, when they adopted as their official name "The Old German Baptist Brethren."

The Progressive element called for adherence to Brethren fundamentals, but adjustment to changed conditions. For example, the Progressives opposed making the women wear a cap as a test of membership. They permitted wearing either a cap or a bonnet provided it was unadorned. In this they were undoubtedly influenced by Paul (1 Corinthians 11:5-16) and Peter (1 Peter 3:1-5) in their eagerness to be biblical Christians. They also believed in freedom of speech and an amicable exchange of views. Thus they tried to follow the New Testament pattern of lifestyle without being "legalistic."

But the Progressives, and Editor Henry Holsinger in particular, were accused of being trouble makers. At his church in Berlin he was accused of insubordination. Although the indictment was without specific charges, the judgment was supported by the Annual Meeting in 1882. Holsinger and his supporters were rejected. The Holsinger group gathered at Ashland, Ohio, and prepared a "Declaration of Principles." They gathered again at Dayton, Ohio, on June 6-7, 1883, and reorganized themselves as the Brethren Church.[38]

The conservatives remained between the Old Order and the Progressives, a centrist position. They were represented by another periodical founded by J. H. Moore in 1876 and called *The Brethren at Work*. After the reactionaries (Old Order) had left and the Progressives forced out, the middle group remained the largest group. They controlled the Annual Meeting and the Standing Committee which sets policy. They approved of education, Sunday Schools, protracted meetings, a paid ministry, and liberty with reference to the single or double mode in foot washing.[39] They differed little from the Progressives in belief, but were more conservative and cautious in expressing themselves. However, in 1876 they made the dress code a test of membership and opposed a "free press."

The Progressives, numbering about 6000 and led by Holsinger, decided to promote Sunday Schools and have a congregational polity. Each local church would be independent in government, but consistent with Brethren doctrines and practices.[40]

The Progressive Brethren then split over the matter of doctrine, and their views of the Bible. The split appeared among the Faculty of Ashland College which was founded in 1878. The institution came under control of the Progressives when they

81

assumed its indebtedness in 1883-1886. Graduated training for the ministry began in 1930 when a graduate school of theology was formed with Alva J. McClain as its director.

A movement towards a liberal theology was initiated by men like J. L. Gillin who trained at Union Theological Seminary in New York and served as President of Ashland College from 1907 to 1911. Gillin proposed that "religious experience," rather than an "infallible Bible," be the basis of authority and that an Arian could be a church member in good standing. In response to Gillin's challenge, McClain prepared a theological statement entitled "The Message of the Brethren Ministry." McClains's statement was endorsed by the National Ministerial Association in 1921 and later by the General Conference.[41]

Tensions developed between the seminary faculty and the students and faculty of the college, the latter being less committed to evangelical Christianity. Simultaneously, the theological tension throughout the Progressives camp was increased by a consolidation of four different church periodicals and a change of administration in publishing. The change left the conservatives in editorial positions, but many were disappointed and vindictive.[42] Published articles on the theological and administrative issues and personalities spread the schism nationwide.

Under the presidency of Dr. Charles L. Anspach (beginning 1935), Ashland sought to become a community college. This caused much distress not only with the Seminary, but with its supporters who wished the college to serve only the church and evangelical Christianity. (They wanted a college similar to Wheaten in its commitment to this constituency.) At the meeting of the college Board of Trustees in April, 1936, two members resigned in protest over this policy on the part of the Administration. The resignations were followed by an "open letter" in June 1936, addressed to President Anspach. This widely circulated communique lodged nine "protests," chief of which was the protest against the alleged trend toward secularism in the Board and among the students. At the General Conference in August 1936, a committee was chosen to investigate the alleged liberalism and lax conduct. In the June 1937 meeting of the college Board of Directors, two members of the seminary faculty (McClain and Hoyt) demanded changes. After interrogation by the Board, their resignation was demanded on the grounds of incompatibility.[43]

Consternation spread through the Church, since these two men were widely known and trusted. This was the catalyst which split the Progressive wing of the Brethren Church into incompatible factions. The Foreign Mission Board, then meeting in Ashland, was profoundly disturbed by this development. At a prayer meeting called that evening in the home of J. C. Beal the first step was taken to form a "new seminary in the Brethren Church.[44]

At a meeting held July 28-29, 1937, the new Brethren seminary was named Grace Theological Seminary. It opened in Akron, Ohio, on October 4, 1931, with thirty-nine students, most of them from the Ashland campus. Ashland Theological Seminary opened with thirteen. Many churches, districts, and conferences threw their support behind the Grace Brethren group. At the General Conference of 1939 held in Winona Lake, Indiana, the split became complete. The Ashland group continued as the Brethren Church; the evangelical wing took the name Grace Brethren. The Home Mission Council also favored the Grace Brethren faction, as did the Womens' Missionary Society, the *Brethren Missionary Herald*, and the National Bible Conference. Grace Theological Seminary moved to Winona Lake at the invitation of Dr. W. E. Biederwolf and operated on the third floor of the "National [International] Headquarters Building owned by the Free Methodist Church."[45]

A building was erected for the seminary at the north edge of Winona Lake in 1951. Later, college buildings were erected on a thirty-acre campus.[46]

A struggle over local church properties occurred in the years following the schism. Both the Ashland and Grace factions professed to retain not only the name Brethren, but also the Tunker traditions. Several lawsuits were brought by the Ashland group to obtain control of local church properties. The outcome in five such suits was about equally divided. The verdict of the Dayton trial was that the Brethren churches were congregational in polity, and, hence, property was locally owned. In a trial at Peru, Indiana, and another at Meyersdale, Pennsylvania, the defendants were accused of departure from Brethren beliefs in the matter of trine immersion, a mode which the

Grace group considered not essential to salvation. The Ashland group won both of these cases.

Struggles in the areas of schools, missions, publications, and real estate left both groups of Brethren divided about equally. The Grace faction, initially in the minority, grew rapidly until it had about the same number of constituents.

The Ashland group claimed to be in the tradition of Pietism and views the Grace group as Calvinistic in such matters as effective calling and final perseverance. They were more irenic, ecumenical, and tolerant of theological pluralism.

The Grace Brethren is presently the more evangelical, mission-minded of the two groups, and tend to be rather rigid fundamentalists. They look to Lewis Shafer of Dallas Theological Seminary as their mentor and use his *Systematic Theology* in basic courses. (In this work Shafer explains the theology of the Lutherans, Calvinists, and others, and then explains the theology of the New Testament!) On mission fields their fundamentalism and separatism make ecumenical activity, even among other evangelicals, difficult.

Which group has the better claim to be in the traditions of the New Testament and apostolic precedents? The truth probably lies between the Calvinistic fundamentalism of the Grace Brethren and the diluted Pietism of the Ashland Brethren. Both may have departed from the original Brethren principles of piety and simplicity. Ashland veered in the direction of "liberalism" with reference to Bible interpretation and application. McClain overreacted by embracing dispensational Calvinism.[47] However, few have grasped more clearly Paul's argument in the Epistle to the Romans than Alva J. McClain in *Romans, Outlined and Summarized* (Zondervan, 1927). The Grace group tend to take the Bible more seriously and, on that important basis, can take a more credible claim to be "primitive."

The central group named (since 1908) The Church of the Brethren, numbers over 200,000 and has its headquarters at Elgin, Illinois.[48] Their ministers are trained at Bethany Theological Seminary at Oak Brook, Illinois (founded 1905), "a moderately liberal institution."[49] The Church of the Brethren has become increasingly free and liberal. Concessions were made on the "dress question" in 1910; a uniformly distinctive dress was recommended, but not enforced. The church leaders sought less isolation and more involvement in issues of the day. Missions were emphasized, as were the "peace witness" and social service. The changes in self-image brought about an "identity crisis" in the 1960's. A unity in theology was sought in vain. A split resulted in the formation of an evangelical movement in 1959 which took the name Brethren Revival Fellowship. The liberals formed the Brethren Action Movement and also the Brethren Peace Fellowship, circa 1968. Today pluralism is accepted, as is the gradual decline in membership. The look now is toward the future rather than to the past.[50]

The Church of the Brethren has reached a stage similar to the United Methodist Church where the majority are concerned primarily with social action and are challenged within by the evangelical Good News Movement. The Conservatives in the center of the Brethren movement have made more "progress" than the Progressives. The identity continues as the Church of the Brethren seeks to conserve her heritage from Pietism, Anabaptism, and the Free Church Movement, while at the same time seeking to be relevant and contemporary.

Few churches has changed more rapidly than has the Church of the Brethren during the last half century.[51] Issues that once seem so important are gradually being forgotten. It is difficult for them to conclude that issues that brought about the origin of the fellowship, such as trine immersion, are no longer important and should not be retained. The concern is first to identify the real issues, and then adhere to them in a situation of pluralism within the fellowship and ecumenicity without. Few have succeeded in living by the maxim of Protestantism's great ecumenicist, Count Zinzindorf: "In essentials unity, in non-essentials liberty; in all things charity."

Another important Brethren group is the United Brethren in Christ, as distinct from Bohemia's *Unitas Fratrum*. P. W. Otterbein migrated from Germany to America in 1752 and preached in the German Reformed groups in Pennsylvania. Like other Pietists, he stressed the importance of a personal spiritual new birth and transformation. Otterbein listened to the Mennonite preacher, Martin Boehm, who also called for an evangelical conversion. After hearing him Otterbein embraced Boehm and exclaimed, "We are Brethren."[52] Otterbein became friendly with Methodists and assisted in Francis Asbury's ordination in 1784. Soon evangelical preachers were meeting informally for fellowship. In 1800 Otterbein and Boehm, with eleven others, formed the United

Brethren in Christ church, a German-speaking group similar in polity and doctrine to the English-speaking Methodists.

A similar movement among Germans with Methodist leanings was organized under the leadership of Jacob Albright, a former Methodist exhorter.[53] They took the name Evangelical Association (later the Evangelical Church). Both of these groups are now merged in the United Methodist Church.

The Plymouth Brethren is another group of Brethren, small in numbers but with a widespread influence. Their origins are to be found in small informal groups gathered for Bible study in parts of England and Ireland. One group met in Dublin, Ireland, from 1825 to 1827 and was led by Anthony Groves (1795-1853). They came to the conclusion that laymen are "free to break bread together as disciples of Christ" and to observe the sacraments without depending on an ordained clergyman.[54] Others joined for mutual fellowship and worship. Those in attendance were asked only that they believe in Jesus Christ and live as a Christian. Meetings were informal. They met weekly for Bible study, prayer, and Holy Communion. (This writer attended a tiny Plymouth Brethren church in Illinois. The congregation gave me a warm welcome, and we studied the Bible cordially in Sunday School. Then I was dismissed courteously as they began public worship which was to conclude with the Lord's Supper. It is not surprising that their congregation was small!)

Among the early leaders of the Plymouth Brethren was John Nelson Darby (1800-1882) who soon became their acknowledged "Patriarch." He moved from Dublin to Plymouth, England, and became leader of their largest congregation (1200 members by 1845). In addition to preaching, traveling, and teaching, Darby wrote a large number of tracts and books, published in Plymouth. Hence developed the name "Plymouth Brethren." Many were attracted to these tracts because of their simplicity, sincerity, and adherence to the Scriptures. Other leaders of the movement included George Muller, head of a large faith orphanage in Bristol, Samuel Tregelles, the New Testament scholar, and George Wigram, compiler of the *Englishman's Greek Testament Concordance of the New Testament*.

Darby wrote extensively. He defined the Church as an assembly of disciples of Jesus who study the Bible diligently and seek to live out its precepts. The most distinctive teachings of Darby emphasized eternal security and dispensationalism. In his view, time is divided into seven "dispensations" or "time periods during which man has been responsible for specific and varying tests as to his obedience to God, from the beginning of history to its end."[55] This scheme has influenced many preachers and teachers, including Dwight Moody, C. I. Scofield, Lewis Sperry Shafer, and Billy Graham, plus the Faculties of Dallas and Grace Theological Seminaries.

Plymouth Brethren have no salaried ministers, observe the Lord's Supper each Sunday, and, unlike the Quakers, permit no women to teach or preach. Like many other Brethren groups, they preach unity and practice disunity. There are now eight different Plymouth Brethren groups with a world-wide membership of nearly one-half million.

D. THE RIVER BRETHREN

Of special interest in this review is the group of Christian Germans in Pennsylvania who called themselves the River Brethren (now the Brethren in Christ). They combine the Anabaptist emphasis on discipleship and simplicity with the Pietist-Methodist emphasis on life in the Holy Spirit.

Like most of the movements in this review this one began as a spiritual awakening among laymen. Among these laymen was a farmer living in Lancaster County named Jacob Engels (1753- 1833). As explained by Bishop Levi Lakenbach, "God's grace and his convicting spirit . . . [were] at work, and finally those two persons [Jacob and John Engel] . . . with others, were led to see themselves as sinners and sought and obtained pardon of their sins and their acceptance with Christ."[56]

Evangelical Pietism and Anabaptism were both influential among German settlers in Pennsylvania. Added to this was "a surge of revivalism" among German-speaking congregations. As one of the early Brethren confessional statements expressed it,

> *Into . . . open, poor sinner's heart the Lord Jesus will come . . . to bestow comfort, peace, love, and trust . . . he receives comfort and forgiveness of sins and eternal life . . . So we confess that to be the new birth, revival of the mind, revival of the Holy Spirit.*[57]

Martin Boehm, who later founded the United Brethren in Christ, was an influential German-speaking evangelist in whom was combined the concern for discipleship with fervent preaching. The River Brethren welcomed Boehm's evangelistic zeal and spiritual maturity, but disagreed with his views of baptism. As a result they gathered a nucleus of those with Anabaptist backgrounds who saw the necessity of a spiritual rebirth.[58] This group did not unite with the Mennonites, because the latter did not believe in the necessity of the "new birth" and the witness of the Spirit. Also, like Dunkers, but unlike the Mennonites, they believed in trine immersion. They considered joining the Dunkers, but chose not to because of their interpretation of baptism. The Dunkers would not administer baptism unless they joined their group. The Dunkers viewed baptism and regeneration as inseparable (although stopping short of baptismal regeneration); the River Brethren believed baptism follows regeneration, as a public declaration of faith and newness of life. Even more basic was the fact that the Mennonites, like the Dunkers, did not regard a personal, heartfelt experience of the new birth as normative for the beginning of the Christian life, at least at this time in Lancaster County, Pennsylvania.[59]

By contrast the River Brethren were convinced that true Christian conversion begins with a conviction of sin, repentance, surrender, faith, and obedience, as did the Pietists and Methodists.

The movement arose because of a spiritual revival among German-speaking residents of Lancaster County. It was reported that the German reformed minister, Philip Otterbein, refused to baptize them (by trine immersion) because they had been baptized before. So like the Brethren in Germany, they decided to baptize themselves. When and where did this occur? The data is scanty. It was probably after the War of Independence and nearly a century after the Brethren movement in German Palatinate under the leadership of Hochmann and Mack.

Several factors contributed to the emergence of the River Brethren. These include the German language, Anabaptist (Mennonite) background, plus Pietist-led evangelism, awakening, and conversion. Like the early Methodists, those who experienced the new birth often felt led to "press on to perfection," but were unclear as to what or how.[60]

The River Brethren's basic convictions may thus be summarized:
They looked to Jesus as Savior and also Lord of all facets of life. Also, like the Mennonites, they believed the New Testament to be more basic than the Old Testament for Christians. They thought of themselves as cross-bearing disciples of Jesus, hence

aliens in a hostile world. They also viewed the Church as a covenant-keeping community united to Christ and to each other.[61]

Their view of the Church, as a community under the Lordship of Christ, and guided by the New Testament, led to a distinctive lifestyle and mode of worship. In addition to baptism (by three-fold immersion), they observed communion in the evening service, including foot-washing, partaking of bread and wine while standing, and addressing one another as "beloved brother" or "beloved sister."

Despite their birth in a period of revivalism they did not stress evangelism; they despaired of trying to convert or reform society. Instead they expected the conflict with the world to continue until the Lord's return. Their task was to watch, wait, pray and obey.

As brethren bound together in covenant, they were obligated to pray for each other, to be subject to discipline, and to dismiss the rebellious. Like Anabaptists, they refused to bear arms. Like other Brethren groups, they did not believe in a paid ministry. They insisted on plainness of attire and life.

Paradoxically, they were committed to Pietist conversion, but rejected revivalism as a means of conversion.[62] Perhaps their view of the world as hostile (like Anabaptists) inhibited a commitment to evangelize the world, despite their own origins, and despite their commitment in theory to the Great Commission (Matthew 28:19-20). They stressed non-conformity more than mission. The "Rules of Government" stated:

Separation should . . . be manifested by our holy lives, and this will lead us to put away . . . everything that is sinful . . . be wholly sanctified . . . our apparel should be sanctified and "made mete [sic] for the Master's use, as well as what we eat and drink."[63]

Since holy living was their goal, separation from the world, modesty in dress, and abstinence from tobacco and alcohol were called for. It is significant that at this time (1880) the Temperance Movement and the Holiness Movement were both gaining in influence. With these Brethren pride was a major problem. To cope with it, plain attire in both men and women tended to be standardized. Deviations from a commitment to simplicity were more easily detected than a lack of inner devotion. "Externals" threatened to take priority over inner piety and Christ-likeness.

Luxury was forbidden and even comfort and convenience were often suspect. When Bishop Lukenback arrived to conduct a love feast, the leaders hesitated to welcome him because he arrived in a carriage which was equipped with the luxury of springs![64]

Separation from the world called for a renunciation of all forms of public amusements and most forms of recreation. Membership in secret societies was forbidden (because of the secretive factor). In ordinances trine immersion, using the forward motion, was the only mode accepted. Attempts were made to find Scriptural basis for this distinctive; doubtless the Dunker precedent, rather than Scripture, was the major factor in this decision. General Conference decided that a candidate for church membership, who had been immersed backward, had to be re-baptized by forward-action trine immersion.[65]

In 1912, the General Conference decided that the single mode of foot-washing was to be used and the double mode discontinued. Prayer veiling for women was made mandatory following St. Paul (I Cor. 10:1-11, because was "in reverence to the man as a token of subjection (10:3, 7-9) and a sign of authority."[66] Apparently they failed to notice Paul's statements about equality and mutual submission (i Cor. 10:11-12; Eph. 5:21). Women were permitted to "prophesy" (testify) in public meetings, but not to teach or to preach. These rules illustrate how determined they were to follow not only the spirit, but also the letter of the New Testament.

In houses for public worship men and women were seated separately and they used separate doors for entrance and exit (as I noticed in 1961). Instrumental music was forbidden in public services. One member, a deacon, was criticized for having a parlor organ in his home. Church choirs were forbidden in order to foster congregational singing. Worship in meeting houses lasted four hours, beginning with a one hour "experience meeting." How many in today's congregations have an "experience" to share?

Formal education beyond the elemental level was feared and discouraged. Novels and drama were forbidden as worse than useless. These Brethren churches multiplied slowly. By 1880 the membership was only about two thousand; today it stands at about eight thousand. They were more concerned with purity than with church growth.

Three schisms rent the Brotherhood during the first century of their existence. The most serious resulted when the congregation near Middletown, Pennsylvania, led by Bishop Brinser, erected a simple meeting house without the consent of the Brethren. Brinser was excommunicated in 1855. They rejected congregations took the name United Zion's Children. A century later the General Conference expressed regret for this action, and in the 1967 General Conference action asked for forgiveness and pardon.

Expansion occurred during the three decades 1880 to 1910 with membership doubling to about four thousand. Geographical expansion occurred as a result of missions and evangelism, especially in the American mid-west. Increasingly, the River Brethren came to grips with a changing environment and sought to respond selectively, endeavoring not to change the "essentials."

1. Doctrinal Issues: Sanctification

Along with many changes in Brethren perspectives with reference to their past and present came a major issue on the subject of doctrine. The early Brethren stressed the new birth as the indispensable mode of entrance into the Christian life. Here they were following the tradition of Pietism rather than that of Anabaptism. They followed Anabaptists in stress on discipleship and growth <u>into</u> grace as well as growth <u>in</u> grace. The acceptance of Sunday Schools, revival meetings, and temperance societies reflected their openness to the need for change in certain areas.

The attitude of openness to other evangelical groups facilitated openness of exponents of "Christian perfection." The Wesleyan doctrine of entire sanctification came in for serious discussion, due to the influence of the American Holiness Movement, the Hepzibah Faith Association, the Free Methodists, and the Salvation Army.[67]

Their hymnal of 1884 included fifty of Charles Wesley's hymns, many of which deal with sanctification. *The Evangelical Visitor* in 1887 published John Wesley's definition of Christian Perfection. Previously the Brethren thought of sanctification as growth subsequent to regeneration, as did most other Protestants. Gradually they came to the conclusion that entire sanctification is a second work of grace subsequent to and distinct from regeneration. Several reasons explain this change:

1. They were in the Pietist tradition which valued inner spiritual life.

2. To these ernest believers who sought to be more Christ-like, the possibility of being delivered from sinful inclinations (as distinct from sinful actions) made perfection (completion) in love (i John 4:12) very appealing.

3. The Brethren saw among the holiness advocates the same separation from the world and simple life-style that they prized so highly.

4. Holiness Associations were multiplying and were calling believers in all denominations to seek holiness of heart and life..

This subject was debated for the first time at the General Conference of 1886. The following year a definitive statement entitled "Sanctification" was adopted and published. After quoting many Bible verses the text reads, "Whereas justification delivers from the *guilt* of sin, sanctification implies:

a. a setting aside apart for God's service,

b. a cleansing from the *pollution* of sin, and

c. deliverance from the power of sin."[68]

Here one notes (1) entire consecration (as distinct from surrender -- the sinner surrenders, the believer consecrates), (2) *cleansing* from sin's pollution (as distinct from *pardon* for sinful *acts*, and (3) deliverance from indwelling sin. This implies a work of grace distinct from pardon. The statement notes the continuance of "inbred sin" in the life of the regenerate and cites biblical promises of full deliverance (e.g., 2 Cor. 7:1; Col. 1:22; 1 Thess. 5:23; 1 John 1:7).

Our part is confession, consecration, and trust; God's part is cleansing and infilling with the Holy Spirit (Acts 4:31). The effects are seen in the permeation of the entire person with the love of God. The Brethren tended to stress spiritual growth more than the instantaneous emphasis in Wesley and in those of the Holiness Movement. Much discussion ensued with some favoring and some opposing what was regarded as a doctrinal innovation. In the Kansas area some over-zealous exponents did a disservice to the cause, but, in spite of hesitation, the view that was in line with Wesleyan interpretation was adopted. Thus Pietism's concern with inner sanctity prevailed over the Lutheran, Reformed, and Anabaptist emphases.

As the discussion of entire sanctification continued the General Conference (which convened at Air Hill, Pennsylvania on May 17-20, 1910) explained that sanctification "destroys all carnality ... and the inclination to sin ... It gives a sense of inward cleanness ... [and] prepares us for the baptism of the Spirit which makes us perfect in love.[69] In this statement the positive aspect is added to the cleansing. The positive note is the condition for the baptism in the Holy Spirit. The latter was stressed by John Fletcher and Asa Mahan of Oberlin College. It was continued in the Holiness Movement in North America. The culmination was seen as divine love made perfect or complete, an emphasis which was favored by John Wesley and was prominent in the First Epistle of John.

By 1910, the Brethren in Christ had officially embraced the doctrine of entire sanctification as a second work of grace, similar to that of the National Holiness Association and other holiness churches. However, they exchanged the term "second work of grace" for "grace of cleansing completed," a change which has merit.[70]

Two decades of debate ensued on the issue of a definition for this particular work of grace. Some objected to the term "eradication," others objected to the expression "saved but not sanctified." (According to Romans 1:4 and I Corinthians 1:2, all Christians are "sanctified" with reference to their new relationship to Christ and to the "world." Some assumed that the Holy Spirit was not given at regeneration. Thus appeared two factors which hindered a clear definition of the subject: the heritage of the past and unscriptural accretions which justifiably brought objections.

In 1919 the change of editors of the *Visitor* resulted in the official publication becoming a strong advocate of the holiness position. Debates continued during attempts of the General Conference to formulate an acceptable definition. Balancing between crisis and process by 1936-1937, the view prevailed that entire sanctification is instantaneous and is subject to regeneration.[71]

Meanwhile Bible Conferences, sponsored by the Brethren in Christ gradually became holiness camp meetings, the most noted of which was at Roxbury, Pennsylvania, where scenes like those at Pentecost occurred. Inspired by the success of the venture at Roxbury, Brethren in Christ camp meetings for the promotion of scriptural holiness appeared nationwide between 1941 and 1963. Seekers after this blessing were thus counseled:

> *When the seeker testified to freedom from past sins, the next step was to "die out," which meant surrender wholly and unreservedly to God for*

all time. The final step was the exercise of faith for the "infilling" or "baptism" with the Holy Spirit.[72]

This is essentially the same as the advice given to seekers in such churches as the Wesleyan, Free Methodist, and Church of the Nazarene, who claim to be in the tradition of the Wesleys.

The debate over the "second work of grace" went on for some fifty years (1890-1940), ending with endorsement of the Wesleyan position. This was the most prominent of the doctrinal change in the history of the Brotherhood. Probably no denomination has struggled with this doctrine and experienced as much as have these Brethren -- not even the Methodists. The Wesleyan position triumphed over the Reformed view, because it seemed based on Scripture and confirmed in the experience of the believers.

The Brethren in Christ maintain their Anabaptist heritage in such matters as nonviolence, baptism of believers only, foot washing, and simplicity. Of all movements who claim affinity with the primitive church these Brethren seem best to have acquired the synthesis of Pietism and Anabaptism; of piety and discipleship.

2. Other Changes

In the history of the Brethren in Christ the period of greatest change occurred during 1870-1910. This period witnessed a shift from emphasis on fellowship in the church to "the individual aspects of the faith."[73]

During this period of transition six major changes occurred: (1) adoption of Sunday Schools, (2) acceptance of revivalism, (3) publication of church periodicals, (4) promotion of missions, (5) addition of Wesleyan holiness, and (6) institution of church schools for higher education. Thus, before 1870 the Anabaptist influence (the church confronting the world) was dominant; after 1870 the trend favored Pietism (the individual in pursuit of godliness).

After 1870 there was a growing acceptance of Sunday Schools and "protracted meetings" for revival. They now believed *children* could and should be saved. The acceptance of entire sanctification helped to clarify their theology of justification -- regeneration.[74]

The change from legalistic "externals" to an emphasis on grace and faith continues to the present. The period of 1910 to 1950 has been termed "the period of adjustment."[75] This period witnessed a plateau of growth. Foreign missions experienced a healthy boost, but the "home base" was near stagnation. The crisis of self-identity and self-justification was widely felt.

The Brethren decided to become more ecumenical at the risk of losing some distinctive "roots." Previously ecumenical moves had been inhibited by Anabaptist-like concerns: "non-resistance," non-conformity in dress, prayer veiling, and foot washing.[76] During the two World Wars Brethren in Christ in Canada and in the United States found common cause with other peace churches. Especially significant was their affirmation with the Mennonite Central Committee.

In Wittlinger's definitive *Quest for Piety and Obedience* fifty pages are devoted to the debate on holiness, and forty-six on non-resistance -- a clue not only to the importance of these essentials among the Brethren in Christ, but also to the near balance between Anabaptist and Pietist influence.

After 1950 a marked growth rate is notable. A major catalyst in mid-century for change among the Brethren in Christ was the influence of the Christian Holiness Association and the National Association of Evangelicals. Brethren who attended such meetings, often as participants, realized that they could learn much from such aggressive and enthusiastic evangelicals.

At the General Conference of 1950 John H. Hostetter's sermon, "The Holy Ghost and Us" (cf. Acts 15:28) called for a change in emphasis from "unproductive legalism" to "aggressive spiritual concern and evangelism." This sermon sounded a bold call for "spiritual revolution."[77] Among the changes that ensued were (1) the acceptance of full-time salaried pastors, (2) setting up of pastoral stationing committees, (3) greater stress given to spiritual renewal and evangelism, (4) easing of restrictions in dress code, (5) tolerance of wedding rings, (6) acceptance of life insurance, (7) addition of musical instruments in worship services, (8) associate membership allowed for divorcees, (9) curtailed requirement for rebaptism and prayer veiling, (10) a shift in architecture from plain meeting houses to "typical Protestant church edifices" with focus of pulpit and altar rail along with (11) the change from a congregational to a modified episcopal polity.[78]

Among the Brethren in Christ, as in patriarchal societies, the role of women was that of a "helpmeet" to the men. However, occasionally women assumed leading roles when the men were absent. In the early mission to Africa eighty percent of the pioneer missionaries were women. In 1905 and again in 1919 the Conference ruled that "sisters shall not preach in public meeting."[79] By 1976 only five women had been officially recognized as deaconesses.

In 1964, for the first time, a woman was elected as a delegate to General Conference. Until 1970 only eight women had been delegates to General Conference; no officials in the womens' missionary society and auxiliary had a vote in Conference.

St. Paul's directives to the churches he had established regarding women in leadership roles certainly shows its influence. This, in turn, reflects the strict literalism with which they interpreted and applied the Scripture and their fear of departure into the ways of the world. Their literalism and fear of "worldliness" kept them from noting and putting into practice the role of women leaders in both Old and New Testaments (Miriam, Deborah, and Priscilla, to mention a few). Nor did they recognize the "new Covenant" in Acts 2:17-18 in which *both* men and women "shall prophesy."

Since 1970 the situation has improved: the long period of male domination of the structures and life of the Brethren in Christ is gradually coming to an end. Their literalism had led them to strict adherence to the *specifics* of the New Testament ("women keep silence" -- I Cor. 14:34) with less emphasis on the *implications* of Scripture such as women will "prophesy" (Acts 2:8; Rom. 16:1,3). It was the recurring problem of all who apply Bible teachings: what was temporal, what was peripheral and influenced by local conditions (such as foot washing when people traveled with sandals), and what were the distinct central, universal principles of servanthood. The early church had to face many "new wineskins" (e.g. circumcision). They decided the issue on the basis of *events* (God's action in giving the Holy Spirit to non-Jews (Acts 10), *conference* (in Jerusalem), and *Scripture* (Acts 15).

Perhaps no contemporary church denomination better illustrates a covenant-commitment to the New Testament as they understood it, while at the same time the maintenance of a conservative, selective response to "new light" and the adjustment to cultural changes in the environment. It demonstrates also the value of an ecumenical attitude toward other believers and a willingness to learn. Probably no church better combines the Anabaptism emphasis on discipleship and the Pietist concern with the Spirit-filled life.

E. APPRAISAL

The Brethren are commendable in that they seek a church closer to the New Testament as they understand it. This involves, among other things, (1) a regenerate membership, (2) separation from sin, and from "the world," (3) a personal and corporate self-discipline, with penalties for rebels, (4) the imitation of Christ in all things, at all times, including non-violence and foot washing, (5) simplicity in life-styles, (6) participation of the laity in church life, including decisions, and (7) evangelism at home and abroad.

This has often been achieved at a high price (as Jesus explained to his disciples): persecution, legalism, slow growth, reluctance to change, and schisms. The Brethren seem especially prone to factionalism. Because of their earnestness they find tolerance difficult. Sometimes a tendency to over-literalize the Scripture leads to a stress of "externals," to the loss of essentials (like the ancient Pharisees). The difficulty of discerning between essentials and non-essentials is experienced by all earnest seekers after truth. Often a fear of higher education inhibited wholesome growth.

What lessons can be learned? (1) the lesson of *Humility* (Who can say, "I am holier than thou"), (2) the difficulty of distinguishing truth from error in doctrine, (3) the need of remaining biblical while at the same time being relevant and effective, and (4) the importance of determining when to follow the literal teaching of Scripture and when to follow the principle -- the problem elucidated by Jesus and experienced by his disciples then and now, (5) the importance of an ecumenical attitude toward other believers, learning and sharing in worthwhile tasks. We can learn much from each of the groups who define the Christian church as believers united by Christ.

Chapter III Endnotes

1. *Johann Walch, Religious-Streitigkeiten der evangelisch-Lutherischen Kirchen* (insubordination) I, 548, cited in D. F. Durnbaugh, "Brethren Beginnings," (Ph. D. Thesis, U. PA, 1960), p . 2 .
2. E. Clifford Nelson, "Pietism," *Encyclopedia Britannica* (15th Edition), (Chicago: 1974), XIV, p. 456.
3. F. Durnbaugh, *European Origins of the Brethren*, (Elgin, IL: Brethren Press, 1958), p. 36.
4. Durnbaugh, *European Origins*, p. 41.
5. Albert Ronk, *History of the Brethren Church*, (Ashland: Ohio Brethren Publishing Co., 1968), p. 29.
6. H. L. Gillin, *The Dunkers, a Sociological Interpretation*, (New York: AMMS Press, 1974), p. 37.
7. M. G. Brambaugh, *A History of the German Baptist Brethren*, (Mt. Morris, IL, 1899), p. 87.
8. Homer S. Kent, Sr., *250 Years Conquering Frontiers*, (Winona L a k e , I N : Missionary Herald, 1958), p. 25.
9. H. R. Holsinger, *History of the Tunkers and the Brethren Church*, (Oakland, CA, 1901), pp. 53-55.
10. Durnbaugh, *European Origins*, pp. 338-339.
11. Kent, *Frontiers*, p. 26.
12. Ronk, p. 37.
13. Ronk, p. 59.
14. Durnbaugh, "The Brethren in Early American Church Life" in F. S. Stoeffler, ed., *Continental Pietism and American Christianity*, (Grand Rapids: Eerdmans, 1976), p. 227.
15. W. W. Sweet, *Religion in Colonial America*, (New York: Scribners, 1943), pp. 279-311.

16. Durnbaugh, "Brethren," in Stoeffler, p. 231.
17. Brambaugh, *German Baptist Brethren*, pp. 155-156.
18. Durnbaugh, *Brethren in Colonial America*, (Elgin, IL: Brethren Press, 1967), p. 61.
19. Brambaugh, p. 198.
20. Durnbaugh, *Brethren in Colonial America*, p. 269.
21. Spangenberg, Nov. 8, 1731 (cited in Durnburgh, *Brethren in Colonial America*, p. 275). Brambaugh, however, (in 1899) wrote that Naas was elder at Amwell "from its inception until his death." p. 124.
22. Durnbaugh, *Brethren in America*, p. 278.
23. Durnbaugh, *Brethren in America*, pp. 280-281.
24. Durnbaugh, "Brethren" in Stoeffler, pp. 251-259.
25. Holsinger, p. 215.
26. Holsinger, pp. 220-221.
27. Brambaugh, pp. 543-546.
28. Durnbaugh, *Brethren in America*, pp. 321-339.
29. Brambaugh, pp. 478-491.
30. Ronk, p. 70.
31. Ronk, pp. 72-73.
32. Brambaugh, p. 551.
33. Ronk, p. 79.
34. Kent, p. 78.
35. Cited in Ronk, p. 92.
36. Ronk, p. 104.
37. Ronk, pp. 127-128.
38. Ronk, PP. 158-160.
39. Ronk p. 141.
40. Kent. p. 115.
41. Kent, pp. 127-128.
42. Ronk, p. 416.
43. Ronk, p. 423.
44. Kent, p. 150.

45. Kent, p. 156.
46. Kent, pp. 199-202.
47. Ronk, p. 447.
48. Durnbaugh, *The Believers Church*, (Macmillan: 1908), p. 130.
49. Durnbaugh, "Recent History," in *The Church of the Brethren, Past and Present*, (Elgin: Bethany Press, 1971), p. 31.
50. Durnbaugh, *The Church of the Brethren, Past and Present*, pp. 36-37.
51. R. E. Sappinton, "Social Involvement, in Durnbaugh, ed., Brethren, Past and Present, p. 107, *et passim*.
52. W. E. Sweet, p. 346.
53. Sweet, p. 347.
54. Durnbaugh, *Believers Church*, p. 162.
55. E. S. English, "Introduction," *New Scofield Bible*, (1967), p. vii.
56. C. O. Wittlinger, *Quest for Piety and Obedience*, (Nappanee, Indiana: 1978), p. 20.
57. Wittlinger, *Quest*, p. 20.
58. Wittlinger, p. 21.
59. Wittlinger, p. 23.
60. Wittlinger, pp. 2-12.
61. Wittlinger, "The Faith of the Founders," (Unpublished essay furnished by its author), pp. 4-5.
62. Wittlinger, "Founders," p. 41.
63. Wittlinger, *Quest*, p. 46.
64. Wittlinger, *Quest*, p. 51.
65. *Church Government*, 1887, p. 7 (cited in Wittlinger), *Quest*, pp. 62-63.
66. Wittlinger, *Quest*, p. 69.
67. Wittlinger, *Quest*, p. 227.
68. Origen, *Confession of Faith*: General Council, Brethren in Christ, (Abilene, Kansas: 1887), p. 57.
69. *Minutes of the General Conference*, (1910), p. 17.
70. *Minutes*, (1910), p. 27.
71. Wittlinger, *Quest*, p. 337.

72. Wittlinger, *Quest*, p. 337.
73. Martin Schrag, "The Brethren in Christ Concept of the Church in Transition," M. A. R., (1978), p. 312.
74. Schrag, pp. 314-315.
75. Wittlinger, *Quest*, p. 475.
76. Wittlinger, *Quest*, p. 477.
77. Wittlinger, *Quest*, pp. 451, 482.
78. Wittlinger, *Quest*, p. 484.
79. Wittlinger, *Quest*, p. 523.

Chapter IV
THE PURITANS

"They did not . . . expend time and money in church architecture, for the more these were absent, reasoned the Puritan, the more the Holy Spirit be present to make his abode in the true temple of the heart."

S. L. Bailey, *Historical Sketches of Andover*, 1880.

Those who seek a church similar to the church of the New Testament must consider the movement in England to go beyond Reformation of the existing Church to the Restoration of the New Testament pattern, to a church independent of the government. The major exponents of the free church movement in Britain were the Puritans. "Puritan" was an epithet of derision which emerged in 1559 and was applied to those in England, during the seventeenth century, who wanted the Reformation to go further than the church of England was willing to go. Puritanism was analogous with Anabaptism on the Continent. When Anabaptism crossed the English Channel, it found points of similarity with Puritanism. However the connection has yet to be clarified.[1] Anabaptists were viewed by most English with horror.

Puritanism was the most influential reform movement in England and Scotland during the sixteenth and seventeenth centuries. "Probably no other religious movement has left so deep an impression on the history of England is the judgment of some historians."[2] Their convictions were similar to those of John Wycliffe and the Lollards of the Medieval Period. They were also influenced by Zwinglians from Zurich, and later, by Calvinists from Geneva.[3]

An anticipation of Puritanism may be recognized, in the fourteenth century, in Chaucer's description of the country parson:

> *first he wrought and afterwards he taught . . . Christ's own lore, and His apostles' twelve He taught, but first he followed it himself.*[4]

Chaucer could discern among his travellers the difference between the true Christian and the nominal Christian -- between the possessor and the professor. In historical perspective Pietism, Anabaptism, and Puritanism are branches of the same stem. That stem is the Bible as made relevant by the Holy Spirit. The variations are due to such factors as time, place, and human leadership.

A. IN ENGLAND

To distinguish the term from kindred movements "Puritanism" usually refers to the religious-political movement in English history from the beginning of the reign of Elizabeth I (1558- 1603):

> *those who wanted **reform from within** the Church as contrasted with the Separatists on the one hand, and those who were satisfied with the established Discipline on the other.*[5]

The basic pattern set before the Marian exile (1553-1558), by Tyndale, Hooper, and others in Tudor England, was the *Covenant theology*. As defined by Tyndale, God's covenant calls for responsiveness, obedience, and a priesthood of all believers.[6] Thus Puritanism in England began with Tyndale before the term "Puritan" was coined.

William Tyndale (1492-1536), in defiance of civil law, went to Germany to promote the Reformation by making the Bible available to English readers. He was supported by laymen (London merchants) and opposed by the clergy. On the basis of the law against "heretics," the Catholics succeeded in having Tyndale executed while in prison. His "heretical" ideas came from the New Testament and from his Oxford teachers, Erasmus and John Colet.[7]

The Reformation began in England under Henry VIII when the English Church separated from Rome (1547). When Edward VI was king (1549-53) Protestantism flourished. He was hailed by many as England's "Josiah" who would lead the Reformation as Josiah led Judah's reformation (2 Kings 22:1--23:25). The English reforms affected doctrine, worship, and discipline, the "external marks of the true church."[8]

After the Marian exodus (1557) and the beginning of Elizabeth's reign (1558-1603), exiles from Zurich and Geneva demanded more reforms. They wanted to "purify" the Church from the remnants of "popery," hence the name "Puritan" was given by their critics. The popularity of John Foxe's *Book of Martyrs* and the Geneva *Bible* accelerated Protestantism. Leaders of these exiles, Humphrey and Sampson, both of Oxford, denounced the use of clerical vestments. Elizabeth opposed this change. In

1566 Archbishop Parker ordered the use of clerical vestments and forbade controversial sermons. Many Puritan ministers, therefore, were forced to leave their pulpits.

The first leader of the explicit Puritan movement was Thomas Cartwright (1535-1603), the last was Richard Baxter (1615-1691). In England the Puritan movement terminated with William and Mary (1689),

Thomas Cartwright, Lady Margaret Professor of Divinity, was expelled from Cambridge University in 1570. Cartwright preached against the priesthood of the Anglican Church. He believed that the rule of the church by elders was more in keeping with New Testament. He denounced the use of the vestments as symbolic of Roman Catholicism. But he criticized those who separated from the Church of England, specifically the Brownists or Independents. By his sermons and writings he gave system and prestige to the Presbyterian form of church government. Cartwright published his *Book of Discipline* which was so influential that Richard Hooker sought to refute it by his *Laws of Ecclesiastical Polity*. Yet Cartwright's book decisively influenced the Westminister Assembly of 1645 and the Long Parliament. Under Cartwright's theses, pastors would have the decisive influence with no dissent tolerated. This failed in England, but found expression in New England in 1630.

1. Growth

Under Queen Elizabeth the Puritans were restricted, but not banished. They were able to preach and publish, but unable to effect changes in the relation of Church and State. Elizabeth adroitly managed to "divide and conquer." She insisted that she was head of the Church. The result was a *new nationalism* in which the throne was supreme and religious pluralism tolerated. This led to a struggle which culminated in the *temporary* triumph of Presbyterian Puritans in the Long Parliament and Cromwell's triumph over the Throne. By the combination of restriction and tolerance the early Puritans became divided and ineffectual as a political factor. Yet they were able to influence the populace by sermons and publications, thus paving the way later for the triumph of Parliament and the execution of Charles I in 1649.

The majority of Puritans wanted the Cartwright *Book of Discipline* to be the pattern for England's churches. A minority of Puritans insisted that church membership be limited to regenerated believers. Later these became Independents or Congregationalists;

they became the founders of the Massachusetts Bay Colony. The more radical Puritans became Brownists or Barrowists and contributed to the Pilgrims who landed at Plymouth after migrating from Holland. All of the Puritans preached and published Bible expositions, but Bible exposition failed to unite them politically.

Cambridge University was the educational center for Puritanism. Puritan preachers, educated at Cambridge, were revivalists and had greater influence than is generally recognized.[9] Oxford, by contrast, was more conservative, less evangelical. The humanist group at Oxford "became the nucleus of the later Anglican Church."[10]

Puritans prepared the way for Milton's *Paradise Lost*, Bunyan's *Pilgrim's Progress*, and Robert Louis Stevenson's *Robinson Crusoe*. The Anglican preachers, meanwhile, steered the middle course between Catholicism and Calvinistic Puritanism, aided by Arminian and Covenant doctrines. It is said that the Anglicans preached the "wisdom of words" while Puritans preached the "Word of wisdom."[11]

The major human influence in the Puritan movement was John Calvin and the theocracy in Geneva.

> "Calvin could state the most contradictory doctrines of divine predestination and human responsibility with such persuasiveness as to make them seem harmonious and palatable to all but the most recalcitrant."[12]

Many Puritans would admit, "We are all Calvinists when we pray, but are all Arminians when we preach."[13]

Puritan writings were very numerous and especially influential during the first half of the seventeenth century, yet they had less *lasting* influence than contemporary writings by Anglican clergymen such as Thomas Hooker's *Ecclesiastical Polity*.

Richard Greenham was a "patriarch" among Puritan preachers and writers. All his pupils, including Separatist Robert Browne (ca. 1550-1633) and Henry Smith, preached about sin and salvation. Most Calvinist preachers from Cambridge were revivalists.[14] Some published writings which actually were diaries of the authors' spiritual struggles and triumphs. One might very well say that "[t]he diary was the Puritan confessional."[15]

In spite of the decision of James I (1566-1625) at the Hampton Court Conference (1604) to "harry the Puritans out of the land," they continued to increase in influence at home and abroad. James I brought to the throne his conviction of the divine right of kings. This was based on the widely accepted platonic doctrine of a hierarchy in which God delegated authority through the king, bishops, legislators, sheriffs, down to the lowest strata of society. When authority was challenged by groups such as the Puritans, tolerance was the more difficult.[16]

The people, however, were thirsty for the Word of God and would travel for miles to hear Puritan preachers and lecturers, often remaining to discuss their teachings. Preachers often were one of the sources of current news.[17] The preachers urged hearers to be more disciplined in their use of time, to be more industrious like the energetic and prosperous Dutch. Their exhortations were directed to those who worked only enough to live and loafed when food was plentiful.

Governor Winthrop of the Massachusetts Bay Colony agreed with the Independents at Plymouth that the Church of England was "unscriptural, arbitrary, and corrupt."[18]

The Boston Bay Colony was not a democracy; it was an *oligarchy*, or rule by the *elders*. John Cotton feared democracy. Said he,

> *I do not conceive that God did ordain "democracy" as a fit government either for church or commonwealth; as for monarchy and aristocracy they are both of them clearly approved and directed in Scripture.*[19]

John Wesley would have endorsed this statement; he once declared, ". . . we Methodists are not Republicans."[20]

The doctrine of Predestination was central in Puritan theology. Preachers were influenced by Calvin, Augustine, and Paul's letter to the Romans. William Perkins advised reading Romans first, then John's Gospel as the key to Christian theology. Many Puritans were introspective, wondering if they were among the elect. Election, calling, justification, sanctification, and glorification were the concern of earnest believers for several generations. The Pauline doctrine of experience aroused,

> *the most active widespread interest in the inner experience of every individual human being and an almost equally active and widespread activity in giving expression to that interest.*[21]

Spiritual health was very important. Typical was John Beadle's *Journal or Diary of a Thankful Christian* published in 1656. Also typical is the *Diary of Michael Wigglesworth* (1653-1657). He taught at Harvard and was pastor at Malden. He wrote,

> *Pride and vain thoughts again prevail over me to the grief of my God. Cleanse me, O Lord, when shall it once be? . . . Again, I had opportunity . . . to discourse with one of my pupils much of the things of God . . . the Lord helping me . . . with much affection . . . what a blessed thing it is to serve and seek the Lord . . . Yesterday morning the Lord gave me a sweet meditation concerning him.*[22]

Earnest Puritans, like earnest Methodists a century later, (and earnest Free Methodists two centuries later who published *The Earnest Christian*), were quite introspective; their over-riding concern was victory over sin and the assurance of divine favor. Likewise while in Georgia (1736), Charles Wesley wrote, "Faint and weary with the day's fatigue, I found my want of true holiness, and begged God to give me comfort from his word."[23]

In 1692 the President of Harvard, Increase Mather, lamented the influence of Arminianism, "That subversive and dangerous promise of divine grace to all good men who sought the Lord."[24]

To the disgust of the Puritans John Leverett, a liberal layman, became President of Harvard in 1707. However in his diary President Leverett deplored the fact that some students were given to "profane swearing, card playing, and riotous actions."[25]

Yet the Puritan influence prevailed among some. Before the Holy Club at Oxford was formed, Joseph Sewall at Harvard College formed for the cultivation of piety "[t]he first college club on record for social prayer."[26]

In Sewall's diary, which he started on April 27, 1707, he moaned over spiritual shortcomings . . . the same ideal of a constant unwearying obedience to God's will, the same yearning to attain a Christ-like perfection in thought, word and deed. Yet before his graduation he had experienced "a comfortably holy state, now God hath heard my prayers . . . O for a thankful heart."[27]

Puritans separated the world of nature from the world of grace.

> *Rebirth is a vivid personal experience in which the individual soul encounters the wrath and redemptive love of God . . . The resulting life-style is one of self- discipline governed by the Scriptures.*[28]

Apparently religious zeal among New England Congregationalists declined thereafter. In 1800 Timothy Dwight, President of Yale College, characterized the typical

"Smooth Divine" as one in whom "that strange new birth, that Methodistic grace, nor in his heart or sermons found a place."[29]

While the English establishment adopted Arminianism, the Puritans chose Calvinism and for three generations sought in vain to finish reformation within the Church of England.[30] They succeeded only in New England. But there the Puritans "were very far from approving in principle the tolerance by which they had profited in England."[31]

2. The Congregationalists ("Separtists")

The more radical wing of Puritanism led by Robert Browne (1550-1633) was among the first to see consciously and affirm "the idea of the church as essentially a redeemed people."[32] As a student at Cambridge (1572-1575), Browne experienced the new birth and sought a church home. Not content with the Anglican or Puritan fellowship, he became convinced that the true church consisted of a personal fellowship of believers. In his words, "The Kingdom of Heaven was not to begin by whole parishes but rather by the worthies were they never so few."[33] In other words a small congregation of real Christians was better than a large one of the less committed.

Their first congregation was at Norwich, England (1581). Although they stressed discipline, they were seen as lawless by other church members, both Anglicans and Puritans. In the Savoy Declaration of 1668 they defined the true church as a *congregation of true believers* -- hence the name Congregationalists. However, the Congregationalists ignored the New Testament pattern of deacons and bishops (overseers), thus reducing the advantage of cooperation among congregations for common goals.

The Queen, the Anglicans, and the Puritans found this anarchical! Henry Barrow, in his *Briefe Discoverie of the False Church*, argued that the established Congregationalist Church was wholly apostate. Finding themselves oppressed on all sides, many fled to Holland, a country which offered a welcome haven to fugitives. Their pastor, John Robinson,

> *charged them before God and His blessed Angels to follow him no further than he followed Christ . . . for he was very confident the Lord had yet more truth and light to break forth out of his holy word.*[34]

Commendably their ideal was Christ in the midst. They sought both to adhere to the faith and also to be prepared to welcome "new light."

> *Congregational Churches are still haunted by the ghost of their essential idea, Christ in the midst. So it was that when Christ came back in the power of His spirit through the preaching of Whitefield and Wesley the Independent Churches were among the first to recognize the fact and give Him welcome.*[35]

B. IN NEW ENGLAND

In New England the Congregationalists were few in number compared with the those Puritans who came in great numbers a decade later. But they knew what kind of a church they wanted.

> *Their worship service was patterned after that of the first century; the reading of the Scriptures, prayers, and words of admonition and instruction. They considered themselves entirely free of all man-made regulations and bound only by the teachings of the New Testament.*[36]

By contrast Puritans of both the Bay Colony and the Salem Colony were loyal to the Church of England. They simply wanted to "set up a purified Church of England" in a place where they would be free to do so. The Pilgrims at Plymouth were considered radicals. "They were not accepted as worthy representatives of the Puritan movement socially, politically, or financially," and thenceforth was considered an "orphan remnant."[37]

Gradually these separate groups in Massachuschets and Connecticut agreed on a free church, in the Congregational pattern as set forth in the Cambridge Platform of 1648. Each church was independent of government or church control. To allay the fears of Presbyterians in Parliament they affirmed their theological agreement with the Westminister Statement of Faith as a "restatement" of Calvinism. They differed on the lesser issue of polity, preferring Congregationalism to Presbyterianism. In this pattern of independence they set a precedent of freedom from Europe which politicians later incorporated into the Declaration of Independence in 1776.

> *"there grew the great tree of religious and civil liberty," which led to the "task of framing a federal constitution which would reconcile the maintenance of local liberties and state rights with the desperate need for national unity."*[38]

The autonomy of the local congregation won out in New England over the rule of state and bishop as well as over the rule by elders, thus setting a precedent for the Baptists and Christians (Disciples). In so doing, they may have gone further than the churches of the New Testament by excluding the rule of elders.

1. The Half-Way Covenant

In New England, the second and third generation Puritans lacked their grandparents' vivid sense of sin and salvation. The Cambridge Platform of 1648 decided that baptized children of regenerate parents were church members and were expected to make a "public confession of personal regeneration, before admission to Holy communion." Parents insisted that their unregenerate children be church members as well. The Synod of 1662 sought a compromise by declaring children could be *church members*, but could not *take communion*. Soon few church members were communicants.[39]

Unlike the Anabaptists and Baptists, the New England Puritans retained infant baptism for children of regenerated parents. Most baptized infants did not later experience the new birth, therefore could not partake of the Lord's Supper even though they were members of the church. Should those who were made members by baptism, though still unregenerate, be expelled? Should their children be baptized?

> *Had they been willing to abandon infant baptism they might at least have avoided the embarrassment of trying to adjust spiritual growth to physical growth . . . Given both infant baptism and the restriction of church membership to visible saints, it was impossible for the Puritans either to evade the question just posed or to answer them without an elaborate casuistry that bred dissatisfaction and disagreement. If they had succumbed to Arminianism it would have been possible for anyone . . . to join the church simply by affirming his possession of a faith that lay within the reach of human volition.*[40]

Because they held *both* infant baptism *and* conversion, as defined by Perkins and Ames, the Half-Way Covenant seemed necessary.

As Calvinists they believed in a limited atonement. Only those predestined to salvation could be members of the true church, therefore, membership was not a matter of individual choice. For Calvin the church was "the totality of all believers whom God from the beginning has predestined to eternal life."[41] William Perkins agreed with Calvin and declared that the church is "the community of those chosen by god for eternal life and established by faith in Christ."[42]

The inconsistency seen in this view is that God alone determines who is regenerate, yet infants were made church members by baptism. They tried to combine both the state-church concept of infant baptism, inherited from Anglo-Catholics, and Calvin's predestination which limited church membership to the elect. The situation in theocratic New England was made worse by the fact that one had to be regenerate in order to have full citizenship in the Commonwealth. And since only one church was tolerated under state control, one had to leave the colony if he wished to join another church.

By 1631 only church members (the elect) could vote. In 1634 a representative government (of free men) was adopted. In 1637 they disagreed concerning the relation of faith to justification. Vane and Cotton advocated free grace (Arminianism), and were accused by Winthrop and others of Antinomianism.[43]

2. The Covenant Theology

"Covenant Theology," as articulated by Tyndale and amplified later by Puritans, was especially influential in New England. While still at sea the "Pilgrims" (Separatists) had entered into the Mayflower Compact with God and with each other. It had affinities both with the Old Testament (God's covenant with Israel) and with the social contract of John Locke and John Ruskin. According to this the people enter into a covenant with God to obey his laws and are assured thereby of his favor. With Calvin the covenant was the "passive reception" of grace by the individual believer; with the Puritans it was an active faith like that between Abraham and the Lord in Genesis 12, 15, 17, and 22. It differed from the individual covenant in that rewards and punishment are in this life and involve the entire community.

When the Puritans were in power in England the conviction that a righteous and sovereign God was in control of national affairs (Covenant Theology) was very influential. The Parliament gave thanks for military victories and repented with fasting during adversities, as in the Old Testament. In his sermon before the House of Commons on August 16, 1645, Thomas Case said,

> *I want time and memory to list . . . the names of those . . . seemingly impregnable fortifications which God hath brought down . . . and*

> *delivered up into the hands of our armies ... General Thomas Fairfax, like Joshua, with a despised army took in order Edgehill, Newburg, York etc. He smote them and showed no mercy as commanded in Deuteronomy 7:2.*

Exhortation followed his thanksgiving. Case urged Parliament to "follow the reformation thoroughly" He continued:

> *When the Lord your God gives them; you must utterly destroy them; you shall make no covenant with them, and show no mercy to them" for the Lord's sake do execution upon all the professed and implacable enemies of the Lord Jesus . . . Behold Christ commands you saying, Bring them hither and slay them before me ... O draw out your sword to execute judgment against such enemies of Jesus Christ, that others may hear and fear, and do no more so wickedly . . . Let us all, both Parliament and people, remember our covenant: let us often read over our covenant, and live up to our covenant; and act up with our covenant, and reform up our covenant.*[44]

John Whincop disagreed:

> *Have we not trusted in our armies, boasted in the multitude of our host, been confident of our strength, prided ourselves in assurance of victory, never looking to the Lord of Hosts all this while?*[45]

The conviction that God was at work in the affairs of England was also reflected in a sermon preached to the House of Commons "at their late Solemn Humiliation" on July 26, 1643.

> *This our day of visitation is a great day. Never in our time and observation was like it being the very time of Jacob's trouble ... God visits his people to this end that they would humble and afflict their souls before Him.*[46]

The language of the Old Testament is woven into these messages reflecting an intimate knowledge of the Scripture by both preacher and listeners. These Puritans, like the Psalmist, so identified themselves with God's holiness that they had to share God's hatred of sin ("Do I not hate them that hate thee; I count them my enemies" Psalm 139:21, 23). Unlike Jesus, however, they failed to distinguish the sinner from his sin -- hence the sinner must be killed. Conversion seemed not to be an option. Cromwell is said to have loved God more than his wife, yet he exulted over the massacre of his enemies."[47]

The covenant relationship seemed effective in the early years of Plymouth Colony. In July 1622 drought was relieved after a "day of humiliation." In 1637 the General Court called for a fast because of the threat of antinomianism. In 1648 the colony was called again to repentance. Increasingly sins were listed as national calamities -- as occasions for repentance and prayer for deliverance.[48]

In a similar manner Wesley found a theological explanation for natural calamities in his sermon "The Cause of the Earthquakes."[49] The same principle is also at work in what has been called "The Moral Majority," the movement that concerns itself with national as well as personal ethics, seeking to bring religion into politics.

After 1660 attention in New England focused more on national sins than upon natural calamities. Spiritual apathy became their besetting sin.[50] On the positive side,

> *Puritanism represents the perennial need of the harsher view of the human nature as a corrective of the too indulgent . . . This increase of the area of felt evil is not the fault of the Puritan, though it is often charged against him. It is dictated by a sense of life which the Puritan should not be charged with inventing, but rather praised for recognizing.*[51]

To this day the President or the Governor may call either for public prayer or public thanksgiving. A relationship between church and state is often recognized today by actions, if not by statute law.

The Puritan awareness of God's holiness and sovereignty caused them to abhor sin. Their awareness of the importance of truth led them to fear its perversion. Since they believed in God's providence and His continuing involvement in human affairs, they identified their commonwealth with ancient Israel. (This occurred especially in New England.) God's enemies were their enemies. Unlike most Anabaptists, they were influenced at least as much by the Old Testament as by the New Testament.

It is understandable that a persecuted minority of earnest Christians would identify with the ethics of the New Testament Church whose mission was to survive and witness. However, when believers were able to determine the function of a modern state they have more in common with ancient Israel than with secular nations. As Emil Brunner pointed out, the Christian must take his insights from the prophets as they viewed their nation, as well as from the New Testament Apostles as they nurtured groups of believers.

It brings up the question of whether any modern nation can function in the same covenant relationship with the Lord of Hosts. Does God rule among the affairs of nations today as the prophets of Israel believed he did then? Do the same principles of right and wrong, good and evil, continue in today's world? Could the Puritans of New England have permitted freedom of conscience and still have kept the faith?

The "Covenant Theology" is often attributed to the influence of Tyndale on Puritanism. This should not be minimized. But the covenant between God and man permeates the Bible and its influence on the Bible readers should be recognized. It would have exerted its influence without Tyndale, as is seen, among other places, in the promises to Noah and Abraham. It is based upon God's influence on human affairs. Specifically it calls for man's obedience to God; in response, God assures man of protection and warns of punishment if he rebels. The principle is *stated* in Deuteronomy 27-30 (obey and prosper OR rebel and be punished). The principle is *applied* during the history of the Kingdom Period, as reported in Judges through II Chronicles.

The Hebrew prophets set the precedent for understanding God's influence on human affairs. Amos viewed drought and disease as divine chastening which called for repentance (Amos 4:6-12). Joel saw the locust plague as divine chastening which called for repentance (Joel 2:1-23). This was based upon God's covenant with the nation as expressed in Deuteronomy 28-30. Those whom the Lord loves may expect discipline and should welcome it (Pro. 3:11,12; Heb. 12:5-7).

In the new Testament Jesus affirmed that the heavenly Father sent rain on both the just and the unjust, treating the latter better than they deserved. But the Old Testament motif reappeared in Jesus' statement that, if we seek first the kingdom, all necessary things would be added unto us (Matt. 6:33). Too few view the Bible in its totality. Rather, they stress the New Testament at the expense of the Old Testament (most Anabaptists) or vice versa (many Puritans).

Few statesmen struggled with corporate evil more agonizing than did Abraham Lincoln. This agony, as witnessed in his Gettysburg Address and in his second Inaugural Address, reflected the influence of the Bible and the Puritan emphasis on God's judgment and grace upon the nation. The influence of covenant theology (which is the influence of the Bible) continued in such statesmen as President Woodrow Wilson (Presbyterian) and President Dwight Eisenhower (Brethren and Presbyterian).

The author of the "Battle Hymn of the Republic" obviously shared with the Hebrew prophets the conviction that national evil calls for divine judgment unless averted by national repentance and reformation. Puritan influence is reflected in the United States pledge of allegiance: "One nation under God." Jefferson's Latin motto on the dollar bill, "ANNUIT COEPTIS (God has smiled on our undertakings"), is a reminder of Covenant Theology and man's subjection to God's will.[52]

C. PURITAN PERFECTIONISM

English Puritans sought to reform the nation and promote holy living throughout the land. The main emphasis of John Wesley and the early Methodists was precisely that. The Puritans were realistic (like Reinhold Niebuhr) in recognizing man's brutality, misery, and sin. The remedy was sought primarily in moral regeneration of the individual and of society. Conviction of sin and repentance were the conditions of renewal.

> *In its insistence upon . . . a new will which should flood and regenerate the total life of the individual, Puritanism contributed significantly to the history of the human spirit. It is this perfectionism which led the Puritan to place the generality of mankind so low and at the same time to exalt saintliness so high.*[53]

While Puritanism remained frustrated, but fruitful, in England, it flourished in Scotland and for several decades in New England.

Puritanism anticipated much of the doctrine of the Holy Spirit which was prominent among the Quakers, the Methodist movement, and modern Pentecostalism. Most Christians think of faith as an assent to deposit of doctrine rather than trust in God's grace resulting in the witness of the Spirit to adoption as a newborn child of God.

> *The Puritans in the seventeenth century England gave more attention to the doctrine of the Holy Spirit than occurred at any other time in history.*[54]

This is seen primarily in the work of John Owen (1616-1693) and his pioneering research on the Holy Spirit in Christian experience. Richard Baxter recognized the importance of the Holy Spirit in everyday living. The work and person of the Spirit is prominent in the many Puritan diaries.

Within seventeenth century Puritanism, the Presbyterians may be seen as the oldest and most conservative wing, the Quakers as the youngest and most radical.[55] George Fox believed that the Spirit is prior to and basic to the written Word. Quakers were accused of circular reasoning by proving the Spirit by the Scripture and the Scripture by the Spirit. Baxter wisely placed priority on the Spirit's illumination of contemporary witnesses. John Howe agreed, as Wesley did later, that the inner testimony of the Spirit was always consistent with the Spirit's inspiration of the biblical writers.[56]

D. PURITANISM AND METHODISM

To what extent did Puritanism influence early Methodism? Puritan influence on George Whitfield was obvious. Whitefield was a Calvinist in theology. He believed in predestination and did not believe in evangelical perfection. He did not expect to be delivered from all sin in this life. Not surprisingly, his influence in Scotland was much greater than Wesley's.

It is obvious that Wesley disagreed with much in Puritanism. He was opposed to the Calvinism of his day and preferred Arminianism, as did members of the Church of England. In justifying his publication of *The Arminian Magazine*, Wesley asked, "Are there not still some Calvinists left in the land?" He asserted, "There never was more need, in the memory of mankind, of opposing the *Horrible Decree*, than at this day."[57]

Wesley viewed the Church of England quite differently than the Puritans. He believed that the rule by bishops was more scriptural than rule by congregation or by the elders. He was autocratic in administration. Only with the greatest reluctance did he ordain bishops for the Methodists in North America.

Like the majority of Puritans, his aim was to reform the Church from within while resisting the demand of his followers for separation. Like Puritans, he favored the class meetings in house churches; he urged pastoral calling, and social service; he wrote and published constantly. Wesley, like the Puritans, remained frustrated by the opposition of the church leaders. And like them, he refused to be bound by the Establishment, convinced that it was more important to obey God than to obey man. Wesley was glad to acknowledge his indebtedness to those in the Catholic, Episcopal, and pietistic traditions. He praised Richard Baxter as an exemplary pastor and writer. In his *Christian Liberty*, many Puritans were listed including R. Sibbs, T. Goodwin, J. Owen,

S. Rutherford, J. Bunyan, and many others. In this library the Puritan influence predominates.

Wesley endorsed the Puritan "Covenant Theology" in his sermon, "Righteousness of Faith" (1742). In it he contrasts the "Covenant of Works" (with Adam) and the "Covenant of Grace" in the gospel. He followed William Ames and Isaac Ambrose "in maintaining a progressively fuller and clearer revelation of this covenant from Adam through Abraham, Moses, David and the prophets."[58] From the Puritans, Joseph and Richard Allen, Wesley borrowed, used, and recommended the "Covenant Service" which is still in occasional use.

From the seventeenth century there was no reconciliation between the Established Church and the Puritans; this came about to some degree a century later through Methodism. For Samuel Johnson, a Methodist was "one of a new kind of Puritan lately arisen so called from their profession to live by rules and in constant method."[59]

Wesley's parents, Samuel and Susanna, charged from Dissenters to High Church Anglicanism. Samuel Wesley shared with seventeenth century Puritans, a disciplined watchfulness to resist temptation and fostered godliness, as seen in a letter to his son John.[60] Susanna, the major influence in the home and parish, did not relinquish her Puritan heritage. Her father, Samuel Annesley, was a distinguished clergyman in London who exemplified Puritan learning and devotion. Susanna became an Anglican at age thirteen, but she read many Puritan authors. In the Epworth Rectory her household resembled the Puritan home of a century earlier. This is seen

> *in times set apart for meditation and self-examination before God, her keeping of spiritual journal or day-book, her observation of the strict Puritan sabbath -- these were part of her 'method' of life.*[61]

Like earlier Puritans, Susanna prepared expositions of the Creed, the Lord's Prayer, and the Decalogue, essays which reflect Puritan influence.[62]

John Wesley decided to follow the advice of his mother rather than that of his father, by choosing "practical piety" rather than "critical learning."

John Wesley's quest for Christian perfection and means of obtaining this goal owed much to Puritanism.

> *The Puritan was taught to approve of no act because it was good enough for the circumstance, to rest with no performance because it was*

> *the best that could be done in this or that situation. He knew indeed that life is imperfect, that the purest saints do not even entirely disentangle themselves from the meshes of corruption, but though perfection was unattainable -- even more so because it was so -- he bent every nerve and sinew to attempting the attainment.*[63]

As Calvinists, the Puritans saw "perfection" as correct obedience -- an impossibility; Wesleyan and the Arminians viewed "perfection" as pure motives -- a possibility to imperfect humans when purified by grace. The former viewed the quest in the light of the Old Testament (The Covenant of Works), the latter in the light of New Covenant (The Covenant of Grace).

> *Unlike the Anglicans, the early Methodists, and the Puritans, did not place high priority on elaborate houses of worship. Puritans in New England, for instance, did not, indeed expend time and money on church architecture, for the more these were absent, reasoned the Puritan, the more would the Holy Spirit be present to make his abode in the truer temple of the heart.*[64]

Wesley praised the Puritans for their emphasis on Christ, the importance they placed on the Scriptures, their self-discipline, their emphasis on growth in grace, sabbath-observance, and extempore prayer.

Non-conformity did not penetrate many rural areas until Wesleyanism. The Wesleyan movement thus resumed a century later the move of Puritanism into the countryside.[66]

Consistent with this observation is the assessment of the historian of Presbyterian Churches in America. "The Great Awakening [in New England] ... terminated the Puritan and inaugurated the Pietist or Methodist age of American church history."[67]

While Puritanism did not succeed in reforming the Established Church, it did accomplish a great deal by fostering family piety (often considered a threat to the hierarchy), personal discipline, and Sabbath observance.

Puritan influence is seen mostly today in Appalachia with its profusion of churches in which the Bible is the guiding light.

Why did not Wesley more openly and explicitly acknowledge his debt to the Puritans? These may have been the factors:

1) His parents were devout Anglicans; his early training (and environment) was conservative.

2) The Puritans of his day were less zealous, more complacent, and less influential than a century earlier. Even in New England their zeal had diminished, their Calvinism was less pronounced.

3) Wesley rejected their idea of a limited atonement, double predestination, and the neglect of love as seen in his sermon, "Free Grace."[68]

4) Wesley disliked a church governed by elders.

The Puritan contribution to the doctrine of the church is far reaching. From their ranks come the two concepts of church polity: the rule by elders (Presbyterian) and by the congregation (Separatists, Congregationalists, Independent Baptists). The latter concept has been the dominant one especially in North America. Both rejected the rule of bishops and preferred rule by laymen.

Methodism drew from three main traditions. In order of importance they appear to be Anglo-Catholicism (the Established Church), then Pietism (*Unitas Fratrum*), then Puritanism.

The influence of the Anabaptists seems to be minimal, chiefly because of their rejection of infant baptism, refusal to bear arms, and noninvolvement in the state. Puritan influence on Methodists may account for one split in Methodism: Wesleyan Methodists and Free Methodists. This influence is seen in lay representation in conference decisions, simplicity in lifestyle and worship, "perfectionism," and the Spirit-filled life.

In short, the influence of the Old Testament was prominent in Puritanism, the New Testament in Anabaptism, while a balance of both influenced Methodism.

Subsequently the Reformed-Calvinistic tradition focused on Bible-study; the Arminian-Pietist-Methodist tradition focused on experience. Calvinists held Bible Conferences; the Methodists held camp meetings in which experience is stressed. The Calvinists stress the Spirit's witness to the Word; the Pietists stress the Spirit's witness to one's adoption into the family of God (Rom.8:16). Both emphases are needed: the *veracity* of Scripture *and* the *assurance* of one's salvation.

Perhaps the early New England leader who best combined the influences of both Pietism and Puritanism was Cotton Mather (1663-1728), pastor of the famed Old North Church in Boston and author of more than four hundred published books. Like Wesley and other pietists, Cotton Mather dwelt on the importance of personal assurance of salvation (Rom. 8:16). He believed in "a double witness: the testimony of our own self-examination and the testimony of the Holy Spirit"[69]

> *Mather and other Puritans magnified the importance of regeneration, the initial stage of sanctification. This does not, however, imply that they neglected the subsequent stages, for Puritan literature offers the most fully developed treatment of sanctification and the Christian life in the English language.*[70]

Pietism and Puritanism are similar in several areas:

1. Both define "church" as an assembly of "the regenerate."
2. Both stress the "new birth" as essential for membership.
3. Both accept the Bible as sole authority for faith and morals.
4. Both agree that episcopal leadership is not essential.
5. Both stress evangelism, including "foreign" missions.
6. Both emphasize holiness: having the "mind of Christ."
7. Both urge the importance of justice in social action.

Pietism and Puritanism present contrasts in other areas:

PIETISTS	PURITANS
Tend to be apolitical	Concerned with politics
Arminian/Lutheran theology	Calvinistic theology
Emphasis on experience	Emphasis on doctrine
Emphasis on faith & love	Emphasis on independence
Lay ministry acceptable	Educated ministry only
More ecumenical	More militant, regimented
Spirit's witness to salvation	Spirit's witness to Bible
Entire sanctification urgent	Regeneration emphasized
New Testament emphasized	Old Testament emphasized
Intention important	Performance important

The above is an over simplification; these are the "brush strokes" of similarity and contrast. It is designed to show how sincere and earnest Christians can differ on some things and be united in others.

E. APPRAISAL

The influence of Puritanism continues to this day in church polity, in the supremacy of the legislative over the executive, and in Covenant Theology. This is noticeable in Canada, in Australia and in the United States of America. In these areas Covenant Theology is reflected in the separation of state and church, in the perceived relationship between God and the nation (as in the Old Testament), as well as in the relation of the individual to God. This agrees with the Anabaptists with reference to the independence of the Church, but differs from them in the role of the State in divine providence. Puritans saw the State, not as demonic, but an instrument in God's purpose.

In seventeenth century England there were five major views of what constitutes the "true" church:

(1) The Roman Catholics continued to insist that the one true church, with the Pope as its head, ministered to the faithful through priest and sacrament -- an international Church.

(2) The Anglican Church renounced allegiance to the Pope and named the monarch as its head. It was *the national* church; its liturgy was more important than doctrine.

(3) The Puritans sought reformation within the established Church by making doctrine more important than ritual; preaching the Word was given priority over liturgy. Most Puritans wanted to remain in the Church of England. They were more numerous and prosperous than the Puritan separatists or Independents.

(4) The Independents and Baptists sought separation of Church and State, a "free" church, with membership limited to regenerated believers.

(5) The Anabaptists, and later the Quakers, were suspicious of the government, clerical vestments, and liturgies. They sought a *"restoration"* (of the New Testament pattern) rather than merely a *"reformation"* of the existing church.

Which of these five groups was nearest to the New Testament ideal and pattern? Perhaps the nearest to the biblical ideal were the Independents or Separatists, the "Pilgrim Fathers" of Holland and later of Plymouth, Massachusetts. Why? They stressed Bible study and expository preaching. They believed church membership should be limited to the regenerate. They loved their neighbors by ministering to the needs of native Americans and by helping their more affluent neighbors in the Bay Colony.

Puritanism had a deep, lasting, and beneficent influence in the land of its origin. But it did not prevail because of the influence of the monarchy and the state church. It did prevail in New England where it was free. Yet even there it was challenged by those like Roger Williams who demanded a free church. Although the Puritans enjoyed limited freedom in England, they denied the same to others in Massachusetts. Second and third generations did not share the spiritual vitality of their ancestors. They had "lost their first love." The revival, under leaders like Jonathan Edwards, challenged latent Calvinism and the "worldliness" of the public. Affluence aided the demise of Puritanism; sophistication helped also. It is said that "proper Bostonians" came to the conclusion that "good" people like themselves would not be sent to hell by a beneficent God. Unitarianism aided the demise of Puritanism, as seen in the Congregational Churches. Many congregations were divided; many became Unitarians with the aid of Harvard College, once the bastion of Puritanism. Its demise was satirically described by Oliver Wendell Holmes in two of his poems, "The Wonderful One-Hoss Shay" (1858) and the novel "Elsie Venner" (1861). Even today in New England "that strange new birth, that Methodist grace" (Timothy Dwight) is more rare than in most parts of this nation. Yet it was from New England that the most effective attack on slavery was launched and the northern tier of states (and Hawaii) was evangelized. Where the Bible is read seriously, both Calvinism and Pietism are likely to flourish.

It is well to remember that both the First Great Awakening (A.D.1726--) and the Second Great Awakening (A.D.1800--) began among those of Puritan descent. Jonathan Edwards in New England led, in the tradition of Robert Brown, among the Congregationalists during the First. The Presbyterians, in the tradition of Thomas Cartwright, led the Second in New Jersey and on the Kentucky frontier. The Colonies, and later the Republic, were profoundly influenced by the revivals which revitalized both religion and social services for several generations, in North America and around the world.

Chapter IV Endnotes

1. F. H. Littell, *The Free Church*, (Boston: Starr King Press, 1957), p. 40.
2. H. G. Wood, "Puritanism," *Hastings Encyclopedia of Religion and Ethics*, X, p. 507.
3. L. J. Trinterud, "The Origins of Puritanism," *Church History*, (1951), XX, p. 37.
4. Chaucer, "Canterbury Tales," *Great Books of the Western World*, R. M. Hutchins, Ed., (Chicago: Encyclopedia Britannica), 22, pp. 167, 168.
5. Christopher Hill, *Society and Puritanism in Pre-Revolutionary England*, (New York: Schocken, 1964), p. 17.
6. *Ibid.*, p, 39.
7. M. M. Knappen, *Tudor Puritanism, A Chapter in the History of Idealism*, (Chicago: University of Chicago Press, 1939), p, 7.
8. J. C. Spalding, "Puritanism," Chicago: *Encyclopedia, Britannica*, (1974), XV, p. 304.
9. W. M. Haller, *The Rise of Puritanism*, (New York: Columbia U., 1957), p. 20.
10. Knappen, p. 36.
11. Haller, p. 23.
12. Knappen, p. 135.
13. Knappen, p. 392.
14. Haller, p. 20.
15. *Ibid.*, p. 38.
16. J. S. Harper, "The Devotional Life of John Wesley," (Ph. D. Thesis, Duke University), pp. 12-19.
17. Hill, p. 33.
18. Alden Bradford, *History of Massachusetts*, (1620-1820), (Boston: Hilliard Gray and Co., 1835), p. 22.
19. Peter Oliver, *The Puritan Commonwealth*, (Boston: Little, Brown & Co., 1956), p. 55.

20. J. Wesley,"Observations on Liberty" *Works*, XI, p. 105.
21. Haller, p. 22 & 95.
22. Compare G. F. Nuttall, THE HOLY SPIRIT IN PURITAN FAITH AND EXPERIENCE. (Oxford, Blackwell, 1846), p. 134.
23. *Diary of Michael Wigglesworth*, (1653-57) Ed. S. Morgan, (New York, Harper, Torch Books. 1940), pp. 3, 81.1940), pp. 3, 81.
24. Charles Wesley, *Journal* (Sun., March 21), I, p. 5.
25. Samuel E. Morrison, *Harvard College in the Seventeenth Century*, (Cambridge: Harvard University Press, 1936), p. 280.
26. S. E. Morrison, *Three Centuries of Harvard* (Cambridge University Press, 1936), p. 61.
27. S. E. Morrison, *Harvard College in the Seventeenth Century*, (1936), p. 457.
28. *Ibid.*, p. 457.
29. Adam Sampson, *Puritanism in Seventeenth Century Massachusetts*, David Hall, Editor, (New York: Holt, Rinehart, Winston, 1968), pp. 28, 29.
30. Timothy Dwight, "The Smooth Divine," in *The World's Great Religious Poetry*, C. M. Hill, Ed., (Macmillian, 1938), p. 369.
31. Sampson, p. 30.
32. Haller, p. 173.
33. F. J. Powicke, The Congregational Churches," in W. B. Selbie, ed., *Evangelical Christianity; Its History and Witness*, (London: Hodder and Stoughton, 1911), p. 87.
34. *Ibid.*, p. 89.
35. *Ibid.*, p. 116.
36. *Ibid.*, p. 120.
37. F. L. Fagley, "The Narrative of the Cambridge Synod," *The Cambridge "Platform of Church Discipline" 1648*, (Boston Commission of Congregational Christian and Unitarian Churches, Boston, 1948), p. 5.
38. *Ibid.*, p. 7.
39. H. W. Foote, "The Significance and Influence of the Cambridge Platform of 1648," *The Cambridge Platform*, (Boston, 1948), p. 49.

40. Herbert Schneider, "A Changing Sense of Sin," *Puritanism in Seventeenth Century New England*, (David Hall, editor) (1968), p. 94.
41. Edward Morgan, "The Half-Way Covenant Reconsidered, in *Puritanism in Seventeenth Century Massachusetts*, pp. 105, 106.
42. *William Ames*, by M. Nethenns, H. Visscher, K. Renter, trans. by D. Horton, Cambridge, H.D.S. Library, (1965), p. 214.
43. *Ibid.*, p. 14.
44. Allen Bradford, *History of Massachusetts (1620-1820)*, (Boston: Hilliard, Gray & Co., 1835), p. 40.
45. Thomas Case, *A Sermon of Thanksgiving before the House of Commons*, (London, 1645), pp. 28, 31, 33.
46. John Whincop, *God's Call to Weeping and Mourning*, (London: Robert Leyburn, 1645), p. 39.
47. John Conant, *The Woe and Weale of God's People*, (London: Christopher Meredith, 1643), pp. 26, 27.
48. Ralph R. Perry, *Puritanism and Democracy*, (New York: Vanguard Press, 1944), p. 234.
49. Perry Miller, "Declension in a Bible Commonwealth" in James Sydney, Jr., ed., *The New England Puritans*, (New York: Harper and Row, 1968), pp. 131-136.
50. John Wesley, Sermon CXXIX, *Works*, VII, pp. 386-399; Likewise Sermon CXXX.
51. P. Miller, *The New England Puritans*, p. 140.
52. P. Miller, *The New England Puritans*, pp. 227, 229, 230.
53. Spaulding, p. 308.
54. R. B. Perry, pp. 242, 248.
55. Geoffrey Nuttall, *The Holy Spirit in Puritan Faith and Experience*, (Oxford: Blackwell, 1946) p. viii.
56. Nuttall, *op. cit.*, p. 14.
57. *Ibid.*, p. 32, 33.
58. *Arminian Magazine*, 1779, cited in Telford, *op. cit.*, III, p. 316.
59. Robert C. Monk, *John Wesley, His Puritan Heritage*, (Nashville: Abingdon, 1966) p. 99.

60. John A. Newton, *Methodism and the Puritans,* (London: W. Williams Trust, 1964), p. 4.
61. Harper, *op. cit.*, p. 50.
62. *Ibid.*, p. 5.
63. Her "Journal" is at the Methodist Book Room at City Road, London.
64. Perry Miller and T. E. Johnson, *The Puritans*, (New York: American Book Company, 1938), p. 284.
65. Sarah L. Bailey, *Historical Sketches of Andover*, (Boston: Houghton, Mifflin and Company, 1880), p. 410.
66. Newton, pp. 12-15.
67. Hill, p. 500.
68. R. E. Thompson, *A History of the Presbyterian Churches in the United States*, (New York: Scribners, 1898), pp. 34, 95.
69. John Wesley, "Free Grace," Sermon CXXVII,. *Works*, 3rd edition, (London: 1872; (Grand Rapids: Baker 1978 reprint.) VII, pp. 373-376.
70. R. F. Lovelace, *The American Pietism of Cotton Mather: Origins of American Evangelicalism*, (Grand Rapids: Christian University Press; Eerdmans, 1979), p. 97.
71. Lovelace, p. 151.

Chapter V
THE METHODISTS

The advent of this "modern mind" as opposed to medieval Augustinianism in both Catholicism and Reformation came in the work of John Wesley. Bible study and experience convinced him that man is free to accept or reject God's offer of Salvation from sin. . . He was an advocate or [of] Armianism, or Semi-Pelagianism. A new age for the church began when men were invited to participate in the most holy enterprises, including that of redemption, and no longer were witless cogs in the machinery of fate. We are yet to estimate how integral was this new idealism to the release of power in western Christendom.

A.T. DeGroot, *Disciple Thought: A History*, (1965), p.74.

A major claimant to be a return to the church of the New Testament is the world-wide Methodist fellowship. The spiritual revival in eighteenth century England resulted in one of the largest and most influential churches in Protestantism.

Methodism was the main carrier of the great tide of evangelical religion which swept through the English-speaking world, reaching its crest of influence in the latter half of the nineteenth century before it began to ebb away.[1]

Methodism differs from the other movements traced in this survey because it is in the mainstream of the Reformation rather than that of the Restoration. John Wesley was conservative; he wanted to renew the Anglican Church, not to replace it. But Methodism's claim to be a return to the church of the New Testament provides enough evidence to justify this claim that its inclusion seems appropriate.

A. ORIGINS OF THE EVANGELICAL REVIVAL

Many assume that the Evangelical Revival in eighteenth century England was initiated by the Wesleys. Before pursuing the Methodist Movement further it will be well to review some contemporary spiritual awakenings.

In 1726 revival came to Dutch churches in the colony of New Jersey under the leadership of Pastor Theodore Frelinghuysen who had been "deeply influenced by the experiential piety of the English Puritans."[2] It was the beginning of "The Great Awakening" along the Atlantic seaboard, which eventually extended from Nova Scotia to Georgia.

The "awakening" spread to the Presbyterians in New Jersey, under the leadership of William and Gilbert Tennent, to the founding of the evangelistic "Log College" (1726), and eventually to Princeton Theological Seminary.[3]

Meanwhile, on August 13, 1727, Pentecost had come to the Herrnhut community of *Unitas Fratrum* (United Brethren) in Saxony under the leadership of Count Zinzendorf. It resulted in the rebirth of the Movement, a century of uninterrupted prayer, and the beginning of foreign missions.[4]

Under the Spirit-anointed preaching of Jonathan Edwards in 1734-37, revival came to the Congregationalists in Connecticut and Massachusetts. America's "Great Awakening" was changing the Atlantic Coast Colonies for the better. George Whitefield's arrival in 1739 vastly enhanced the "Awakening" and its extension. Typical of the influence of Whitefield was his impact upon a Connecticut farmer who, with his wife, hastened on horseback to Middletown where a marker now commemorates the event. The farmer wrote in his diary:

> *He looked almost angelical a young slender youth . . . with a bold countenance . . . . He looked as if he was Cloathed with authority from ye great god and a sweet collome Solemnity sat upon his brow and my hearing him preach gave me a heart wound by gods blessing . . . my old foundation was broken up & i saw that my righteousness would not save me.*[5]

Isaiah, and Saul of Tarsus would have understood how he felt, as would millions of believers since then.

Simultaneously in Wales a revival, independent of the movement called Methodism, occurred under the impassioned preaching of Howel Harris, a layman who had received the *assurance* of salvation by faith. Ejected from churches, he preached to large crowds several times a day. His converts formed small societies. Deplorable moral conditions were transformed into God-fearing communities extending over seven counties with "nearly thirty societies" flourishing. "A wide-spread reformation followed.

Public diversions became unfashionable, and religion became the theme of common conversation."[6] Despite fierce persecution by religious leaders Harris continued preaching (1736-42), beginning nearly two years before the itinerant preaching of Whitefield and the Wesleys.

> *Meanwhile a similar revival occurred in Calvinistic Scotland(led by James Robe) where young converts held prayer-meetings in fields, barns, schoolhouses, and the manses of their ministers . . . . Some suffered such distress of mind . . . that they not only shrieked aloud, but . . . convulsed in their bodies . . . . On finding peace . . . had their countenances so lit up with serenity and brightness, that their neighbors declared they had obtained not only new hearts, but new faces.*[7]

In each instance a low state of religion led to a concern on the part of a few who prayed for spiritual life of the churches and country. God answered by sending his Holy Spirit for renewal. Thus in Germany, America, Wales, and Scotland God was working in preparation for renewal in England in which Whitefield and the Wesleys were used so effectually.

While Cambridge University was the "Mother" of Puritanism, a century earlier Methodism was "born" at Oxford University, older than Cambridge and under the influence of the Anglican Church. Although later than the University of Paris and after some quarrels with Scotland, Oxford became a mature University in 1274 A.D. During the 14th century Oxford became superior to the older universities on the Continent. Among the most influential Christian leaders from Oxford there were Wycliffe, Wesley, and John Henry Newman, founder of the Tractarians and the one who prayed "Lead Kindly Light" finally to the Roman Catholic Church. Of these three leaders, wrote S. Parkes Cadman, "John Wesley expressed the spiritual aspirations and transformed the character of his age more profoundly and permanently than did any other contemporary Englishman."[8]

Methodism began in the mind of a few students who spent six evenings each week together "reading the Scriptures and provoking one another to love and to good works." The term "methodist" apparently began as a term of derision by some students at the University as they observed the "Holy Club" as a small zealous group strict in prayer, Bible study, Eucharist, concern for the poor, and who pursued these priorities very methodically. Beginning "as a company of people associating together, to help each other to work out their own salvation," they saw Methodism as "the religion of the Bible, the primitive Church, and . . . the Church of England."

This religion, as Wesley defined it, is

> *no other than love, the love of God and of all mankind; the loving God with all our heart, and soul, and strength, . . . and the loving every soul God hath made, every man on earth as our own soul . . . . Ever showing itself by its fruits.*[9]

Twenty years later Samuel Johnson defined "methodist" in his *Dictionary* (1755) as "one of a new kind of Puritans lately risen, so called from their possession laying great stress on method."[10]

What followed from the "Holy Club" at Oxford: was a spiritual awakening, or religious renewal, evolving a group called "Methodists." More than once spiritual awakenings occurred at this famous old University. It was at Oxford that Wycliffe (1330-84) dared to call the Catholic Church back to the Bible before they interred his dust, where Erasmus lectured on the New Testament and anticipated the Reformation, where the Anglican Church opposed the Puritans, where Methodism originated, and also the Oxford MOVEMENT led by John Henry Newman.

William Penn was rejected at Oxford because his piety opposed the Anglican formalism. Yet there Frank Buchman (1878-1961) founded the Oxford GROUP which in 1938 became the world-wide Moral Re-armament.

Beginning with Wycliffe, Oxford's influence permeated the British Isles in a way similar to the origins of the Pietists, Anabaptists, Moravians, Brethren in Europe and the Puritans (Edwards), Disciples (Stone), and Pentecostals in America.

B. THE QUEST FOR HOLINESS

For John Wesley the quest for "holiness" began in 1723 when he was age twenty-two, during his third year at Christ Church College, Oxford. This determination to be a fully committed Christian became his obsession to the end of his life. This led him and some of his friends to make what they called "Christian perfection," or "the mind of Christ," their first priority.

Before this Wesley thus described his spiritual condition:

> *Till I was about ten years old I had not sinned away that 'washing of the Holy Ghost' which was given me in baptism . . . . At school I was*

> *almost continually guilty of outward sins . . . . However, I still read the Scriptures, and said my prayers, morning and evening . . . . Yet I had not all this while so much as a notion of inward holiness; nay, went on . . . very contentedly, in some or other known sin . . . . When I was about twenty-two, my father pressed me to enter into holy orders. At the same time, the providence of God directed me to Kempis's "Christian Pattern." I began to see that true religion was seated in the heart, and that God's law extended to all our thoughts as well as words and actions.*[11]

In a letter to his mother dated May 28, 1725, Wesley said that he was "lately advised to read Thomas Kempis," and sought advice from his mother. She urged him to "press after greater degrees of Christian perfection."[12]

Strangely in his "Plain Account of Christian Perfection," he states that he read Kempis a year after reading Bishop Taylor's "Rule and Exercises of Holy Living and Dying." The date of the "Letter" indicates the error of date in "Plain Account."

In any case he learned from the Roman Catholic the importance of *"inward religion,"* from Anglican Bishop Taylor the imperative of intention, and then from William Law's "Christian Perfection" and "Serious Call" the importance of *entire devotion to God.*

The most determinative event occurred in 1729, as he narrates in "Plain Account," when he began "not only to read but to study the Bible." The result was an intense pursuit of scriptural holiness. He then realized that he must have 'the mind which was in Christ,' and the priority of 'walking as Christ also walked,' . . . in all things . . . an entire inward and outward conformity to the Master.[13]

This concern for holiness ("Christian perfection") is seen in his sermon, "The Circumcision of the Heart," which he preached at the University of Oxford in 1733. In it he defined the holiness he sought as that [which] . . . in the sacred writings is termed holiness; and which directly implies, the being cleansed from all sin, . . . the being endued with those virtues which are in Christ Jesus; and being so 'renewed in the image of our mind,' as to be 'perfect as our Father in heaven is perfect,'. . . . Love is the fulfilling of the law.[14]

Wesley's purpose was to prove that in 1777 his view of holiness ("entire sanctification") was consistent with his insight at the age of twenty-three. Some changes in the interim, which he does not mention, include the relation of justification to sanctification, sin in believers, the twin perils of placing the ideal too high or too low, how to experience this "perfection," when to expect it, and the matter of losing and keeping this experience. But these were amplifications and clarifications more than deviations from early convictions. Thus it is apparent that Wesley thought that the Christian defined in the New Testament is one who by faith and obedience can be made by grace "as perfect as our Father in heaven is perfect" (Matt. 5:48).

This conviction is the cutting edge of early Methodism, the most distinctive and most criticized feature of the movement. It is often an embarrassment to those who claim adherence to Wesleyan theology. It was an embarrassment in Wesley's day, hence his repeated efforts to define and defend it. When tempted to abandon this quest he was constrained by Scripture to make no concessions to indwelling sin, to continue to "press on to perfection" (Heb. 6:1), to answer critics, to publish credible witnesses to this experience, and to urge his preachers to include it in every sermon.

Part of the problem is the nomenclature of this doctrine. "Perfect" is a biblical term synonymous with "mature," as modern versions recognize. It is a relative term, not a designation of something with no defect as in current language. Wesley's defense by proof texts leaves much to be desired; he often took them out of context, overusing some of them (Deut. 30:6; Ps. 130:8; Ezek. 36:25-27) and making too little use of others (Acts 1:5,8; Romans 6:1-22; 2 Cor. 7:1; Col. 1:22; 1 Thess. 5:23). But he dwelt essentially and courageously on the major areas of biblical evidence (Matt. 5:48; 22:37-40; I Cor. 13; Phil. 2:5; Eph. 3:16-21; I Pet. 1:16; 2:21-24; 1 John 1:7, 9). He dared not "water down" Scripture to conform to experience, but stressed the importance that one's experience and conduct mirror the pattern of the New Testament, not by human achievement alone, but by God's Grace. There would be no occasion for pride.

While most Christians agree that sanctification should follow justification and be progressive, the Wesleys insisted that this sanctification process begins at conversion and may be consummated in this life to the extent of giving victory over besetting sin and enabling the believer to love God with all one's being (Matt. 22:37- 40). To the many detractors Wesley would appeal to the Word of God and persevere.

The grand purpose of this evangelical revival was to "reform the nation and spread scriptural holiness" throughout the world. This came to be the most *distinctive* message of the Methodists. After more than two centuries this emphasis is alive in many who bear the name Methodist or Wesleyan: in many Holiness missions, the Keswick movement, the Holiness associations in North America, South Africa, and Japan, the Pentecostals, and several denominations who trace their roots to the early Methodists.

C. PERSONAL ASSURANCE

Beginning in 1723 the Wesleys sought holiness, *assurance* of their salvation, and acceptance as God's children. This goal eluded them until May 1738, when Charles, and then John (at Aldersgate) received the "witness of the Spirit" which gave them *assurance* of salvation. The need for that assurance was made more acute by Wesley's earlier encounter with the Moravians on the Atlantic and in Georgia. Spangenberg had asked Wesley,

> *Have you the witness within yourself? Does the Spirit of God bear witness with your spirit, that you are a child of God? . . . Do you know Jesus Christ? . . . do you know he has saved you? . . . . Do you know yourself? Wesley, surprised, could only answer, "I hope he has died to save me." When Spangenberg pressed him for a personal assurance, Wesley answered in the affirmative, but later commented, "I fear these were vain words."*[15]

This poignant encounter, in which this Anglican cleric was nonplussed as to how to answer, is a clue to the rarity of personal assurance, even by those intimately acquainted with Scriptures and church tradition. This inner witness of the Spirit to one's new birth (Rom. 8:16; cf. 1 John 3:19-24), exemplified by the Moravians, and experienced by the Wesleys, is Methodism's contribution to Protestantism. By contrast Reformed theology views the witness of the Spirit as a witness to the veracity of Scripture. Is this why Calvinists have Bible conferences, while Wesleyans have camp meetings? This doctrine of *assurance* of one's salvation, of the forgiveness of sins, and acceptance by God, was anathema, especially to the Church of England. In 1739 Joseph Butler, the Bishop of Bristol rebuked John Wesley, charging that his doctrine of assurance ("enthusiasm") was "a very horrid thing."[16] Such claims of "assurance" were regarded as presumptuous, as having a "holier than thou" attitude. The Catholics based their assurance or faith on the sacraments, and the absolution by their priests. It was an inference, not the "witness of the Spirit." Consequently they could not witness with assurance.

The Calvinists, by contrast, hoped they were among the chosen, or "elect" but could not be sure of it. For the Reformed theologians this personal "witness" was too subjective and tenuous, as contradictory to their most tenacious doctrine, final perseverance. Modern neo-Calvinists now accept this doctrine, which was considered fanatical when first articulated by the Wesleys in sermon, writing, and song.

> *This great doctrine, the statement of which was one of the most important services rendered to the Church by Wesley, had been obscured by the Sacramentalian teaching of the Romish Church and exaggerated by the Mystics.*[17]

John Wesley's quest for assurance after Aldersgate led him to the Moravians at Herrnhut where he eagerly recorded living witnesses to entire sanctification.

Upon his return to England Wesley reported that while walking from London to Oxford on October 9, 1738, he read Jonathan Edward's, *A Faithful Narrative of the Surprising Work of God in the Conversion of Many Hundred Souls in Northampton . . . in New England.* Wesley was profoundly moved by this account, and it served to reinforce his own faith. As Outler observed,

> *The crisis which followed ranks with Aldersgate in importance if not in drama. . . . It is not too much to say that one of the effectual causes of the Wesleyan Revival in England was the Great Awakening in New England.*[18]

Soon after reading this report Wesley published an edited portion of this tract and also Edward's *Treatise Concerning the Religious Affections.*

Even after Aldersgate (on May 14, 1738) the "witness of the Spirit" was not constant. A letter from a friend on October 14 threw him into "great perplexity . . . . I have not that joy in the Holy Ghost; no settled, lasting joy."[19]

Assurance came gradually and decisively after Wesley consented, with great reluctance, to follow Whitefield's example by preaching in the streets and open fields. The response was so overwhelming that "blessed assurance" remained for the remainder of his life. Thus the subjective inner witness was confirmed by the objective "fruits" which Wesley thereafter used as *verifying* the "witness of the Spirit." L. R. Marston finds the sudden change in Wesley after Aldersgate, from introspection to spiritual power, as the clearest evidence of his "enduement of power from on High," or his "second work of grace." It followed his reluctant decision to leave the Fetter Lane Society and accept Whitefield's request to continue the field preaching in Bristol.[20]

Some twenty years later in a sermon entitled "The Witness of the Spirit" Wesley explained the basis of "assurance."

> *By the testimony of the spirit, I mean, an inward impression of the soul, whereby the Spirit of God immediately and directly witnesses to my spirit, that I am a child of God; that Jesus Christ hath loved me, and given himself for me; that all my sins are blotted out, and I, even I, am reconciled to God.*[21]

In the context of Protestantism, as a whole, Methodism's theological contribution may be viewed as four-fold: (1) personal *assurance* of salvation, (2) the *witness of the Spirit* to that change, (3) *entire sanctification*, as distinct from, and subsequent to, justification-regeneration, and (4) **love for God and neighbor.**

D. THE LOVE OF NEIGHBOR

Methodism, especially in the early decades, can claim kinship with the Quakers, Mennonites and Salvationists, with respect to love of neighbor. Wesley professed and practiced the "great commandment" (Matt. 22:38) that love for God must be matched by love for neighbor. During the earliest years at Oxford care for the poor was prominent in the spiritual disciplines of the "Holy Club." Wesley always insisted that assurance of salvation must prove itself by the "fruit" of social service, of ministry to the needy. The Class Meeting always added to spiritual self-examination a collection for the poor. They took time to visit those in prison and to ride with convicts to the gallows with prayer for their eternal destination. No portion of the Bible influenced John Wesley more than I John where he read, "Those who say, 'I love God' and hate their brothers or sisters, are liars; for those who do not love a brother or sister whom they have seen, cannot love God whom they have not seen?" (1 John 4:20). He called slavery in the American Colonies "the vilest that ever saw the sun." He and Whitefield added schools and orphanages to their evangelistic labors. Wesley founded health care clinics and wrote a book on medicine. This "home doctor book" was used for a century.[22]

A major factor in the growth of the Temperance Movement in the United States, during the nineteenth century was the Methodist Church. Although in later years the Wesleyans often failed to balance love for God with love for neighbor, the Methodist message is actually close to the New Testament in the emphasis on assurance of salvation, the witness of the Spirit, the mind of Christ and love for God and neighbor with *love* the capstone.

John Wesley was convinced that Methodism was a return to primitive Christianity. His sermon at City-Road Chapel in 1777 entitled "What Hath God Wrought," provided supporting evidence of his claim that "Methodism is the religion of the Bible."[23]

The results seem to justify this claim. During his long ministry John Wesley (1703-91) witnessed a change in most of England, from the moral and spiritual decadence (resulting from the collapse of Puritanism and the Restoration of 1662) to a nation where Methodism was honored and its founder acknowledged as a revered churchman rather than a dangerous fanatic. England was changed for the better.

Methodism had a solid basis for its claim that it represented a return to early Christianity. It did so by emphasizing a membership limited to *believers*, a radical departure from the national churches of Europe. By necessity, as well as by choice, it became a "free" church. The effort to become a church within a church *(ecclesiolae in ecclesia)* failed because the Anglican hierarchy refused to ordain Methodist ministers.[24] Rather than a nominal assent to creeds and liturgy, Methodists, like the Puritans and Quakers, demanded evidence of a spiritual transformation, effected by the Spirit of God, with Jesus as Lord in fact as well as in name.

Methodists took seriously the command to "love thy neighbor" by giving to the poor and the orphans as well as ministering to prisoners. They believed in loving God by their diligence in the "means of grace," private and family prayer, witnessing to their salvation, taking the sacraments, seeking the "mind of Christ," and visiting "the fatherless and widows in their affliction" while keeping themselves "unspotted from the world" (James 1:27).

While their separation from "the world" was not as radical as that of the Anabaptists and Quakers, the early Methodists avoided alcoholic beverages, dance halls, theaters, gambling, and the like. They were positively active in witnessing to God's grace and helping the needy. Methodism is a part of Pietism, a religion "of the heart."[25] Despite their liturgical background, the Wesleys discovered the truth of justification by faith with the help of Luther, the Puritans, the German Pietists (Moravians or United Brethren), and the Scriptures.

Notwithstanding its founder's political conservatism, Methodism in North America was even more influential than in the British Isles. Nearly all historians applaud the positive changes resulting from Methodism's contribution to life among English-speaking peoples in the eighteenth and nineteenth centuries.[26]

The enormity of the conditions in England during this period is becoming ever more horrible as viewed in recent studies. Wesley's London was two cities: the affluent West End, and "the old rotting East End." Until 1790 there was so little room for burials that cadavers of the poor were left to decay in open pits. In London there was one gin shop for every 120 persons; English workers consumed eight millions of gin annually. Working conditions in factories gave scant attention to the health of the laborers. Child labor was a scandal; many "went to work after their sixth birthday" and worked in 14 hour shifts day and night. Legislation in the House of Commons prescribed public hanging for over two hundred offenses, such as cutting down an ornamental shrub. When the jails became overcrowded felons were transported to Georgia (until American Independence), and then to Australia,[27] alleviating, to some extent, the ruthlessness of England's policy of consigning felons to penal colonies:

The Wesleyans did particularly good work at the foot of the scaffold with condemned criminals ... one preacher ... helped fourteen men to lament and exult their way ... into the portals of eternity.[28]

In the 1830's, Tasmania was dotted with Anglican Churches and Methodist meeting houses. Methodism also followed the English to South Africa in the same decade. Today South African Methodists exceed in number even the largest of the Dutch Reformed denominations, as indicated in the census of 1970.

This moral and spiritual transformation in eighteenth century England was in contrast to the low ebb of religion in Deist-led America before and after the War of Independence (1775-1783).[29] It was also in contrast to the French Revolution (1789-1799) led by humanists and neo-pagans.[30] As many historians have observed, the Evangelical renewal in England was in contrast to the Revolution in France. In a sense the Wesleys built more wisely than they knew!

To what extent, if any, did Wesley and his associates come short of a full return to Apostolic Christianity? In other words, to what extent did the Wesleys' heritage and environment inhibit their grasp of the basic principals of the church set forth by Jesus, Peter, John, and Paul?

The area in which John Wesley wrote least and was the least controversial was in the area of sacraments: baptism and the Lord's Supper. In this area he found little to debate. He accepted quite readily the teaching of his church - the Church of England - which differed little from the views of Martin Luther and John Calvin.

E. THE SACRAMENTS
1. Wesley on Baptism

Baptismal Regeneration

The Church of England, like Roman Catholics and Lutherans, accepted the Augustinian doctrine of baptismal regeneration. Wesley accepted this position of his church as defined in the *Articles of Religion*.

Said Richard Hooker (1554?-1600), the first great Anglican churchman after the Reformation,

> *The infusion of grace . . . is applied to infants through baptism, without either faith or works, and in them it really taketh away original sin and the punishment due to it.*[31]

The Anglican "Office for Baptism" affirmed baptismal regeneration. It reads in part, "Give Thy Holy Spirit to this infant, that he may be born again." After baptism the priest declares, "seeing this child is regenerate and grafted into the body of Christ's church, let us give thanks to Almighty God . . . . It hath pleased Thee to regenerate this infant with thy Holy Spirit." Sugden comments, "Wesley was trained up to accept this view."[32]

In 1756 John Wesley published a "Treatise on Baptism," which his father had published originally in 1700. Wesley made a few omissions in his father's treatise but did not mention its author. They wrote:

> *By baptism, we who were 'by nature children of wrath,' were made the children of God. And this regeneration, which our Church, in so many places, ascribes to baptism, is more than barely being admitted into the church, though commonly connected therewith; being 'grafted into the body of Christ's church, we are made the children of God by adoption*

> *and grace.' This is grounded on the plain words of the Lord: 'Except a man be born of water and of the Spirit, he cannot enter the kingdom of God.' By water then, as a means, the water of baptism, we are regenerated or born again. Herein a principle of grace is infused, which will not be wholly taken away, unless we quench the Holy Spirit of God by long wickedness.*[33]

A similar statement occurs in his 1756 sermon entitled "The New Birth" (XXXIX):

> *It is certain our Church supposes that all who are baptized in their infancy are at the same time born again; and it is allowed that the whole Office for the Baptism of Infants proceeds from this supposition. Nor is it an objection of any weight against this, that we cannot comprehend how it is wrought in infants. For neither can we comprehend how it is wrought in a person of riper years. But whatever be the case with infants, it is sure all of riper years who are baptized are not at the same time born again.*[34]

Elsewhere in the same sermon he emphasizes, "baptism, the sign, is spoken of as distinct from regeneration, the things signified." In the rest of the sermon it is obvious that he does not accept baptismal regeneration except for infants, and here he accepts the Church's statement as final with neither Scripture or reason to defend it. His ambiguity in the matter is obvious.

Baptism of Infants

In most of the treatise the emphasis is on the baptism of infants. In a prefatory statement Wesley states, "Three things are essential to Christian baptism: an episcopal administrator, the application of water, and the naming of the Trinity" (cf. Matt. 28:19).[35]

The basis for the first, Wesley explained, is that the Lord commissioned "his apostles only." This factor invalidates "dipping" (immersion) by Anabaptists and other independents, because, said Wesley, "They want episcopal administrators which are essential to Christian baptism."[36] Here Wesley's high church convictions are in evidence. However, this preamble was omitted when the essay was printed in 1758.

At great length the Wesleys, father and son, argued for sprinkling rather than "dipping" or immersion. In support they cited such precedents as the 3,000 in Jerusalem and the baptism of the Philippian jailer with his family during the night, both situations in which immersion seems less likely, if not impossible.

In support of sprinkling in Jerusalem he quotes Mr. Fuller - "no water mills in Jerusalem because of insufficient water." Wesley may not have known of the existence of Hezekiah's Pool, near the Joppa Gate, and the pool of Bethesda (John 5:1-10). Also he ignores the Pauline metaphor of being "buried with Christ in Baptism" (Rom. 6:1-3; Col. 2:12), and being risen with Christ into newness of life, where immersion seems to be the mode envisioned. The Apostolic fathers recommended baptism in "living" (running) water and reserved pouring or sprinkling ("clinical baptism") for those unable to be immersed.[37]

The benefits of baptism are said to be more than a public testimony to a new life in Christ. "Primarily," affirms Wesley, "it is the washing away of the guilt of original sin by the application of the merits of Christ's death."[38] Authority for this is to be found in the *Book of Common Prayer* (Article nine). Obviously infants share this "guilt:"

> *The free gift . . . is applied to us in baptism . . . the ordinary instrument of our justification. [The proof of this lies] in the rubric at the end of the office . . . children who are baptized, dying before they commit actual sin, are saved . . . this is agreeable to the unanimous judgment of all the ancient Fathers.*[39]

Wesley overlooked the testimony of Tertullian (fl. A. D. 200) who opposed the baptism of infants.[40]

Omitted here is any reference to repentance and faith as the conditions for baptism. It must be by ordained clergymen, and water must be applied, otherwise the merits of Christ's death are not applicable. Such are his underlying assumptions. Here Wesley writes as the high churchmen in the Anglo-Catholic "tradition of the fathers," not as an evangelical revivalist in the New Testament tradition. On what basis is water necessary to make Christ's atonement applicable and effectual? Where is this stated in Scripture? How can they come from "east, west, north, and south to sit down in the kingdom" (cf. Matt. 8:11; Luke 13:29) if they have not been "properly" baptized?

Wesley apparently never doubted that by baptism infants are truly regenerated. However he was quick to admit that subsequent sin nullified the benefits (sermon on the "New Birth").[41] He does not envision parents dedicating infants and deferring baptism until the candidate is mature enough to make it a personal decision, thus giving baptism its maximum significance. The question is: does the application of water do more than dedication without water? If so, how or on what biblical grounds?

Wesley, like many others, saw baptism as a continuation of circumcision which admitted infants into the patriarchal covenant-relationship with God. This was superficially based on only one text (Col. 2:11-13), which, in metaphorical language, described Christians as having a "circumcision made without hands," once dead, buried, and now raised with Christ. When Paul used circumcision positively, as here, he invariably meant a spiritual transformation, an ethical renewal, not something physical. In this he agreed with Deuteronomy 10:16; 30:6 and the prophet Jeremiah 4:4; 6:10; 9:24, 25.

For Paul to indicate that physical baptism (of infants) bestowed grace would destroy his central thesis that grace came by faith in Christ and not through physical acts and ordinances. The only circumcision Paul urged was "of the heart" (Rom.2:25-29). Paul came "not to baptize but to preach the gospel" (1 Cor. 1:17; 1 Cor. 7:19; Gal. 5:6; 6:15; Phil. 3:3; Col. 2:1; 3:11).

In his "notes" on Colossians 2:11-13 Wesley did not argue that baptism replaced circumcision. Curiously, he admitted baptism by immersion is implied here, contrary to his statement in the "treatise on baptism" but he balanced it by an allusion to sprinkling in Hebrews 10:22. He overlooked the fact that in Colossians 2:12 the term was "baptism" (*baptismas*) while in Hebrews the term was "sprinkled (*eloumenos*), a term often linked with washing the whole body (in contrast to feet only) before entering the temple.[42]

In further elaboration on the fit subjects for baptism, Wesley was eager to prove it included infants. As noted previously he wrote,

> *Infants are guilty of original sin . . . they cannot be saved unless this is washed away by baptism . . . they are children of wrath and liable to eternal damnation.*[43]

The only exceptions were those for whom Christian baptism was not available, but he did not elaborate. The contrast with Jesus' statement and attitude is evident (cf. Mark 10:13-16). He continued "infants are capable of making a covenant" and hence, are fit subjects for baptism. Again, casuistry prevailed over common sense. Since baptism replaced circumcision and since infants were circumcised, it follows he argued, that infants are fit subjects for baptism.

Wesley acknowledged that original guilt originated with Adam and that the remedy was provided by the second Adam (cf. Rom.5:12-21; 1 Cor. 15:22-49). He added the unscriptural dogma that baptism was the means by which the remedy is made effective.

The third reason given was that Jesus invited children to come. Children could not be brought to Jesus except by baptism. Again what is the scriptural basis for this? Can this be effected by parental dedication? Is water essential in bringing them to Jesus?

Fourth, he argued on the basis of inference that apostles baptized infants since they baptized entire families. Presumably infants were included. He cited "the unanimous testimony of their most ancient learned and authentic (Jewish) writers," as evidence that male infants were both circumcised and baptized.[44] Actually, the only evidence of Jewish practice prior to John the Baptist is the testimony of the medieval philosopher Maimonides that proselytes were accepted into Judaism by circumcision for males and baptism for females.[45] Both males and females were accepted by immersion.[46]

Wesley made the unwarranted assumption that the Jews accepted infants as proselytes. The reverse seems to be the truth. Finally, he concluded that since "the Christian Church in all places and in all ages" baptized infants as its "general practice" then the practice must have been apostolic, hence authorized by Jesus. Thus he argued from Christian history to apostolic practice rather than vice versa. He ignored Tertullian (A.D. 200), perhaps because he was not considered "orthodox?" Tertullian advised that "a postponement of Baptism is most advantageous, particularly in the case of children . . . let them become Christians when they have been able to know Christ."[47]

Ignored also were the Quakers, the Anabaptists, and Brethren movements of the previous two centuries (perhaps because they were not "regular churches"). Obviously, he had these exceptions in mind. Because he felt that he had the burden of proof, he spent much space and effort in his defense of infant baptism. He did not face the question of what infant baptism does that the dedication of infants by parents failed to do (reserving baptism to those who repent and believe, thus giving baptism maximum significance).

He sought to make void the argument that repentance and faith preceded baptism by insisting that since circumcision was preceded by repentance, the same was true of baptism which replaced circumcision. Of what do infants repent? Such is the casuistry by which a distorted logic is forced to defend an absurdity, set forth by Samuel and repeated by his son John.[48]

This argument ignores the emphases in both Gospels and Epistles that in the New Covenant, group morality of the Old Testament is replaced in the New Testament by individual responsibility for one's actions, not that of parents' or ancestors (Deut. 10:16; Jer. 32:9; Ezek. 18:30; Luke 3:8; John 8:39-41; Rom.2:1--3:31; Gal.3:15-29).

How could Wesley remain to the end of life oblivious of the contradiction between his high-church Anglo-Catholic view of infant baptism and the gospel's emphasis on conscious regeneration prior to baptism? The tension between the sacramental and the evangelical (biblical) view of baptism continued to plague British Methodism for decades.

However, Frank Baker observes that,

"Strand by strand the ties of doctrine and practice binding Wesley to the English establishment frayed or loosened . . . . Wesley's earlier advocacy of the doctrine of baptismal regeneration had somewhat softened . . . baptismal regeneration was possible but not guaranteed.[49]

After much discussion, British Methodists in 1882 made revisions in the Book of Offices in which language supporting baptismal regeneration was omitted, thus "repudiating the view that the infant is born again in baptism."[50]

Should we not agree with Sugden that Methodism should either abandon infant baptism (in favor of dedication) OR reintroduce confirmation as having at least equal importance?

The struggle in American Methodism to interpret and explain infant baptism is paralleled in the Free Methodist Church which separated from the Methodist Episcopal Church North in 1860. Revisions in the baptismal liturgy made in 1860, 1866, 1882, and in 1914 were all away from baptismal regeneration.

C. Wesley King, in a 1975 study of Free Methodist pastors, found that about one half preferred dedication of infants by believing parents, with baptism later after a personal confession of faith.[51]

In response to a question by a student at Asbury Theological Seminary Bishop L. R. Marston defined a mediating position:

THE COVENANT OF BAPTISM is that which

1. witnesses to the infant's inclusion in the "covenant of grace" (Acts 2:39).

2. witnesses that the child is accepted by God . . . "until he comes of age."

3. "admits the child to . . . the Christian community."

*4. The parents **dedicate** their child to the church, **pledge themselves** to live an exemplary life, and rear the child as a Christian.*

5. This covenant "is witnessed by water baptism as sign and seal of the covenant of grace, according to which the child is now . . . in the body of Christ."[52]

This explanation evokes several questions:

1. With reference of the first item, are unbaptized infants outside the "covenant of grace"? Does God make the provisions of the atonement contingent upon the parents' dedication of the infant (Acts 2:39)? The context of this text implies not infants, but all descendants of those who heard Peter's sermon. The "promise" alludes to the effusion of the Holy Spirit on believers (Joel 2:28).

2. Is baptism that which makes the infant "accepted by God"? Are unbaptized infants not accepted (Matt. 19:13-15; Mark 10:13-15)?

3. Does the application of water do something that dedication alone fails to do in admitting the child to the Christian community?

4. In what way does water *baptism* do more than *dedication* of infant by parents to God and the church?

5. The witnesses to the dedication of the parents are God and the community, not the water as such. It is the dedication of the infant's parents which makes the event significant. The child is already in the Kingdom (by prevenient grace) as Jesus declared.

After carefully reviewing with appreciation nine reasons against baptism of infants, a contemporary Anglican clergyman who favors the baptism of infants concludes:

> *I would even be willing, in recognition of the failures in our paedobaptist churches, to give up infant baptism for one generation if that were possible! It would clear the ground, and enable us to have a fresh start, with the sign of the covenant marking out believers, and their children.*[53]

He considers baptism of infants God's act and believer's baptism man's response to God's act. This is hard to square with the New Covenant interpretation of baptism as a response of the believer to God's grace of pardon and adoption.

Admittedly neither Scripture nor early church tradition can answer the question. But to give baptism its *maximum* efficacy as a witness, it should follow repentance and a confession of faith by the candidate (Acts. 2:38-39; Rom. 6:3-4; cf. Col. 2:20; 3:1). Since water connotes washing or cleansing, it is more appropriately applied to those who *need* cleansing from sin than to innocent infants.

Today in the United Methodist Church, Christian parents or guardians are urged to present infants for baptism and train them in discipleship. The children become preparatory members until they are confirmed after training in Sunday School or Pastor' Class. Omitted is the mode of baptism, or its theological implications, about which the Wesleys were so explicit. An alternative of dedication, to be followed by baptism at confirmation, is not mentioned (*Discipline*, 1984).

2. The Lord's Supper

Outler observes that with reference to the Lord's Supper, Wesley followed a "middle way between an extreme eucharist realism . . . and its allegoristic opposite."[54] For the Wesleys the eucharist was "God's love in action, the actual means of grace," hence, "indispensable" for Christians.

Wesley urges that communicants "'prepare themselves for this solemn ordinance by self-examination and prayer.'" But, he added, "'this is not absolutely necessary.'" What is important, he continues, is a resolve "'to keep all the commandments of God . . . . and to receive all his promises.'"[55]

In the Anglican-Methodist ritual the communicant is bidden to come, as a sinner, to repent, thus making the sacrament a channel of pardoning grace. Is not this more in the Roman Catholic tradition in which the mass is the indispensable channel of grace? In the New Testament, and in evangelical perspective, Holy Communion is a feast of gratitude by saints whose sins are previously "covered with the blood." Compare "This do in remembrance of me," (Luke 22:19; 1 Cor. 11:24,25); the "cup of blessing," (1 Cor. 10:16); "You proclaim the Lord's death till he come" (1 Cor. 11:26.). Also the term "communion" connotes fellowship of those already reconciled, rather than a means by which the sinner receives pardon. Believers, of course, need to remember that they are "sinners saved by grace," and need the merits of Christ's blood constantly. The Eastern Orthodox seems closer to the New Testament than the Anglo-Catholic liturgy. They refer to the Lord's Supper as the Eucharist (thanksgiving).

The Anglican liturgy assumes a life of continual sinning and repenting with no real lasting victory over sin in this life.

Wesley believed that those "in Christ" may have continued victory over acts of sin, but he never seriously attempted to harmonize the sacramental theology he inherited with the evangelical theology which he rediscovered and which he articulated so effectively.

Wesley skillfully and judiciously sought to give both sacraments validity without succumbing to "cheap grace" (Bonhoffer). He did so by insisting that neither sacrament by itself brought assurance; that faith in Christ, and the transforming work of the Spirit are indispensable.

Commendably, Wesley interpreted the Eucharist as significant in three ways:

*(1) As a **memorial** of Jesus' death and vicarious atonement: "Ye do show forth the Lord's death; do this in remembrance of me" (Luke 22:19): "You proclaim the Lord's death" (cf. 1 Cor. 11:26). The communicant is reminded of Calvary and its significance personally, now.*

*(2) A "means" or **avenue** of present grace and spiritual renewal. In Wesley's word, He will meet me there, because He has promised so to do. I do expect that He will fulfill his Word, that he will meet and bless me in this way. Yet, not for the sake of any works which I have done ... but merely through the merits, and sufferings, and love of His Son.*[56]

Faith is essential, if the sacraments are a means of grace. As Wesley continued:

The opus operatum, the mere work done, profiteth nothing; ... there is no power but in the Spirit of God; no merit but in the blood of Christ ... consequently, even what God ordains, conveys no grace to the soul, if you trust not in Him alone.[57]

*(3) The Eucharist looks forward to the **future** (cf. "the Lord's death until he comes," (1 Cor. 11:26). It anticipates participation in the "marriage*

supper of the Lamb," ("I shall not drink again of the fruit of the vine until that day when I drink it new with you in my Father's kingdom," Matt.26:29).

Wesley differed from the Puritans who stressed self-examination prior to communion and Low-churchmen who took communion thrice yearly. Instead, with the High-churchmen, he stressed frequent or "constant" communion. Wesley would have none of the casual or infrequent communicant. In his advanced years he exhorted (or commanded) his Methodists to commune at every opportunity. Years before he had exhorted students at Oxford to commune daily or at least every week. He rejected the "frequent" and insisted on "constant" instead.

He dwelt at length on the sacrament as a command of God and also as an expression of God's mercy. In pursuit of this theme, the young cleric ignored the fact that grace came by faith from Christ and that the Sacrament reflected inward grace rather than an essential channel of that grace. The veteran revivalist found no reason to change or qualify the language of this pre-conversion theology. Wesley never resolved this tension between sacramental theology, and evangelical or biblical theology.[58]

Part of this theological concern was for reasons of expediency. First, Wesley wanted to integrate his evangelical piety with liturgical piety and to resist the inclination of many Methodists who cherished independence from the State Church. Second, his brother Charles insisted on adherence to the National Church. Third, he was being true to his heritage. Fourth, he needed no more controversy which would imperil the Evangelical Revival. He was not in a position to make an objective decision based on Scripture alone. If there had been less at stake, he might have agreed with those evangelicals who demanded a free church, and individual conversion, as many of his spiritual heirs did later.

Theological tensions about these sacraments were muted during Wesley's lifetime. They surfaced soon after his passing. Infant baptism was challenged and debated in the latter half of the following century. Holy Communion was usually observed four times each year rather than "constantly." Free from these restrictions, Methodism flourished in North America more than in the country of its origin. As Methodism became less episcopal, it became more evangelical and vigorous. Conversely, as the movement later became less evangelistic it gradually became more ritualistic. This is the phenomenon common to virtually all groups and is in evidence even among the recent new Pentecostal groups.

F. METHODIST INFLUENCE TODAY

A new look at Wesley was introduced in 1977 at the Sixth Oxford Institute of Methodist Theological Studies. Thor Hall is one of the voices challenging students of Wesley to differentiate themselves from "triumphalistic-denominational and idealistic-ideological" viewpoints which have characterized Wesleyan studies thus far. By contrast "tradition criticism" is said to seek a more objective appraisal of the man and his heritage, rather than the usual "pietistic individualism."

The new challenge is based on the conviction that Wesley was so much a creature of his own times that he cannot be a "model for Christian theology and Christian social ethics today."[59] Advocates of this "new view" point out that while Wesley knew of no "holiness" apart from "social holiness," this was in relation to people, not to the social structures of his day. While this approach to Wesleyan studies is at "an early stage," it is already obvious to them that no tradition-critical scholar can any longer consider Wesley's thought and practice the model for Christian social-ethics in our or any other era. Wesley was not even a mature social ethicist or political theologian for his own time . . . . his was not an adequate social ethic for contemporary Christians.[60]

Hall challenges the claim that Wesley was ecumenical by pointing out his criticism of Calvinism, the Quietists, Catholics, and Independents. His defenders may declare that he was a "contender" for the truths he found in Scripture and in his Anglican Church. He was motivated by a concern for sound doctrine, as was St. Paul, and against any theology that hindered the truth of the Gospel. His ecumenicity is best seen in his Sermon XXXIV, "Catholic Spirit." In this sermon he disclaims insistence on *opinions*, or *mode of worship* but rather "is thy heart with God?" As a pietist he stressed holy living as more important than controversy over doctrines. At Harvard Divinity School Wesley's sermon on a "Catholic Spirit" was read in chapel to an appreciative "liberal" audience which included very few evangelicals and even fewer disciples of Wesley. Hall might have been disappointed by their favorable response!

Hall then challenges Wesley's claim that Methodism was "nothing but scriptural Christianity . . . the true Christian doctrine of the Church of England." From this he concludes that "those he separated himself from, *by that very move*, were categorized as non-scriptural, even non-Christian."[61] This judgment seems less than objective! Wesley did not separate himself from the Church of England; he was thrust out of their pulpits. Actually Wesley, in this context, was defending his position against those who accused him of "separatism." Wesley simply affirmed his allegiance to Scripture and to his Church.

Next Hall questions whether Wesley really loved the poor. Was his merely, "a sentimental response to . . . their simplicity, receptivity, and teachableness?"[62] Instead, Hall says that Wesley failed to demand a restructuring of society to help the poorest. Quoting frequently from Porter's (1982) *English Society in the Eighteenth Century*, he faults Wesley for not demanding a political "war against poverty" instead of merely ministering to the poor out of Christian love, and admiring those who were "content with their lot." Thus he finds Wesley not addressing the social evils that cause poverty. Despite his disclaimers, Hall judges Wesley by the perceptions of today rather than of his day and age. Few of Wesley's contemporaries did more than he to help the impoverished.

Hall also doubts whether Wesley, a clergyman, had enough real righteous anger over a society which tolerated exploitation to serve as a model today. He discounts Wesley's tract on the evil of slavery in the colonies and his demand that Parliament outlaw slavery. But let Wesley speak for himself on his "mature" (age 88) thoughts on the subject. Wesley wrote to Wilberforce in Parliament on February 24, 1791, four days before his death, commending:

> *Your glorious enterprise, in exposing that execrable villinay, which is the scandal of religion, of England, and of human nature. Unless God has raised you up for this very thing, you will be worn out by the opposition of men and devils . . . . Go on, in the name of God, and in the power of His might, till even American slavery, the vilest that ever saw the sun shall vanish away before it . . . . a man who has a black skin, being wronged or outraged by a white man, can have not redress; it being a **law**, in our colonies, that the **oath** of a black, against a white, goes for nothing.*[63]

Yet even this evidence of righteous wrath and demand for social reform is not sufficient to convince Hall of Wesley's concern for the oppressed and his demand for political action! It is at least plausible that Methodist influence helped England to be the first European nation to outlaw slavery, and to even suppress, on the high seas, the African slave trade.

After noting Wesley's concern for the spiritual welfare of condemned felons Hall wonders why Wesley did not demand prison reforms and repeal of laws which specified death for shoplifting. Are we sure that he condoned these laws?

Wesley is found wanting because he was an evangelist and not also a social reformer like Benthem and Edmund Burke. Hall might have strengthened his thesis by asking why Wesley did not join with Quakers, and Anabaptists, in renouncing the bearing of arms. Wesley seemed more concerned about profanity among the soldiers than the subject of warfare itself.

Hall's insistence on "tradition criticism" in Wesleyan studies needs to be taken seriously and not dismissed. However, in disregarding Wesley's demand for "reforming the nation" as having little relevance for today's social problems, he overstates his case. Jesus, Peter, and Paul could be subjected to the same criticism, of being evangelists rather than social activists. Is the New Testament not relevant today?

We have much to learn from Wesley. He was not only a man of the eighteenth century, but, because of his acquaintance with Scripture and with the religion of the heart, he was far ahead of his time, even a model for our time.

Hall does not claim to be a Wesleyan scholar and, therefore, begins his thesis with the insights of Outler, "the leading light in the renewed study of Wesley."[64] Yet Outler himself, in the context of the Wesleyan heritage and our future, summarizes his assessment on a positive note: Wesley's way of "doing theology" is still relevant in several respects; these are

> *To ground it all in Scripture; to match it all against the centuries and the Christian consensus; to keep . . . grace **and** agency together; . . . effective mission . . . effective service to the world for which Christ died . . . is there a conceivable alternative more promising?*[65]

Most of the participants in Oxford Institute of Methodist Theological Studies seem to be more positive than Professor Hall with reference to the relevance of Wesleyan theology in today's world. Their "Working Group Paper" reflects a hopeful note:

> *The time is ripe, we believe, for fresh studies of Wesley in the contexts of cultural history as well as church history . . . it would see his constant emphasis on salvation by grace through faith . . . from the first stirrings of conscience [prevenient grace] on to the fullness of grace in holiness . . . to appreciate . . . his multiple ministries to the needy and oppressed . . . his interests and involvements in the issues of economic justice and human rights.*[66]

In many of the authors in this series attention seems focused more on Wesley and his relevance to today's problems than on Wesley's adherence to Scripture. In this review the concern is Wesley's claim that Methodism is a return to the religion of the Bible and his influence on the world of today.

Wesley can hardly be blamed for the social accompaniments of England's initiation of the industrial revolution. The specialist on Wesley and early Methodism is Henry D. Rack, *Reasonable Enthusiast John Wesley and the Rise of Methodism.* Recent assessments of this work vary. One recent positive assessment concludes, "This monumental biography of John Wesley joins the relative small cluster of superior works which rank at the top of the numerous biographies of Methodism's founder."[67]

Another specialist evaluates less positively in "Wesley on the Rack: Rack on Wesley." Ben Witherington III comments, "There is a certain tendency in *Reasonable Enthusiast* to downplay the importance for Wesley and his movement of certain of the essentials of doctrinal orthodoxy." Witherington also wonders "why only about 10 pages out of some 554 pages of text are directly devoted to the development of American Methodism," since the book includes "the Rise of Methodism."[68]

His assessment concludes that "Rack gives insufficient attention to the interface between the revival and reformation and how Wesley related one to the others."[69]

Some readers may conclude that Rack is eager to present Wesley in his humanity rather than his "triumphs" as many biographies have been eager to present him.

> *It was precisely this combination which accounts . . . for early Methodism's broad appeal. There can be little doubt that even in the later days Charles Wesley's "Jesus Lover of my Soul" has had as much*

(if not more) influence within American Protestantism as John Wesley's sober discourse "On Christian Perfection".[70]

APPRAISAL

To what extent was Wesley correct in viewing early Methodism as a return to New Testament Christianity? His judgment is valid, despite the retention of the hierarchical elements previously noted. It is seen in several respects: early Methodism emphasized a life transformed by Christ, victory over sin, and service to humanity. It is significant that the Methodists adopted the doctrines of the English Reformation as preserved in the Anglican Church. Yet the Methodists devised a *discipline*, not a *creed*; it formed a pattern of *life* more than a pattern of *thought*. The doctrine was there, but subordinate to a lifestyle consistent thereto.

The most *distinctive* doctrines of early Methodism were (a) *assurance* of personal acceptance in Christ, (b) *holiness* of heart and life, and (c) *love* of God and neighbor. The Methodists initiated some practices reminiscent of the Lollards in the time of Wycliffe. These include (1) the establishing of laymen (and women) as exhorters (to follow the sermon), evangelists, "elders," and pastors, (2) invading a parish but not invited by the State Church, (3) providing services to the needy, and (4) spreading the gospel through world evangelism. In defence to his Bishop Wesley replied, "The world is my parish." They broke new ground in these areas, or at least brought into prominence what earlier saints had discovered and witnessed.

Methodism transformed England more effectively than Puritanism, because it was less dogmatic. It did not directly challenge the institution of the State and did not resort to force to advance its aims.

Primitive Christianity sought to transform the Roman world through suffering and faith rather than political or military force. Methodism, unlike Puritanism, relied on both preaching and social service alone to affect its leavening influences on society.

It was in the area of holy living that the Wesleys were most distinctive and nearest to the genius of the New Covenant. To have the "mind of Christ," to "walk as He walked," to love God with all one's being and one's neighbor as one's self were their central concerns.

They differed from many Calvinists in offering free salvation to *all*, not just to the elect. Unlike the Established Church, they brought good news to the poor and unwashed rather than wait for them to attend houses of worship. The innovative Class Meeting served admirably to foster personal holiness, social concern, and spiritual discipline.

Many streams formed a confluence in the Methodist Revival. In order of influence they included Pietism, Puritanism, Protestantism, Anglicanism, and Catholicism. Like the Anabaptists, they insisted on *discipline* for the individual as well as for the group ("class" or "society"). They insisted on personal regeneration - - sanctification, like the Pietists. And as the Quakers, they went beyond progressive sanctification to entire sanctification, verifiable by a holy life. Methodists, like the Moravians, liked to sing the gospel.[71]

With the reservations listed previously, the claim of early Methodism to be a return to the church of the New Testament is convincing.

Chapter V Endnotes

1. Winthrop S. Hudson, *Religion in America*, (New York: Scribners, 1981), p. 59.
2. Hudson, p. 62.
3. W. W. Sweet, *Religion in Colonial America*, (New York: Scribners, 1942), pp. 275-281.
4. A. W. Schottschneider, *Through Five Thousand Years*, (Bethlehem, PA: Comenius Press, 1956), p. 54.
5. Sweet, p. 286.
6. Luke Tyerman, *Life and Times of John Wesley*, (London: James Sangster, 1976), I, pp. 222-223.
7. Tyerman, I, 221.
8. S. Parks Cadman, *The Three Religious Leaders of Oxford and Their Movements*, (Macmillan, 1916), p. xv.
9. John Wesley, "Sermon" CXXXI, *Works*, VII, 423-424.
10. Richard P. Heitzenrater, *Mirror and Memory* (Kingswood, Nashville, TN, 1989) p. 15.
11. John Wesley, "Journal" (May 1738), *Works*, 1, 98.
12. Susanna Wesley, "A Letter," *Arminian Magazine*, John Wesley, Editor, (London: J. F. & Co., 1778), Vol. 1, p. 35.
13. J. Wesley, *Works*, XI, 367.
14. J. Wesley, "Circumcision of the Heart," *Works*, V. p. 203.
15. John Wesley, "Journal" for May 1738, *Works*, I, pp. 98, 99.
16. A. C. Outler, *John Wesley*, (New York: Oxford, 1964), pp. 346-367.
17. E. H. Sugden, "Annotation," in J. Wesley, "The Witness of the Spirit," in Sugden, *The Standard Sermons of John Wesley*, (Nashville: Lamar & Barton, Agents, nd.), I, 200.
18. Outler, p. 15-16.
19. John Wesley, "Journal" (October 14, 1738); *Works*, I, p. 162.
20. L. R. Marston, *From Age to Age A Living Witness*, (Winona Lake, IN: Light and Life Press, 1960), pp. 54-59.
21. John Wesley, "Sermon XI," *Works*, V, pp. 98, 99.

22. J. W., *Primitive Remedies*, (Santa Barbara, CA: Woodbridge Press, 1975), pp. 1-142.
23. J. W., *Works*, VII, 419 ff.
24. This tension is treated at length in Colin W. Williams, *John Wesley's Theology Today*, (Nashville: Abingdon, 1960), pp. 207-242.
25. A. W. Nagler, *Pietisim and Methodism*, (Nashville: Publishing House of Methodist Church South, 1918), F. E. Stoeffler, ed., *Continental Pietism and Early American Christianity*, (Grand Rapids: Wm. B. Eerdmans, 1976), pp. 211-212.
26. For example, J.W. Bready, *England Before and After Wesley*, (London: Hodder and Stoughton, 1938).
27. A chilling description of England at his period is detailed in Robert Hughes, *The Fatal Shore*, (New York: Knopf, 1987), pp. 20-31.
28. Hughes, p. 389.
29. A discerning history of people and events leading up to this War is in A. J. Langguth, *Patriots*, (New York: Simon and Schuster, 1988), pp. 13-637.
30. A new perspective on the French Revolution is in Simon Schama, *Citizens*, (New York: Knop, 1989), pp. vii-948.
31. Richard Hooker, "A Learned Discourse of Justification," *Ecclesiastical Polity, Everyman's Library*. Edited by Ernest Rhys, (London: J.M. Denton and Sons, 1925 reprint), I, p. 19.
32. Sugden, I, pp. 280, 281. It is strange Bishop Ole Borgen in "No End Without the Means: John Wesley and the Sacraments," *The Asbury Journal*, Spring, 1991, makes no mention of the inconsistence of regeneration before the application of water. Scripture says, "believe and be baptized," (Acts 2:38; 8:36-37).
33. J. W., *Works*, X, pp. 191, 192.
34. J. W., Sermon "The New Birth," *Works*, VI, p. 74.
35. From Wesley's manuscript in Epworth House, cited in A.E. Outler, *John Wesley*, (New York: Oxford University Press, 1964), p. 318.
36. Op. cit.
37. *Didache*, VII, 1-4; cf. *Barnabas* XI, 8-10, *The Apostolic Fathers*, translated by Kirsopp Lake, (London: Wm. Heinmann, 1930), I, pp. 321, 383.

38. J. Wesley, "Treatise on Baptism," *Works*, X, p. 190.
39. *Book of Common Prayer*, p. 388, cited in *Works*, X, p. 191.
40. Tertullian, *De Baptismo*, C. xviii. *Documents of the History of the Church*, edited by B.J. Kidd, I, pp. 149, 150, (citing A. Souter, *Tertullian's Treatises on Prayer and on Baptism*), (New York: MacMillan Co., 1938), p. 69.
41. J. Wesley, *Works*, VI, pp. 75, 76.
42. William F. Arndt and F. Wilbur Gingrich. A Greek-English Lexicon of the New Testament and Other Christian Literature. Second edition, revised and augmented by F. Wilbur Gingrich and Frederick W. Danker. (Chicago: University of Chicago Press, 1979), p. 481.
43. J. W., "Treatise on Baptism," *Works*, X, p. 193.
44. *Works*, X, p. 197.
45. G. F. Moore, *Judaism,* (Cambridge: Harvard University Press, 1946), I, pp. 330-335.
46. After a "confession of faith" the candidate was "then immersed completely," and then later given "exhortations and benediction" -Eidersheim, "Baptism of Proselytes" in *Life and Times of Jesus the Messiah*, (New York: Longmans, Green and Co., 1899), II, p. 746.
47. Tertullian, *De Baptismo*, C. xviii, Kidd, p. 150.
48. *Works*, X, p. 199.
49. Frank Baker, *John Wesley and the Church of England*, (Nashville, Abingdon, 1970), pp. 142, 246.
50. *Ibid.*, p, 282. In his doctoral dissertation Dr. Chong Nahm Cho carefully came to the conclusion that even in his directives for American churches, John Wesley retained most of the language of Angelical Church, including baptism regeneration. Chong Nahm Cho, "A Study in John Wesley's Doctrine of Baptism in the Light of Current Interpretations," (Emory University: Doctor of Philosophy, 1966), p. 149.
51. C. Wesley King, "Infant Baptism in Biblical and Wesleyan Theology," M. Th. Dissertation, Asbury Theological Seminary, 1975 (in The B. F. Fisher Library), p. 331.

52. L. R. Marston, "Letter" in the Free Methodist Historical Center, Winona Lake, Indiana, cited in King, p. 331.
53. Michael Green, *Baptism*, (Intervarsity Press, 1987), pp. 98-99.
54. A. Outler, p. 333.
55. Cited in Outler, p. 337.
56. Sermon: "The Means of Grace," Sugden, I, 254.
57. Op. cit. 259.
58. See also Irwin Reist, "John Wesley's View of the Sacraments: A Study in the Historical Development of a Doctrine," *Wesley Theological Journal*, (Wesley Theological Society, Spring, 1971), pp. 41-55.
59. Thor Hall, "Tradition Criticism: A New View of Wesley," at the LeRoy A. Martin Lectureship at the University of Tennessee at Chattanooga, 1987, p. 6.
60. Hall, p. 17.
61. Hall, p. 9 (citing *Works*, I, pp. 225, 232).
62. Hall, p. 11.
63. J. W. "Letter to a Friend" (Wilberforce), *Works*, XIII, p. 153.
64. Hall, p. 6.
65. Outler, "Methodism's Theological Heritage: a Study in Perspective," *Methodism's Destiny in an Ecumenical Age*, Paul M. Minus, Jr., editor, (Nashville: Abingdon Press, 1969), p. 70.
66. M. Douglas Meeks, Editor, *The Future of Methodist Theological Traditions*, (Nashville: Abingdon Press, 1985), p. 55.
67. Kenneth Cain Kinghorn, *The Asbury Theological Journal*, Spring 1991, Volume 46, pp. 131-133.
68. *Ashland Theological Journal*, (Ashland, Ohio, 1991), pp. 77, 79.
69. *Ibid.*, p. 80.
70. Stoeffler, "Pietism, the Wesleys, and Methodist Beginnings in America," *Continental Pietism and Early American Christianity*, F.E. Stoeffler, Editor, (Grand Rapids: Wm. B. Eerdmans, 1976), pp. 210-211.

71. Timothy L. Smith, *The Pentecost Hymns of John and Charles Wesley*, (Kansas City, MO: Beacon Hill Press, passim.), p. 22. *See also John and Charles Wesley*, Frank Whaling, Ed., (New York: Paulist Press, 1981), p. 285.

Chapter VI
IN QUEST OF UNITY: DISCIPLES (CHRISTIANS)

The First "Campmeeting"

"This memorable meeting came on Thursday or Friday before the third Lord's Day in August, 1801. The roads were literally crowded with wagons, carriages, horsemen and footmen moving to the solemn camp. The sight was affecting. It was judged, by military men on the ground, that there were between twenty and thirty thousand collected. Four or five preachers were frequently speaking at the same time, in different parts of the encampment, without confusion. The Methodist and Baptist preachers aided in the work, all appeared cordially united in it--of one mind and one soul, and the salvation of sinners seemed to be the great object of all. We all engaged in singing the same songs of praise--all united in prayer--all preached the same things--free salvation urged upon all by faith and repentance." ("Autobiography of Barton W. Stone").

The Cane Ridge Meeting House, James R. Rogers, (Cincinnati, The Standard Publishing Company, 1910), pp. 157-158.

One of the few denominations to originate in the New World is that which is known by the name provided by pagans in Antioch: simply "Christians" (Acts 11:26) or, as some prefer, "Disciples" (Acts 19:1). To trace their origins and proliferation leads to one of the most complex trajectories in American Church history. But their importance is indicated by the fact that, world-wide, they number some five million communicants. Their bold claim to have no other creed than the New Testament demands recognition in a study of those who claim to be nearest to the Church of the New Testament.

The quest for origins leads to Bourbon County, Kentucky, and the "Shrine" at Cane Ridge a few miles east of Paris. It was here, in the beautiful "Bluegrass" region of central Kentucky, that the "Second Great Awakening" made its most remembered impact. The influence of the "Second Awakening", in extent and length, was far greater even than the "First Great Awakening" along the Atlantic seaboard seventy years earlier. The most recent (1975) and definitive history of this denomination chronicles "the sweep and direction of Disciples history from Cane Ridge to the present."[1]

Why begin at Cane Ridge? The "Shrine" there provides an explanation. Here, on a county road, a modern steel structure covers the primitive log meeting house where Pastor Barton Stone served two Presbyterian churches, the other at nearby Concord. In a nearby building, a museum preserves much of the memorabilia concerning Pastor Stone and the origins of the "Christians." The warden, housed nearby, welcomes the numerous visitors and conventions which frequent Cane Ridge, especially in summer months. Here one can envision the moving of God's Spirit, like that at Pentecost, an event which launched not only a new denomination, but even more importantly, the "Second" religious "Awakening," the effects of which still linger.

Here, on August 7-12, 1801, occurred the climax of a series of revivals in Kentucky, beginning in Logan County the previous year.

> *The rising tide of religious awakening reached its climax in a union meeting of Presbyterians, Methodists, and Baptists at Cane Ridge in August, 1801. The immense throngs that gathered from all parts of Kentucky and from many parts of Ohio . . . choked the roads, and exhausted the food supply. They came in wagons, buggies, on horseback, and on foot. . . . They were housed in tents erected in rows in the woods and lit by torches and campfires at night. Preachers from the three communions addressed groups simultaneously from stumps, logs, and improvised pulpits, as many as seven preaching at one time. . . . People in a sea of sound were praying, weeping, shouting, and calling on the Lord for mercy. Skeptics who came to witness these strange phenomena themselves succumbed to their influence. There were some 3,000 converts . . . Members of the three denominations found a common ground of unity in a profound shared experience and the simple, nontheological preaching of faith and repentance . . . a practical demonstration of Christian union.*[2] *An estimated 20,000 were in attendance.*

This was the origin of "camp meetings" which began among Presbyterians, and continued in Methodism. Those familiar with the Reformed doctrines of election were amazed and elated that the gospel was intended for *all*, not only for the "elect." Consistent with the Pentecost in Jerusalem (Acts 2:17-21) the "good news" on this western frontier became eclectic, and democratic; ALL were welcome to participate!

The overt expressions of spiritual renewal included "the jerks," prostration, groaning for deliverance from guilt, joyous shouting in relief, and singing "in the Spirit." Pastor Stone, amazed at these unexpected developments, tried to describe them:

> *This is more unaccountable than anything else I ever saw. The subject in a happy state of mind would sing most melodiously, not from the mouth or nose, but entirely in the breast . . . . Such music silenced everything and attracted the attention of all. It was most heavenly . . . . Dr. J. P. Campbell and myself . . . concluded it to be something surpassing anything we had known in nature.*[3]

These strange phenomena caught and kept attention, but were peripheral to the central fact of new birth and spiritual renewal. It was "probably the greatest demonstration of revival power ever seen in America . . . . one of the great events in the history of religion" in North America.

A brief review of events which culminated at Cane Ridge is appropriate. Periodic "awakenings" haad occurred in what is now the United States since Colonial days, beginning with Frelinghusen, and Gilbert Tennent, in New Jersey. Both pastors, like Spener and Franke in Germany, "insisted that no one ever became a Christian without first being subjected to the terrifying realization that he was not a Christian."[5]

In Connecticut the "Great Awakening" was led by Jonathan Edwards and intensified, after 1739, under Whitefield and others associated with Calvinism. Graduates of the Tennent "log college" at Neshaminy fanned out with evangelistic zeal in the southern states and on the western frontier. "The first Methodist revival in America was the one which occurred in 1772 in Devereux Jarratt's parish in Virginia and spread to neighboring counties."[6]

A. WILDERNESS REVIVAL

At Harrodsburg, Kentucky, a bronze roadside marker erected by the Kentucky Historical Association reads thus:

WILDERNESS REVIVAL

Scene of the First of a series of religious revivals conducted in Kentucky during April and May in 1776. The Rev. Thomas Tinsley, a Baptist minister, was assisted by William Hickman in meetings held here under a spreading elm tree. The tree was only a short distance from the "Big Spring" where Captain James Harrod and men started Kentucky's first settlement. [A marble marker nearby adds] The spreading elm was the Pioneers' first Sanctuary.

In Kentucky Presbyterians were more numerous than Baptists or Methodists. Revivals in Logan County and in the Lexington area were led by Presbyterians, especially James McGready and William McGee. These revivals resulted in 340 additions to Presbyterian Churches in a few months. A half century after the Cane Ridge campmeeting Presbyterians grew to 487,691 members, Congregationalists to 197,197, the Baptists to 815,212, and the Methodists to 1,323,631.[7]

Even more significant was the impact on the moral life of the nation. Bible Societies were formed, the Temperance Movement began, mission societies proliferated, duelling was outlawed, the Holiness Movement was accelerated by Finney and continued by the Methodists, the role of women was enhanced, and numerous church colleges were founded.

A wave of Protestant revivals known as the Second Great Awakening swept the country during the first third of the nineteenth century. . . . this evangelical enthusiasm generated a host of moral and cultural reforms. The most dynamic and divisive of them was abolitionism. Heirs of the Puritan notion of collective accountability that made every man his brothers keeper, these Yankee reformers repudiated Calvinistic predestination, preached the availability of redemption to anyone who sought it, urged converts to abjure sin, and worked for the elimination of sins from society.[8]

The ethos of the nation improved until the end of the century.

B. THE STRUGGLE FOR UNITY

However, as with the first Great Awakening, the revivals on the Kentucky frontier had their opponents. Those who welcomed revivalism were called the "New Light" group, the conservative, negative side were the "Old Lights." Several Presbyterian ministers complained that preaching was done by unordained, untrained laymen. This was not a problem with the Baptists and Methodists if the gospel was being preached with positive effects.

Also the revivalists were "proclaiming salvation for all in utter disregard of the Calvinistic doctrine that Christ died only for the elect." Presbyterian elders accused their pastor, Richard McNemar, of declaring "that a sinner has power to believe in Christ at any time."[9] Order in worship, theology, and ordination were seen by some clergy as threatening; the status quo was being disturbed by revivals. Preaching without training and ordination became such an issue that in 1810 the formation of the Cumberland Presbyterian Church resulted, after repeated appeals to the General Assembly were in vain.

Tensions mounted until six Presbyterian pastors, who had been accused of forsaking Calvinism for Arminianism and of teaching that Christ died for all, rather than only for the "elect," withdrew from the Synod of Kentucky at Lexington in 1803. Earlier at his ordination, Barton Stone had stated that he had reservations about the Westminster Confession, yet was approved for ordination because he affirmed his commitment to Scripture.

1. Barton Stone and the "Christians"

The six who withdrew from the Synod of Kentucky still insisted that they were Presbyterians and, consequently, organized the "Springfield Presbytery," loosely organized but committed to revivalism. Included in their *Apology* was Barton Stone's listing of errors in the Presbyterian interpretation of Scripture. Stone and the other five insisted that atonement was for *all*, that *anyone* may believe, and be regenerated. They rejected Calvinistic elements in the Westminster Confession, because they seemed inconsistent not only with Scripture, but also with what God seemed to be doing in winning souls via revivalism. It was not unlike the situation in Acts when God's action in admitting non-Jews to the Covenant seemed contradictory to both tradition and the Old Testament (Acts 10-15). They were placing Scripture above creedal statements, something intolerable to the Old Light majority of Presbyterians.

Less than a year after these New Lights separated from the Synod and prepared their subsequent *Apology*, the Springfield Presbytery, decided to dissolve itself. To explain this action they prepared what they called their "Last Will and Testament."

Their "Will" was drawn up like any last will. It contained some of the following elements.

Their decease was (1) to permit their merger into "the Body of Christ," consistent with their aversion to schism; (2) to adopt "the law of the Spirit of life in Christ Jesus" [Rom. 8:2]; (3) "to obtain license from God to preach the simple Gospel"; (4) to recognize those who speak when under God's authority, with or without ordination; (5) to maintain the right of the congregation to choose its pastor; (6) to accept the Bible as the only authority; (7) "to pray more and dispute less"; (8) to require the Synod of Kentucky to liberate those who do not agree with the Confession of Faith (9) to "*will that sister bodies read their Bibles and prepare for death.*"[10] Six pastors signed the document on June 28, 1804 and published it, accompanied by an "Address." Three *major* concerns emerged: the appeal to Scripture over creeds, a return to what they considered the primitive church and the need for unity among Christians. Since they were no longer Presbyterians, what were they? In spite of their abhorrence of divisions, on June 28, 1804, they chose as a name for their group the term "Christian" (to which any of the denominations had equal claim.) This decision resulted in still another denomination, despite their concern for unity.

Following these six "New Light" pastors, several Presbyterian congregations became "Christian" in Northern Kentucky and Southern Ohio. New churches were planted which shared these views. Even today some of the United Churches of Christ in southern Ohio refer to themselves as New Lights, since they came into being because of the early Nineteenth Century revival resulting from the events in Kentucky.

> *Religious meetings inspired by Cane Ridge were held in people's homes and in groves of trees. Among these visiting preachers was the reverend Barton Stone, instrumental in the Cane Ridge revivals . . . . Followers of the Christian Faith . . . . organized the Christian Church, called by some "The New Light," in Russellville Ohio, on the 26th day of June, 1827 . . . . "The Christians receive Christ as their only leader; Christian as their only name; the Bible as their only creed, and all Christians as their brethren.*"[11]

Meanwhile in Virginia, James O'Kelley, in protest against Asbury's insistence on Episcopal polity, formed the "Republican Methodists" (December 1793) with a congregational polity. Later on August 4, 1794, at the suggestion of O'Kelley's associate Haggard, they decided to change their name to the "Christian Church." It was Haggard who suggested this name for the seceders in Kentucky.

Later Haggard, influenced by Samuel Davies, published an essay, rediscovered in 1953, entitled, *An Address . . . on the Sacred Import of the Christian Name.*[12]. While insisting that Christians should be known by no other name, he accused other denominations of neglecting the Bible and focusing on non-essentials. The basic desire of the new denomination was the *restoration* of the primitive church, a motive prominent at the origins of Anabaptists, Puritans, Brethren, Methodists, and Pentecostals. In this they were part of the Pietist movement through the centuries.

As the historian of Presbyterians in America viewed it, "the Great Awakening . . . terminated the Puritan and inaugurated the Pietist or Methodist age of American church history."[13] The Christians in the Ohio Valley were partakers of this "Pietist age." The "New Light" or "Christian" groups multiplied rapidly. By 1805 they counted more than fifteen churches on both sides of the Ohio river, some at the expense of Presbyterian churches and others as the result of evangelism.

Both Presbyterians and the Christians suffered at the hands of enthusiastic Shakers from New York. The perfectionism and zeal of the Shakers, aided by the revival atmosphere, served to wean two of the six founding fathers of the Christian church, with their congregations, to the Shaker movement. They founded a community at Pleasant Hill, between Harrodsburg and Lexington, which flourished until the Civil War; their stone buildings have recently been restored to become the Shakertown of today.

Of the six founding fathers only Stone remained. He labored in desperation to save the Movement he headed. The remnant continued to evangelize and increase, as did the Baptists and Methodists; the Presbyterians lagged. Membership among the Christians by 1830 had increased to about 12,000.[14]

Growth of Christian churches resulted from the efforts of converted laymen who, with little training, began preaching while still continuing with their occupation, which usually, like that of Stone, was farming. Dedication to their task gave them energy to evangelize effectively, like the Apostle Paul, early Methodist circuit riders, and Pentecostals of the present century.

Early in his ministry Stone struggled to test prevailing theologies with Scripture. In 1804 his mind "became embarrassed on the doctrine of Atonement."[15] He objected to the doctrine of the substitutionary death of Christ, as it seemed to imply that God the Father needed to be reconciled to sinners and that the death of Jesus paid the ransom of all sinners, all mankind. In this he overlooked the principle of satisfying the demands of the Law, as argued by Paul in Romans 3:20-28 and elsewhere. He lacked time and opportunity to articulate an alternative view, but contented himself with stating the views he rejected, and simply affirming the truth of John 3:16. He failed to find in Scripture the doctrine of the Trinity, but the failure did not emerge in his teaching.

After opposing a Presbyterian minister's decision to adopt believers' baptism, the minister's defense was so convincing that Stone also refrained from baptizing infants. Baptism was not a problem during the revival "excitement," but later it became an issue. Sprinkling seemed inadequate, many preferred immersion. After a conference among the Christian elders and pastors, it was agreed to permit either. Who would baptize? They agreed that the authority to preach implied the authority to baptize.

As public interest intensified Stone came to the conclusion that baptism was ordained for the remission of sins and ought to be administered in the name of Jesus to all believing penitents . . . Into the spirit of the doctrine I was never fully led, until it was revived by Brother Alexander Campbell, some years later.[16] Stone's eagerness to avoid sectarian strife led to his willingness to modify his view of baptism, and prepared him for the more strident and hence divisive theology of the Campbells.

Stone's continued leadership included his publication of the *Christian Messenger* beginning in 1826 and extending throughout his life. This journal kept the Movement alive and was the major link among the independent Christian churches which lacked both the cohesiveness of a conference, like the Methodists, or a Synod, like the Presbyterians.

Although the Cane Ridge Campmeeting is the best remembered of the events which launched the Christian Churches, and Barton Stone was the pastor-host of the event, he was not the "Founder" of the movement. Most initiatives came from others. But he was the most steadfast of the early revivalists, as noted earlier. Most of his theological essays were his own and did not necessarily embody the distinctive convictions of the Movement.

> But there was a firmness, a sweetness, and a saintliness in Stone's character that gave him the growing influence among his brethren. Moreover, when the movement was a little more than twenty years old, Stone began to edit and publish a magazine, the **Christian Messenger**. . . . the chief instrument of such unity as they had. In the absence of any actual "ecclesiastical head," the editor, who was the outstanding elder statesman of the group, and the sole survivor of those who initiated it, became the most influential personality among the Christians in the West.[17]

Stone was most effective as an evangelist. In Northern Kentucky and in Southern Ohio many Christian Churches resulted from his labors. Typical of Stone's work as evangelist, with R. Dooley, in Ohio is this excerpt from his *Autobiography*.

> We preached and baptized daily in Eaton for many days. No house could contain the people that flocked to hear. We had to preach in the open streets to the anxious multitude. At night, after service, the cries and prayers of the distressed in many houses around were truly solemn. Almost the whole town and neighborhood were baptized, and added to the Lord. We left this place, and preached and baptized in many other places. We were poorly clad, and had not money to buy clothes. Going on . . . a limb tore brother Dooley's striped linen pantaloons very much. He had no other, nor had I another pair to lend him. We consoled ourselves that we were in the Lord's work, and he would provide. He tied his handkerchief over the rent, and we went and preached to the people. That night we lodged with brother Samuel Wilson, whose wife presented brother Dooley a pair of homespun linen pantaloons.[18]

His account reports conversions at night and baptisms illuminated by flaming torches. Obviously they followed the New Testament precept; "repent and be baptized" quite literally, with little emphasis on a follow-up or the *didache*, the instruction which should follow conversion (Matt. 28:19-20).

This picture of lay-evangelism reflects graphically the far-reaching influence of the "Awakening" and is a poignant reminder of similar scenes in the Gospels, of the mendicant Friars in medieval Europe, of the Lollards in Wycliffe's England, of Wesley's lay-preachers, and of the Methodist circuit riders contemporary with Stone.

2. The Campbells and the "Disciples"

> *In 1807 there came from Ireland to America a man of great humility and deep Christian convictions, who was destined to initiate the greatest*

> *religious movement of peculiarly American origin in the history of the Christian Church . . . . to state in the earliest and a most important document . . . the basic Biblical principles by which the union of all Christians might be accomplished.*[19]

Thus historian Murch introduces Thomas Campbell who, in his judgment, was the real founder of the Christian (Disciples) denomination. The debate between those of the Stone tradition and those of the Campbells, as to the real founder of the denomination, has never been fully settled, hence the the dual name: Christians (Disciples).

Born in Ireland of Scottish parents in 1763, Campbell experienced an evangelical conversion after a period of "misgivings and a sense of sin." He was graduated from Glasgow University in liberal arts and began his study for the Christian ministry. Licensed by the Presbytery in Ireland, he began a ministry of preaching and teaching. His home, with his wife Jane and six children, was one of devotion and spiritual disciplines, like those of early Puritans and Methodists.

Several issues disturbed him as pastor and principal of the school at Rich Hill, Ireland: (1) quarrels about doctrine among the Presbyterian factions, (2) the influence of the Puritan congregation at Rich Hill, which was warm, evangelical, and open to all of kindred spirit, (3) their observance of the Lord's Supper each Lord's Day, (4) membership in the Evangelical Society, which was open to all denominations, and (5) the rebuke he received in Pennyslvania for serving communion to those Presbyterians who were not of the Associate Synod of North America. He resigned from his denomination and was without ecclesiastical credentials.

Campbell asked his son Alexander, then principal of the school his father had headed, to come to Pennsylvania. Determined to continue his ministry, he preached in any church that invited him. He urged listeners to cooperate, rather than compete with other Christian groups, and he held meetings under trees, like the Evangelical Societies in England. In 1809 a large gathering of those with similar concerns gathered to hear him. After his message concerning the importance of Scripture and unity among Christians, he ended by an appeal destined to become the slogan of the new movement: "WHERE THE SCRIPTURES SPEAK, WE SPEAK; AND WHERE THE SCRIPTURES ARE SILENT, WE ARE SILENT."[20]

Soon after this meeting the "Christian Association of Washington" [western Pennsylvania] was organized on August 17, 1809, with only twenty-one members!

After further reflection Thomas wrote his "DECLARATION AND ADDRESS," one of the three doctrinal statements of the Disciples (the other two being the "Apology for Renouncing the Jurisdiction of the Synod of Kentucky" and "The Last Will and Testament of the Springfield Presbytery."[21]

Four essential principles of the "Declaration" were the right of private judgment, sole authority of the Bible, avoidance of sectarianism, and Christian unity (based on Scripture alone). Included in this doctrine is an important definition of a church that is Christian. He wrote:

> *The church of Christ upon earth is essentially, intentionally, and constitutionally one; consisting of all those in every place that profess their faith in Christ and give obedience to him in all things pertaining to the scriptures, and that manifest the same by their tempers and conduct.*[22]

The thirteen propositions of the *Address* may be condensed into six:

(1) the essential unity of the Church of Christ.

(2) the supreme authority of the Scriptures.

(3) the special authority of the New Testament.

(4) the fallacy of human creeds.

(5) the essential brotherhood of all who love Christ and try to follow him.

(6) the conviction that if human innovations could be removed from the church, followers of Christ will unite upon the scriptural platform.[23]

The first, fifth, and sixth propositions all stress unity; if these are combined the list is reduced to four. So the gist of the *Address* is this: if Christians unite on the basis of Scripture alone, and forget "human creeds," Christ's prayer for unity will be fulfilled. This is true. The paradox is that in the effort to dispense with "human creeds" the Campbells created still another "human creed" to the exclusion of all others. This commendable quest for unity among Christians in America had been sought in vain by Count Zinzendorf in the years 1742-46. Both were unsuccessful in healing the frequent quarrels over doctrine and polity; hence competition instead of cooperation prevailed.

Before coming to America, Alexander had come to the same conclusions as had his father with reference to the Seceder [Presbyterian] church and the Lord's Supper. When he read his father's *Declaration and Address* he found himself fully in accord with these principles. Urged by his father, he spent the next six months in a disciplined study of the Bible.

Meanwhile, by 1810 Thomas had come to the conclusion that the Christian Associations he sponsored were not multiplying. His message was not gaining attention and support. In desperation he applied to the Synod of Pittsburgh for membership in the regular Presbyterian Church. His request was denied.

> *The Synod are constrained by the most solemn considerations to disapprove the plan (of association) . . . and further . . . Mr. Campbell's request to be received into christian and ministerial communion cannot be granted.*[24]

Later the Synod was more specific in listing reasons for the rejection:

> *such a merger would be destructive of the whole interest of religion by promoting divisions instead of union, by degrading ministerial character, by providing free admission to any errors of doctrine and to any corruptions of discipline . . . . his belief that there are some opinions taught in our Confession of Faith which are not founded in the Bible, and avoiding to designate them; for declaring that the administration of baptism to infants . . . is a matter of indifference . . . for encouraging and countenancing his son to preach the gospel without any regular authority; for opposing creeds and confessions as injurious to the interests of religion.*[25]

Obviously, the relationship of the Campbells to the Presbyterians was, in many respects, similar to that of Barton Stone.

At a meeting of the Christian Association on November 1, 1810, Alexander gave a ringing and convincing explanation of the principles of the "Reformation." On May 4, 1811, the group, numbering thirty, organized itself as the "Brush Run Church." They had become an autonomous church, congregational in polity. The Lord's Supper was served then and every Lord's Day thereafter.

The issue of baptism soon arose because three of the charter members had not been baptized. Alexander's first child brought up the question of mode. After he had studied the Bible further, Alexander was convinced that immersion was the biblical mode. He requested rebaptism for himself by a Baptist preacher "on a simple confession of faith." His infant was not baptized. The Campbells were confronted with what others had discovered, that Scriptures must be interpreted by "human means," in which honest opinions differ. The naivete of "where the Scriptures are silent we are silent" must have been apparent.

Later members of the Brush Run church were accepted in the Redstone Baptist Association and, despite some tensions, remained Baptists for seventeen years, until paradoxically, as a separate denomination, they pursued their goal of Christian unity.

3. The Merger of Christians and Disciples

A major event in the on-going revival was the arrival on the Kentucky frontier of Alexander Campbell. Barton Stone and Alexander Campbell met for the first time in Georgetown, Kentucky. Campbell's fame had preceded him. Stone noted that, "Some said, He is a good man; but others say, nay: for he deceiveth the people."[26] Stone, eager for unity, heard him in public and in private and came to this conclusion:

> *I was pleased with his manner and matter. I saw no distinctive feature between the doctrine he preached and that which we had preached for many years, except on baptism for remission of sins . . . . I thought then that he was not sufficiently explicit on the influences of the Spirit, which led many honest Christians to think he denied them . . . . In a few things I dissented with him, but was agreed to disagree . . . . I will not say there are no faults in Brother Campbell . . . over these few my love would throw a veil, and hide them . . . . I am . . . constrained to acknowledge him to be the greatest promoter of this reformation of any man living.*[27]

In Stone's words, "He boldly determined to take the Bible alone for his standard of faith and practice, to the exclusion of all other books as authoritative."[28] Stone gladly welcomed this addition to what he called the "Reformation."

Campbell differed from Stone in his emphasis on "baptism for the remission of sins [baptismal regeneration] for believing penitents." His followers also stressed weekly communion. Because of Stone's eagerness for Christian unity and their common commitment to the "Bible only," the two groups became one in spirit.

One note of difference which caused concern among Stone's associates was Campbell's perceived neglect of the "influences of the Spirit." Some got the impression that he believed that the written Word was sufficient, that prayer and the work of the Spirit were unnecessary for salvation.[29] This perception was confirmed later.

> *Alexander Campbell in his **Christian System** almost makes the Holy Spirit identical with God as creator and revealer. . . . Contrary to the teaching of popular revivalism in the early nineteenth century, Disciple evangelists said that men are not converted by direct action of the Holy Spirit upon their wills, but by their own voluntary response to the saving Word. . . . The fact is that Disciples of Christ have never known quite what to say about the Holy Spirit. . . . When Campbell said that "there is God and the Spirit of God, just as there is man and the spirit of man," he did nothing to clarify the concept of the Holy Spirit as in any sense a distinct personality.*[30]

After consultation and prayer, Stone, J. T. Johnson ("than whom, there is not a better man," said Stone), evangelists John Smith and John Rogers, agreed that a merger with the Reformers would be desirable. This was recommended in pages of *The Christian Messenger*.

Alexander Campbell was excited and wrote, "I will, with the help of God, co-operate in any measure which can conduce to the furtherance of the gospel."[31] A merger of the Christians and Reformers was effected in 1832 in Lexington, KY. Later Stone was on the defensive for this move. He lamented the negative voices among both the Christians and the Reformers. In his last recorded "Biography," intended for his children, he refers to "darts from both sides," which he will patiently endure until the "the resurrection to immortality."[32] But the majority were convinced that this move was "a Restoration of the New Testament Church in doctrine, ordinances, and life."[33]

4. Walter Scott's Contribution

Another charismatic Scotchman then entered the picture as a "reformer." Walter Scott, born in Scotland in 1796, is recognized as one of the four Founding Fathers of the Movement. After studying in the University of Edinburgh, he arrived in New York in 1818. He taught Latin on Long Island, then went "west" to Pittsburgh and joined a "free church" where immersion, foot washing, and the "holy kiss" were practiced. He was favorably impressed by the eagerness of this group to follow the New Testament practices literally. He read a pamphlet written by Henry Errett and published by "Scotch Baptists" in New York.

173

> *It connected baptism so definitely with remission of sins and salvation that, in this view, it became highly questionable whether any of the immersed, regardless of their possession of the fruits of the Spirit, could be "acknowledged as Disciples, as having made the Christian profession, as having put on Christ, as having passed from death to life."*[34]

Further reflection led him to the conclusion that anyone is a Christian who could affirm that "Jesus is the Christ." In this rational approach to the gospel, his acceptance of John Locke's insistence on the rational, as distinct from the emotional aspect of conversion, was seen as a major contribution to the idea of primitive Christianity.

Meanwhile the Campbells perceived that their interpretation of primitive Christianity was not spreading rapidly. The arrival of Scott in Ohio and his success in evangelism demanded a fresh review of Scriptural teaching. He preached that a sinner can do three things in order to be saved: (1) believe (on evidence) that Jesus is the Messiah, (2) repent, and (3) receive the baptism for the remission of sins ["baptismal regeneration"]. In response God would do three things: (1) pardon the penitent, (2) impart the Holy Spirit, and (3) give eternal life.[35]

This simple message evoked such response that Eastern Ohio experienced a revival with many additions to the churches. Unlike the Second Great Awakening in Kentucky and elsewhere, it was a "blending of rationality and authority" (of the Bible). Little emphasis was placed on the work of the Holy Spirit in convicting sinners and regenerating the believer. The awakening was largely limited to Baptist churches. The theology and strategy of the Mahonging Baptist Association was changed to the degree that they resolved to dissolve the Association and become an independent group of autonomous churches. Without Scott's success in evangelism on Ohio and Stone's Christian movement (in Ohio) "the Campbells' dream of Christian union on a biblical basis probably would have been passed over quickly on the rapidly changing frontier."[36]

Thomas Campbell acknowledged that Scott's message brought a needed addition to their movement. He was convinced that the restoration to a New Testament pattern, which the Campbells presented, was correct, but that their method of presenting it needed Scott's emphasis on evangelism and simplicity. This became the accepted procedure for many years thereafter.[36]

However not all Disciples saw Thomas Campbell's assessment of revivalism thus: "Most Protestants had been caught up in the excitement of the new emotionalism of campmeetings and revivals, to which Mr. Campbell gave no support."[38]

Scott described his discovery of "the gospel in its original terms":

> *The publication of the gospel in the express form given it by the Apostles on Pentecost, and the public ministration of its spirit on their inspired plan, viz. in immersion, are facts which in the development of reforming principles, are perhaps more connected with the body of Christ, and the abolition of sects; the destruction of systematic theology, and the conversion of the world, than any other piece of solid knowledge which had been recovered to the church during the progress of three hundred years' reformation.*[39]

This raises several questions. Were those immersed actually regenerated, "born of the Spirit"? What were the "fruits" of those who joined the churches on this basis? Why did the Campbells, who did not believe in revivals, so readily accept this new technique and its results? Why did the Campbells and Scott, who stressed the Word more than the work of the Spirit, accept so uncritically the popular response as the vindication of message and its method? How would the disciples of Stone have responded *prior* to their merger with the disciples of the Campbells? How could Scott and the Campbells, well trained in the Bible, accept one verse of Scripture (Acts 2:38) as alone definitive and neglect not only the Epistles, but even the warning of John the Baptist against immersion without repentance (cf. Luke 3:7-14).

> *"The Disciples considered baptism one of the steps in the saving process [baptismal regeneration] , while the Baptists insisted that baptism was a **sign** of the forgiveness of sins and a regeneration which had already taken place . . . the argument has never subsided.*[40]

Scott's understanding of baptism is reflected in his endorsement of his colleague Joseph Gaston as "the very first Christian minister who received the gospel after its restoration and who argued for the remission of sins by baptism." The rejection of this "gospel" by the Baptists is not surprising!

In addition to being an evangelist, Scott emerged as editor of *The Evangelist* (1832-44), then educator: as President of Bacon College (1836) and of Covington Female Institute (1852-55).

Despite their sincere and ardent quest for unity the Disciples found it necessary to sever connections with the Baptists and to form yet another denomination. The division was initiated almost simultaneously by both sides. An early indication of the split came with Alexander Campbell's "Sermon on the Law" in 1816. The Apostles, declared Campbell, "were authorized to preach the gospel, not the *law*, to every creature. They were constituted ministers of the New Testament, not the Old."[41] This was not unlike the viewpoint of the Anabaptists. To regular Baptists this was "anathema."

In 1829 the Beaver Association of Baptists issued a statement of their objection to followers of the Campbells:

> *They teach "that there is no promise of salvation without baptism; that baptism should be administered on belief that Jesus Christ is the Son of God, without examination on any other point; that there is no direct operation of the Holy Spirit on the mind before baptism; that baptism procures the remission of sins and the gift of the Holy Spirit; . . . that no creed is necessary for the church; that all baptized persons have the right to administer the ordinance of baptism.*[42]

Later the Tate's Creek Association added: no special vocation for ministers, the Law of Moses "abolished," "experimental religion is enthusiasm," and the Scriptures contain no "mystery."

The differences between Baptists and the Reformers emerged gradually and were numerous: (1) Baptists were less interested in unity, (2) Baptists had a (Philadelphia) Confession of Faith, (3) The Reformers objected to *Associations* of Churches, (4) Reformers considered the name Baptist sectarian, (5) Baptists did not observe the Lord's Supper weekly, (6) Baptists required candidates to give a testimony to their conversion, and be accepted by the congregation before baptism, (7) Reformers insisted that baptism and conversion were simultaneous (hence were termed "water regenerationists"), (8) among Baptists only ordained ministers could serve Communion, and (9) Campbells downgraded the Old Testament.[43]

The three *major* factors which led the Disciples to become an independent and separate denomination were (1) the attacks by Alexander Campbell on other "sects" (including the Baptists) in his role as "Iconoclast and Reformer" while Editor of the *Christian Baptist*, (2) his downgrading of the Old Testament, and (3) the emphasis by Scott on baptism.[44]

In his mature years Campbell was more moderate and conciliatory. He is recorded as saying "the term *Christian* was given first to immersed believers and none else, but we do not think it was given because they were immersed, but because they had put on Christ."[45]

The severance with the Baptists was complete, but the merger with the Christians was firm, due largely to the irenic spirit and eagerness for unity, on the part of Stone. As noted previously, the Christians (Disciples of Christ) number about five million world-wide, this despite the departure of some conservatives who formed the Church of Christ and the Churches of Christ.

One criterion of the influence of the New Testament on those who bear the name of Christ is one's attitude toward slavery, a major issue in the decades prior to the Civil War. Barton Stone freed the slaves he owned "from a sense of right." In 1833 he wrote,

> *There is no intelligent man in our country who does not confess that slavery is anti-Christian, . . . that it is ruining our country, and the morals of our children; and will ultimately, if persisted in, be the plague and destruction of the white population.*[46]

Stone was not an abolitionist; he favored facilitating the return of slaves to Africa. His concern in the above quotation, was more for the country than for the oppressed. Yet his compassion for the slaves was real and sincere. The same may be said for Thomas Campbell. Walter Scott "deplored slavery" but did not work for immediate emancipation. Alexander Campbell freed his slaves but was ambiguous about the emancipation of all slaves. He supported the Fugitive Slave Law.

> *Shifting his emphasis according to the mood of the nation and special circumstances in the church, he sometimes appeared to be antislavery, sometimes proslavery . . . . Without question, the welfare and unity of the Disciples were more important than either the amelioration or eradication of slavery.*[47]

Such was the gist of his articles in *The Millennial Harbinger* in 1845. His influence was not sufficient to avoid a split among the between the Disciples of the North and those of the South. Their congregational polity did not permit any official separation; each congregation was independent. Some Disciples defended slavery; others violently opposed it. Among the latter was John G. Fee, founder of interracial Berea

College in Kentucky and author of *An AntiSlavery Manual* (1848). The College he founded still benefits from this courageous tradition of justice.

The first generation of leaders, especially the Campbells and Scott, were trained in theological schools. The second generation of preachers and editors "moved into positions of power without the benefit of theological education."[48] Bethany College, headed by A. Campbell, used only the Bible, because he was determined to ignore "human creeds."

In 1865 under the leadership of Robert Milligan, The College of the Bible was formed in Lexington, Kentucky, as part of Transylvania University. Milligan's interest in biblical studies began at the historic Cane Ridge Church.[49] This interest culminated in his *Scheme of Redemption* published in 1875, still the Disciples' nearest thing to a "definitive theology." Here the first students, thirty-seven in number from a wide geographical territory, studied biblical languages and doctrine, church history and dogmatics, and homiletics.

Divisions soon plagued the University, the College of the Bible, and the churches. After earlier skirmishes involving both politics and religion, the first major theological crisis for the Bible College occurred in 1917 between the conservatives and theological liberals on the faculty. The two main Disciples magazines became involved with the *Christian Standard* defending the conservatives and the *Christian Century* favoring the liberals. Eventually two theological schools resulted: the conservative or evangelical churches sought graduates from the Cincinnati Bible Seminary (1924), the "progressives" or liberals depended on the Lexington School, which in 1965 became the Lexington Theological Seminary.

Paralleling these developments, the Kentucky churches, which reflect the Barton Stone or conservative wing, are now *Christian* Churches headed by the historic Broadway Christian Church in Lexington and affiliated with the Seminary in Cincinnati. The more liberal *Disciple* Churches, headed by the historic Central Christian Church, are affiliated with the Lexington Theological Seminary. The latter is accredited and has nation-wide influence, especially in the ecumenical movement.

The difference between the two groups is displayed in the church announcements each Saturday in the *Lexington Herald-Leader*. Under the caption "Christian" thirteen churches are listed; under "Disciples of Christ" are three; under "Churches of Christ" are two. Nearly all except "Disciples" have Sunday evening meetings and several a mid-week service. The evangelical (conservative) churches are multiplying.

As an example of the continued growth of the Christian churches (in the tradition of Baron Stone) is the move of the South Christian Church in Lexington, Kentucky. Despite the objections of several members the majority moved to a new location, south of Lexington, to a site just north of the Jessamine County border. Now it is the largest building in the area. It accomodates 2200 attendants in the sanctuary; morning worship services are held three times on Sunday. In addition it has a Christian school adjacent to the sanctuary. At pageants during Easter and Christmas multitudes gather from the area; an appeal to the gospel terminates the drama. During Easter week on 1992 a total of 22,249 were in attendance. Church membership here is 4,200. "The Southland Hour" is on TV and radio. The leadership of this church (Dr. Wayne B. Smith) challenges Christian morals to permeate the community.

By contrast, the "liberal" wing of Denomination (Christian/Disciples) recommended the Dean of Lexington Theological Seminary to be the leader of the entire Denomination. But he was voted down by the majority; the conservative influence in 1992 prevailed.[50]

Perhaps none of the major Protestant denominations has made a greater effort at the unity of Christians than this one, yet their stress on independence developed into what James H. Garrison, Editor of *The Christian*, called a "morbid fondness for controversy." This was especially true of the Campbell side. Their initial rejection of "man-made creeds" did not deter theological debates that were often heated and divisive. In the later years the controversy was between liberals and conservatives. Earlier it was the alternative of Calvinism or Arminianism.

This conviction (of man's freedom of will and hence responsibility) was what led Barton Stone and Charles G. Finney to leave Presbyterian theology and welcome this (Wesleyan) influence of the Second Great Awakening on the western frontier. As W. S. Hudson concluded, the continued influence of this "evangelistic urgency [during]. . . the decades immediately preceding the Civil War witnessed the triumph of the distinctive emphases of Methodism in practically all the denominations."[51]

The Campbells and Scott carried the truth of man's freedom and responsibility further than Wesley, resulting in less stress on sin and the regenerating work of the Spirit, with more influence on the quick and easy "five steps" including immersion. This commitment to evangelism, after Scott and the merger with Stone in the Ohio Valley, led the Disciples to the Pacific Coast from 1830 to 1860, their greatest era of expansion. The revival resulted in the publication of many magazines and books. Simultaneously the emphasis on higher education witnessed the emergence of colleges and academies.

As noted earlier, more controversial than baptism in the Disciples' theology was the doctrine of the work of the Holy Spirit. Here, like Stone, the Campbells differed from both the Methodists and the Christians. In his *Christian System* Campbell wrote what caused the most misunderstanding:

> *Now we cannot separate the Spirit and the word of God ... What ever the word does, the Spirit does; and whatever the Spirit does in the work of converting men, the word does. We neither believe nor teach abstract Spirit nor abstract word - - but word and Spirit, Spirit and word.*[52]

This worried Stone and was challenged by the Baptists. It was contrary to the activity of the Holy Spirit in the Book of Acts and also to the influence of the Spirit in the revivals.

Campbell's view was influenced by his studies of Locke in Glasgow. He arrived in America retaining "the spirit of enlightenment philosophy" and the "efficacy of reason." While not denying the existence of the Spirit, he concluded that emotionalism in the conversion experience was not from the Holy Spirit. He saw the work of the Spirit only in obedience to the written Word; later, however he acknowledged the work of the Spirit in regeneration as distinct from immersion.[53]

His view of the emotion in revivals was negative, yet he welcomed the revivals of Scott and others in the movement because of their results. Disciples do not consider it necessary to struggle to repent and beg for mercy like the publican (Luke 16); the "penitential struggle," of Pietism (and Methodism) is absent. Christian Churches in Southern Ohio report that traditionally the pastor or evangelist would say, "come forward; give your hand to the preacher and your heart to God." This provided a "passport to heaven."[54] "Disciples are probably in the rear of most of the larger communions in producing literature related to the devotional and spiritual life."[55]

> *The Disciple position is a catholic view (more than it is a protestant position) because it says that the Holy Spirit operates through the church . . . . the tendency of the American religious environment encouraged Disciple evangelists to identify themselves with Protestantism. The result was a strong swing toward individualism as preached in then current revivalism. This featured salvation "sole fide" -- by faith alone -- and lessened the concern for the agency of the community, the church, in the continuing work of redemption.*[56]

In response to the *Report* of the Third World Conference on Faith and Order (Lund, Sweden, 1952) the Disciples had this objection,

> *The soalfidian [sic] which is suggested by such expressions as "all who believe in Him die and rise again to a new life" is foreign to the thought of the Disciples, who would generally modify this to read, "all who believe in Him and who become obedient to his will die and rise again to a new life."*[57]

It is unlikely that the evangelical wing of Disciples would accept this and the preceding quotation. Faith alone is not only the keynote of Protestantism, it is also the keynote of Pauline theology. Could not conservative Judaism today make the same affirmation as that of "Disciples generally": "all to believe in Him [Father or Son?] and who become obedient to his will . . .."? Obedience is imperative to the believer; but to substitute obedience for "die and rise again to a new life" is a betrayal of the essence of the gospel of Christ. Unless the believer is transformed and becomes a "new creation," he cannot claim to be a Christian in the New Testament meaning of the term (cf. John 3:5-8; 2 Cor. 5:17; Col. 3:1-3; Jas. 1:18; 2 Pet. 1:4).

The commitment to Christian unity is reflected today in the Disciples' commitment to the ecumenical movement. This is especially true of the more "liberal" wing of the Christian (Disciples of Christ) movement.

5. The Church of God (Anderson)

Another denomination with an equal aversion to diverse "sects" deserves attention. The Rev. Mr. John Winebrinner was a member of the German Reformed Church and pastor at Harrisburg, Pennsylvania. His preaching resulted in a revival in his parish. This led to his expulsion from that denomination, but he continued his evangelistic preaching. His idea of the true church was like that of Barton Stone and the Campbells: no human creed, the Bible alone, a church which consisted of believers only, and an abhorrence of "sects." Excluded from one "sect," he determined to lead in fostering the *true* Church of God, which he founded in 1830.[58]

> *He adopted the apostolic plan, as taught in the New Testament, and established spiritual, free, and independent churches, consisting of believers or Christians only, without any human name or creed or ordinances or laws . . . . The local church was the unit. It possessed perfect autonomy.*[59]

The similarity in motives to those of Stone and the Campbells is obvious. His Church had no written creed, but accepted the "Word of God as their only rule of faith and practice." And he was determined not to form another "sect." David S. Warner, a pastor in Ohio, and a member of this Church of God, was licensed in 1867. The Holiness Revival of the Nineteenth century was in full swing. Warner was opposed to those who preached entire sanctification. His diary records his reaction to a holiness meeting.

> *Nearly all blew loudly the horn of sanctification but manifested little of its fruits, such as travail of soul for the sinner and sympathy for the one soul at the altar, to whom none gave a word of encouragement, but each in turn arose and boasted of his holiness. Oh the delusions of Satan! How manifold they are!*[60]

His attitude changed radically later as he saw that holiness was Scriptural. The Keller family and Warner's wife Sarah experienced entire sanctification. He was convinced by seeing the change in others: "Since seeing every day the change in my dear wife I thought I was beyond doubt of the second work."[61] Soon he confessed his need, abandoned his doubts, accepted inner cleansing by "naked faith," and two days later received his own experience of entire sanctification. In another excerpt from the Diary:

> *The Lord wonderfully baptized my soul . . . . Oceans of love flow through my soul. Oh, how inexpressibly sweet and joyful! . . . Praise the Lord, he so abundantly fills my mouth with holiness that I can not get to anything else to say.*[62]

This led to his expulsion from the Church of God. As explained by a historian of the Church of God:

> *The Eldership was contending against inroads of heresies advocated by D. S. Warner. It had finally to resort to the old remedy of excision in order to prevent the spread of the disease and restore the body to health.*[63]

This action and his fellowship with those of the holiness movement led to a prominent place in the new fellowship. However his aversion to "sects" and his own expulsion from his own "sect," led to his discomfort with the numerous divisions within the Holiness Movement. But he continued his commitment to the doctrine and experience.

His Diary discloses his reaction:

> *On the 31st of last January, [1878] the Lord showed me that holiness could never prosper upon sectarian soil, encumbered by human creeds, and party names, and he gave me a new commission to join holiness and all truth together and build up the apostolical [sic] church of the living God.*[64]

Warner saw the Holiness Movement as the vehicle by which his vision of a united Church of God could be realized.

> *Warner called for each sanctified individual to reject sectarianism in his own heart and leave his denomination "to join the one holy Church of the Bible, not bound together by rigid articles of faith, put perfectly united in love, under the primitive glory of the Sanctifier, continuing steadfastly in the Apostles's doctrine and fellowship, and taking captive the world for Jesus."*[65]

Warner pursued avidly the goal of a church free from sectarian divisions. He asked the Indiana Holiness Association to modify its membership statement to permit him to continue in its activities.

> *Warner was already in contest with men like Thomas Dody, and especially with the Free Methodists, who under B. T. Roberts, were avidly trying to rally their own reform movement to a single denominational loyalty, Warner's suggestions were rejected.*[66]

Paradoxically, while Warner was calling for Christian unity he was also calling for Christians to leave their respective denominations. Even his wife Sarah rejected these efforts at "come-outism." She wrote,

> *I feel it my duty to say to all of God's children, that he has opened my eyes to see the evils of come-outism. I am free from it and praise God that he has so completely delivered me from the spirit of it. It simply cuts off a few members by themselves, who get an idea that none are*

> *clearly sanctified unless they see as "we" do; and then, they have a harsh grating that is the very opposite of love.... They hold and teach that no one can be entirely sanctified and belong to a "sect."*[67]

Warner and his wife divorced.

In spite of his rejection of "sects" in the interest of Christian unity and his commitment to Wesleyan doctrines, a trace of Warner's Anabaptist tradition remained from his association with Winebrinner's church.[68] However, his preoccupation with Old Testament prophecies, Ezekiel's in particular, was inconsistent with the Anabaptists, as well as with the Campbell concept of the "Restoration."

The appeal to the advocates of holiness to "come out " of sects and join an independent movement resulted in the Church of God (Anderson) becoming third in size among the Holiness denominations. As with the Disciples, the crusade for unity led to yet another denomination, often in competition with other holiness groups. The emancipation from "man made creeds" was an illusion. When this author sought to enlist the Church of God (Anderson) in a projected non-denominational Bible Commentary enterprise, the answer was negative, because of their commitment to Amillenialism! (Later by request, this author contributed a series of articles for the *Gospel Trumpet*). Those affiliated with the Church are not "members" since they are averse to being another denomination. But the dream lives on.

The dream of Stone and the Campbells unfortunately remains a dream. The Church of Christ is a spinoff of the Disciples, as is the Churches of Christ. In southern Ohio, where this author served as pastor of the Congregational-Christian Church, United Methodists and Presbyterians cooperated in a city-wide evangelistic crusade. The Church of Christ alone could not participate because their view of baptism differed from that of the other three churches!

As historian Murch explains, the vision of Stone and the Campbells has divided into three main branches: the liberal wing (Disciples), the conservative or right wing (Church of Christ), and the centrist group (Christians).[69]

> *The extreme left in Discipledom may be characterized as having abandoned the authority of the New Testament and its normative pattern .... Having undermined this foundation pillar of Thomas Campbell's platform for Christian unity, this school of thought further denies that fellowship is predicated upon a common body of doctrine. Its theology*

> lies in the realm of expediency and opinion, consequently exalting the liberty of the human mind. Leftists favor the universal practice of "open membership" as a practical demonstration of "Christian Unity." Leftists having lost the distinctive message of the Disciples have become apologists for the "historic position" of the Disciples on Biblical authority and practice, and seek to convince the religious world that they alone represent the true spirit of the communion.[70]

The "Rightists," or the most conservative group (Church of Christ) are evangelical and have much in common with the "Centrist" group. They seem to "major on minors." Centered in Nashville, Tennessee, they proclaim to the world "Christ did not found the Lutheran or the Methodist Church. If you wish to join the church that Christ founded you should join the Christian Church." Impeccable logic! Their most distinctive features include avoidance of instrumental music in public worship and avoidance of the "silences" of the Bible, such as modes of conducting the Lord's Supper, Sunday School, colleges, choirs, method of choosing elders, missions, millennial views, church discipline. Even in this conservative group there are marked divisions.[71]

> The Church of Christ sees denominationalism as a sin, because . . . it fails to give full honor to Christ as the head of the church . . . puts human authority ahead of the divine . . . is in conflict with the plain teachings of Scriptures on the nature of Christian unity, postpones the fulfillment of Christ's prayer that all His **disciples** might be one . . . that the world may believe.[72]

The "Centrist" includes some views held by both left and right segments of the Restorationists.

> They accept the Holy Scriptures as divinely inspired, alone and all-sufficient as the revelation of the will of God for mankind and of Christ as His gospel . . . that the basic pattern of the church is revealed in the New Testament and that it is the duty of every faithful follower of Christ to restore and maintain that pattern. In the midst of a divided Christian world they consider themselves to be "Christians only, but not the only Christians."[73]

As viewed by Tucker and McAllister, the "Christian Churches and Churches of Christ" claim to stand squarely in the great tradition of Stone and the Campbells. So do Disciples and Churches of Christ. Yet the existence of three distinct communions, sharing a common past, provides vivid testimony that the Stone-Campbell movement itself failed to overcome the forces of divisiveness let alone lead a fragmented church into a new day of unity.[74]

One is left to wonder what would have happened if the revivals associated with Stone would have continued without the merger with the Campbells who were more doctrinaire and prone to assume the role of "iconoclast."[75] Stone was more in the tradition of Pietism in which Christian experience and conduct is more important than "man made creeds."

C. APPRAISAL

Pietism, at its best, is in the best position to promote unity without union. For "born-again" Christians unity in Christ is not something to be achieved; it is part of the new birth. Unity of spirit and of goals flows from this corporate relationship. Paul's analogy of the human body portrays the church as a unity with diversity, her head being Christ (1 Cor. 12:4-31). Those with strong convictions and commitments find unity more difficult than those without. Schism was a problem, even in the primitive church. It surfaced in Jerusalem (Acts 6:1-6), in Antioch (Acts 15:36-40), in Corinth (1 Cor. 1:10-13), and even in Philippi (Phil. 2:1-5; 4:2).

Unity is especially difficult when doctrine or polity is given priority. When evangelism is given primacy united action is easier, as witness the cooperation between Whitefield and Wesley and the evangelistic crusades of Finney, Moody, and Graham. A common enemy also unites defendants. Catholics and Protestants united when Vienna was threatened by Moslem armies. In many mission fields comity agreements (cooperation rather than competition) exemplify this principle. A common challenge invites cooperation.

The quest for unity (as distinct from union and uniformity) is even more urgent now than in the early nineteenth century. It is achieved by being Christ-centered. As spokes in a wheel, the closer to the center (the hub) the closer to each other; the closer believers are to Christ the closer to each other. Only thus will the pastoral prayer of Jesus, with its five-fold appeal for unity, be answered. The vision of Stone, the Campbells, and Warner must not be abandoned.

In summary, which of these quests for Christian unity came nearest to the New Testament pattern? No one can honestly claim objectivity, but some are less biased than others. The Church of God is commendable in its emphasis on a holy life. By failing to admit it is another denomination and that it has members, its ideal of unity remains illusionary. The factions among the Christians (Disciples) demonstrates the difficulty of unity amid diversity so prominent in Acts and the Epistles. Those who were associated with Stone seem to have more in common with the primitive church, if only because their early appearance on the scene. During times of spiritual renewal (revivals) the similarity to the primitive church is most apparent. When a church loses its "first love" (Rev. 2:4) the similarity fades.

The quest for unity leads to a definition of "church," which in itself involves problems. Thomas Campbell's famed definition of "church" seems clear and convincing:

> *The church of Christ upon earth is essentially . . . one; consisting of all those in every place that profess their faith in Christ and give obedience to him . . . and that manifest the same by their tempers and conduct.*[76]

But in the implementation of this principle the Disciples discovered that the doctrine of the church, long the central theological concern of the movement, became a problem of the first magnitude for them. As they pondered the nature and structure of the church in the light of the biblical record and their own self understanding, they found themselves split into contentious parties.[77]

The result was different views of "where the Scriptures are silent, we are silent." Some wished to enlarge on the great commission by adding Sunday Schools; others objected that this innovation meant a betrayal of their historic legacy. The Campbells had brought to the fellowship the philosophy of John Locke on "Human Understanding." If they had followed Scripture, as illuminated by the Holy Spirit and Christian experience in the tradition of Pietism, perhaps their quest would have been more successful. But we can learn much from their efforts at unity.

Chapter VI Endnotes

1. W. E. Tucker & L. G. McAllister, *Journey in Faith*, A history of the Christian Church (Disciples of Christ), (St. Louis, MO: Bethany Press, 1975), p. 37.
2. W. C. Bower, *Central Christian Church*, (St. Louis: Bethany, 1962), pp. 23-24.
3. Barton W. Stone, "Life", in *The Cane Ridge Reader*, H. S. Dickinson, editor, (Cincinnati: J. A. & U. P. James, 1847), pp. 41-42.
4. J. D. Murch, *Christians Only*, (Cincinnati: Standard Publishing, 1962), pp. 29, 86.
5. W. S. Hudson, *Religion in America*, (New York: Scribner's Sons, 1981). p. 64.
6. W. E. Garrison & A. T. DeGroot, *The Disciples of Christ*, (St. Louis, MO: Bethany Press, 1948), p. 98.
7. Murch, p. 31.
8. J. M. McPherson, *The Battle Cry of Freedom*, (Oxford, 1988), p. 8; see also pp. 20, 35, 88-91, 191. Note W. W. Sweet, *The Story of Religion in America*, (Grand Rapids: Baker, 1975) pp. 231- 257; M. E. Marty, *Righteous Empire*, (New York: Dial Press, 1970) pp. 81-110; T. L. Smith, *Revivalism and Social Reform*, (Nashville: Abingdon Press, 1957), pp. 34-113.
9. *Journey*, p. 73.
10. C. N. Thompson, ed., *Historical Collections of Brown County, Ohio*, (Piqua, OH: Hammer Graphics, Inc., 1969), pp. 963-964. (The author served as pastor of this "New Light" Church 1948-58).
11. Summary from *Disciples*, pp. 109-110.
12. *Journey*, pp. 80-81.
13. R. E. Thompson, *A History of the Presbyterian Churches in the United States*, (New York: Scribners, 1895), pp. 34, 95.
14. *Journey*, p. 83.
15. Barton Stone, "Life," in J. Rogers, Editor, *The Cane Ridge Reader*, (Cincinnati: J. A. & U. P. James, 1847), p. 56ff.
16. Stone, p. 60, 61. Until recently a marker on Main Street, Lexington recalled the eight-day debate between A. Campbell and Rice of the subject of baptism, so great was public interest in this subject in the 1830's.
17. *Journey*, p. 123.

18. Stone, p. 73.
19. Murch, p. 35.
20. Murch, p. 40.
21. *Disciples*, p. 145.
22. *Journey*, p. 113.
23. F. D. Kershner, *The Christian Union Overture*, (St. Louis: Bethany Press, 1923), p. 26; cited in *Journey*, p. 113.
24. *Journey*, p. 116.
25. *Disciples*, pp. 154-155.
26. Stone, p. 75.
27. Stone, p. 76.
28. Stone, p. 77.
29. Stone, p. 77.
30. A. T. DeGroot, Disciple Thought : A History, (Fort Worth, Texas: Texas Christian University, 1965), pp. 12-13.
31. Murch, p. 95.
32. Stone, p. 79.
33. Murch, p. 95.
34. *Disciples*, p. 181.
35. *Disciples*, pp. 187-188.
36. *Journey*, p. 133.
37. *Journey*, p. 134.
38. *Disciple Thought*, p. 76.
39. Walter Scott report to the Mahoning Association (1828) cited in *Disciples*, p. 190.
40. Howard E. Short, "The Christian Church (Disciples of Christ)," in M. D. Strege, Editor, *Baptism & Church, a Believers' Church Vision*, (Grand Rapids: Sagamore Books, 1986), p. 41.
41. Alexander Campbell, "Sermon on the Law," *Millennial Harbinger*, 1846), pp. 513, cited in L. E. Lair, *Christian Churches and Their Work*, (St. Louis: Bethany Press, 1963), p. 50.
42. *Disciples*, p. 194.

43. *Journey*, pp. 139-140.
44. See *Disciples*, pp. 173-185.
45. A. Campbell, *Millennial Harbinger*, Nov. 1887, p. 507 (cited in *Journey*, p. 158).
46. B. Stone, *Christian Messenger*, September 1833, p. 274, cited in *Journey*, pp. 191, 192.
47. *Journey*, p. 230.
48. *Journey*, pp. 193-194.
49. Dwight E. Stevenson, *Lexington Theological Seminary*, (St. Louis: MO, 1964), p. 24.
50. See "Restoring Mainline Trust: Disagreeing in Love," *The Christian Century*, July 1-8, (Chicago, IL, 1992), pp. 645-648.
51. Hudson, p. 180.
52. A. Campbell, *The Christian System*, (Pittsburgh: Forrester and Campbell; 3rd. ed., 1840), p. 5; cited in *Disciple Thought*, pp. 46, 47.
53. *Disciple Thought*, p. 48.
54. As reported by an older member of the Congregational-Christian Church pastored by this author.
55. *Disciple Thought*, p. 52.
56. *Disciple Thought*, p. 77.
57. *The Shane Quarterly*, July, 1953, pp. 93, 94, cited in *Disciple Thought*, p. 78.
58. A. L. Byers, *Birth of a Reformation*, (Guthrie, Oklahoma: Faith Publishing House, 1921, 1966), p. 52.
59. C. H. Forney, *History of the Churches of God*, cited in Byers, p. 53.
60. D. S. Warner, "Diary," cited in Byers, p. 62.
61. Warner, "Diary" for July 5, 1877; Byers, p. 120.
62. Warner, "Diary," July 29, 1877, cited in Byers, p. 138.
63. From Forney, *History*, cited in Byers, p. 137.
64. Warner, in his journal for March 7, 1878, cited in M. E. Dieter, "The Holiness Revival of the Nineteenth Century," (Ph.D. Dissertation at Temple University, 1973), pp. 277, 319.
65. Warner, *Bible Truths*, p. 429, cited in Dieter, p. 281.

66. Dieter, p. 287.
67. Cited in Byers, p. 320.
68. Dieter, pp. 285-287.
69. Murch, pp. 279. 309, 293.
70. Murch, p. 279.
71. Murch, pp. 310-312.
72. Murch, p. 320. Murch adds: "This Right-wing group may be characterized as *Biblical Exlusivists*, in contrast to Centrist *Biblical Inclusivists* and Left-wing *non-Biblical Inclusivists*.
73. Murch, p. 293.
74. *Journey*, p. 386.
75. *Disciples*, pp. 167-175.
76. *Journey*, p. 113.
77. *Journey*, pp. 236-237.

Chapter VII
THE PENTECOSTALS

> *"When you come together, each one has a hymn, a lesson, a revelation, a tongue, or an interpretation. Let all things be done for building up. If any one speaks in a tongue, let there be only two or at most three, and each in turn; and let one interpret. But if there is no one to interpret, let them be silent in church and let them speak to themselves and to God .... For God is a God not of disorder, but of peace .... So my friends, be eager to prophesy, and do not forbid speaking in tongues; but all things should be decently and in order."*
>
> Paul: (I Cor. 14:26-28; 33; 39-40)
> A.B. Simpson: "Seek not; forbid not."

Another claim to the distinction of being the church closest to the New Testament pattern comes from the movement called Pentecostalism. Adherents often refer to themselves as the "Latter Rain" which heralds the advent of the "Messianic Age." Most believe themselves to be "a renaissance of Apostolic Christianity. Standing alongside Catholicism and . . . Protestantism as a 'Third Force'."[1] The main distinction between modern Pentecostals and other holiness and evangelical believers is the conviction that after conversion the promised Baptism of the Holy Spirit is verified by the gift of tongues.

In this review the emphasis is on history more than on theology. Space permits attention only to the main segments of this multifaceted movement. When one presents a viewpoint other than his own it is best, as Plato advised, to present the other viewpoint in its best light, before challenging it.

Pentecostalism generally, like second century Montanism, reflects a desire to return to the dynamism of earliest Christianity, especially as described in the Acts of the Apostles. Like the Montanists and the early Quakers, Pentecostals emphasize the experience (of the Holy Spirit) as more immediate and relevant than the words of the Bible. They prize spiritual fervor more than formal education. Charismatics are more democratic, less hierarchal, less concerned with contemporary mores, committed to a more literal interpretation and application of Scripture than most of their contemporaries.

As in other assemblies where the influence of the Holy Spirit is pervasive, they tend to be more ecumenical, to welcome "outsiders" as fellow worshipers. History shows that where distinctions of race, sex, status, and the like are minimal (see Joel 2:28-29; Acts 2:17-21) it is due to the influence of the Spirit. Church history, including the Pentecostal movements, tend to bear this out. Conversely, it can be argued that where patriarchal and hierarchal mores prevail there is less concern for the "freedom of the Spirit" and the participation of women, blacks, and minorities.

During the sixteenth and seventeenth centuries attention was focused on justification by faith; the next two centuries stressed sanctification and missions. During the present century attention has turned to the gifts of the Spirit to the extent that President Henry Sloan Coffin of Union Theological Seminary (New York) termed Pentecostalism a "second Reformation" or, as its adherents would prefer, a "Restoration."[2]

Most Pentecostals have little interest in theological development during Christian history. They are interested mainly in "primitivism" rather than seeking historical and theological links between the biblical "Early Rain" and their "Latter Rain."[3]

It is now widely regarded as the fastest growing movement in the Christian church. By 1970 the World Council of Churches estimated its world-wide adherents as numbering 30,000,000. The largest of the numerous Pentecostal denominations, The Assemblies of God, alone numbers more than 15,000,000.[4]

One adherent lists these five reasons for the Movements's "remarkable growth": Bible study, quest for holiness, substitutionary atonement, "free and exuberant worship," and "evangelistic zeal."[5] (The Free Methodist Church, in 1860, was among the first to leave the parent body on these issues, especially the Wesleyan focus on entire sanctification).

A. ORIGINS

Historians and theologians trace the roots of the movement to the "holiness revival" in England, Wales, and in America during the nineteenth century. Frederick Bruner is among the many who trace the origins of Pentecostalism to early Methodism:

> *The major influence, then, of Methodism on Pentecostalism has been . . . an experience subsequent to conversion . . . requiring the meeting of certain conditions beyond conversion or justifying faith for its attainment . . . . Since Wesley almost all those who have embraced this doctrine have been wittingly or not, Wesley's children . . . and today the most prominent of these is Pentecostalism.*[6]

Early in the Methodist movement John Fletcher, despite John Wesley's caution, taught the Baptism of the Holy Spirit as simultaneous with entire sanctification, thus adding the Luke-Acts statements to the Wesleyan doctrine. Recent Wesleyan studies focus on Fletcher's addition to John Wesley's explanation of "Perfection" as significant for the North American Holiness Movement and its influence on Pentecostalism.[7]

Later Charles G. Finney, and especially his associate Asa Mahan, taught the need for the Baptism of the Spirit. This Baptism of the Holy Spirit is equated with entire sanctification in the doctrinal statement of the Church of the Nazarene and is the title of a book by H. C. Morrison, founder of Asbury Theological Seminary.[8]

Speaking in tongues was said to have occurred in London at Pastor Edward Irving's Presbyterian Church on Regent's Square as evidence of "receiving the Holy Ghost."[9] During the Moody revival in England some were reported to have spoken in tongues. Also during the world-renowned Welsh revival of 1904 speaking in tongues was reported: young men and woman who knew nothing of Old Welsh were said to have spoken in that language.[10] But glossolalia did not accompany the work of the major evangelists: Whitefield, Wesley, Finney, Moody, Billy Sunday (or lesser known preachers).

The Pentecostals usually trace their origin to "a Los Angeles revival in which speaking in tongues was regarded as a sign of Baptism in the Spirit."[11] Others point to Topeka, Kansas, at Bethel Bible College on January 1, 1901, as Pentecostalism's origin.[12]

1. Revival in Appalachia 1886--

Other historians trace the modern Pentecostal movement to the mountain counties in East Tennessee and western North Carolina under the leadership of two Baptist preachers, R.G. Spurling, Sr. and R. G. Spurling Jr.[13]

> *The elder Spurling participated in a holiness revival in Monroe County, Tennessee, and . . . organized an independent body called The Christian*

> Union, which he regarded as a "reformation movement" to restore primitive Christianity.[14] Information on this "holiness revival" is hard to come by, but Free Will Baptists, who from the beginning accepted the basic premises of Methodism," reached this area in 1855, and at "the height of the holiness crusade of the 1880's . . . adopted a strictly Wesleyan perfectionist creed.[15]

The Christian Union, headed by Spurling, consisted of only nine members who agreed to "take the New Testament, or law of Christ" as their "only rule of faith and practice." This occurred on August 19, 1886, at the Barney meeting house near Coker Creek, Monroe County, Tennessee.[16]

Two years later Spurling Sr. died and was succeeded by his son Richard, who was also a licensed minister in the Baptist Church. Spurling Jr. shared his father's burden for revival. For a decade, at the church and in the mountain counties of eastern Tennessee, he preached repentance in the tradition of the Reformers. He, with his father, had "searched the Scriptures for greater light on the subject of holiness." But for all his zeal for righteous living, Richard had but a "nebulous conception of positive holiness" and the Wesleyan emphasis on entire sanctification as a "second work of grace."[17]

Revival did come, however, by way of three laymen, influenced by the New Testament call to holy living and Wesley's emphasis on entire sanctification. William Martin (Methodist), Joe Tipton (Baptist), and Milton McNabb (Baptist) experienced the new birth and the infilling of the Holy Spirit. They became preachers of sanctification. These men traveled together through the mountains preaching the same clean living and holiness that Spurling had preached for ten years -- with one difference. Instead of viewing the subject in a negative way by condemning the lack of holiness among professed Christians, they urged the people to seek a definite spiritual experience of [entire] sanctification which would make holiness not only possible, but natural.

Denied access to church buildings "they hailed those they met, Bibles in hand, and expounded to them the necessity of Christian perfection -- obtainable through an experience of sanctification such as they had received."[18]

Meanwhile a group of Baptists in Cherokee County, North Carolina, were praying for revival in their homes. Soon they met together in the Scherer (one-room) schoolhouse, where they were joined by these three itinerant lay preachers -- Martin,

Tipton, and McNabb -- who exhorted them to seek the experience of entire sanctification. The result was astounding. Sinners repented, believers experienced sanctification, and lives were transformed. People came from as far as thirty miles in wagons throughout the mountains to hear from these untutored men "this new doctrine of holiness." Spurling and his associates then joined this revival movement in 1896, ten years after the formation of their Christian Union.

Despite hostility the doctrine of holiness swept the mountain region . . . it was grace from which no man was excluded. Revival came to the mountains because a few simple folk appropriated what the larger churches had discarded.[19]

Opposition came from the churches: "about thirty were excluded from the Baptist church at one time because they professed to live a holy life."[20] It is ironic that the Wesleyan-Arminian call to holiness of heart and life was welcomed in communities predominantly Calvinistic.

In the revival "demonstrations in the Spirit" were not uncommon. Spontaneity in prayer and witness became prevalent, often accompanied by shouts of praise and sometimes by walking in the aisles in ecstasy. They were afraid of quenching the Holy Spirit.

After the three evangelists had gone the revival continued in the Scherer schoolhouse. Upon reading the book of Acts they concluded the gift of tongues was normative in those who had received the baptism in the Holy Spirit.

> . . . *like a cloud from a clear sky the Holy Ghost began to fall on honest, humble, sincere seekers after God. While the meetings were in progress, one after another fell under the power of God, and soon quite a number were speaking in other tongues as the Spirit gave them utterance.*[21]

This occurred in 1896 near Camp Creek, North Carolina, under the leadership of a layman, W. F. Bryant, and is documented from interviews with participants in the revival (taken some time later than the events) by Charles W. Conn "the accurate and talented historian of this Church."[22] Glossolalia is said to have appeared here four or five years before the similar phenomenon in Topeka, Kansas.

In 1896 . . . before either the appearance of the Pentecostal phenomena at Topeka, Kansas, or the massive outburst at Los Angeles, at least one hundred people, who at

Carolina, received the baptism of the Holy Spirit and spoke in tongues. There were members of an organization called the Christian Union whose name was changed to the Holiness Church in 1902 and finally to its present Church of God in 1907.[23]

While not the first recorded instance of "tongues," it was the first time its influence led to the formation of a Pentecostal denomination. "The revival that began in the Scherer Schoolhouse in 1896 formed the nucleus of what later became the 'Church of God' of Cleveland, Tennessee."[24]

Persecution intensified after this "gift of tongues." Most of the opposition came from leaders of denominations which had experienced severe persecution in their own formative years. Rowdies took up the challenge and their anger turned to violence. Lay leader, W. F. Bryant, was wounded by gunshot, and the new church building was burned to the ground. Violence continued until Mrs. Emiline Allen immobilized an angry mob by offering to feed them. But, said she, "We won't stop serving the Lord."[25]

Unfortunately some fanaticism followed revival, enough to give it a bad name. Fanaticism took several forms: one was asceticism (prolonged fasting), another was legalism, still an other "eternal security" which led to antinomianism (nothing the believer does is sinful). Some believers abandoned their faith and joined the "outside" in repudiating the faith they once espoused.

The leaders, Spurling and Bryant, protested these developments in vain. The church was reorganized under the name "The Holiness Church at Camp Creek" on May 15, 1902, and soon after accepted as pastor a colporteur for the American Bible Society, A. J. Tomlinson, who later became the Overseer. Rules were drawn up and a creed was formulated as a safeguard against deviations by extremists. This provides another demonstration that the church normally formulates creeds only when threatened with heresy.[26]

In January 25-27, 1906 representatives of the four "holiness churches" met in a mountain cabin for their first "Annual Conference." They decided not to serve as a legislative, or as an executive body, but only as a judiciary. The use of tobacco was initially discouraged and later forbidden. Foot washing was done annually. Family worship was urged, and mid-week prayer meetings were recommended. Sunday Schools, campmeetings, and missions were, in time, adopted as regular features of their assemblies. This first General Assembly of a score of delegates meeting for days in the mountains in January, 1906, set the pattern for the next half-century.

Increasingly emphasis came to be placed on spiritual gifts, especially divine healing and glossolalia. At length the Baptism in the Holy Spirit, subsequent to regeneration, received by faith instantaneously and authenticated by the "gift of tongues," came to be their most distinctive doctrine.

At their third General Assembly on January, 1908, during the visit of G. B. Cashwell, from the Azusa Street Mission in Los Angeles, Moderator Tomlinson received the baptism of the Holy Spirit, twelve years after several laymen had experienced this "baptism." In Tomlinson's words,

> *I yielded myself up to God . . . . great joy flooded my soul, my hands clapped together without any effort on my part . . . . The Holy Ghost spoke through my lips and tongue beyond my control . . . . the very language of Indian tribes there.*[27]

During the summer of 1908, in Cleveland, Tennessee, a tent campaign, lasting several weeks, resulted in some 300 conversions, while 250 were said to have been "baptized with the Holy Ghost." Among the latter was F. J. Lee, a Baptist layman, who later succeeded Tomlinson as General Overseer.

Tomlinson, accompanied by T. L. McLain, evangelized in Florida, eighteen miles from Tampa, at the Pleasant Grove campground, operated by the South Florida Holiness Association (where L. L. Pickett and Bud Robinson had preached). Tomlinson's party conducted a meeting, apparently at the invitation of R. M. Evans, a retired Methodist minister. The meetings "were blessed by great manifestations of the Spirit" with many "falling under the power" and giving expression in "weeping, praises, tongues, interpretations, dancing, leaping, and other demonstrations."[28]

At the close of the meeting 174 joined the Church of God, as it was now called. Twelve leaders were "ordained" and "went in all directions to preach and witness."

By 1910 the Church of God had evolved an outline of its basic doctrines -- mostly a list of the Scriptural passages on which faith and practice were based. These included repentance, justification, regeneration, new birth, sanctification subsequent to justification, holiness, water baptism by immersion, baptism in the Holy Ghost subsequent to cleansing, speaking in tongues as evidence of the baptism in the Holy

Ghost, abstinence from liquor and tobacco. Added later were avoiding jewelry, secret societies, and swearing, each with biblical references.

Nearly all of these twenty-eight "Teachings" were similar to other evangelical churches in the Wesleyan-Arminian tradition. The exceptions were: foot washing, divine healing for all in the atonement, and tongues as evidence of baptism in the Holy Spirit. Absent was a statement of church polity, yet in practice they ordained "bishops" (pastors) and "elders" (leading laymen). Unlike most creedal statements. There was, for instance, no attempt to correlate biblical statements: no recognition, for instance, that "new birth" and "regeneration" were synonymous, no attempt to relate "sanctification" to "holiness." Obviously these earnest laymen had little acquaintance with biblical theology.

In practice, healing and baptism in the Spirit, as evidenced by "tongues," became the hallmark of authenticity for the Church of God which has its headquarters in Cleveland, Tennessee. Emphasis on entire sanctification, the fruit of the Spirit, and perfect love receded into the background.

As with other Pentecostal groups, the Spirit became more prominent than the Father or the Son in devotional life and in preaching. In this writer's hearing at a Nebraska church, a young woman testified that at first she was on the ground floor with the Father, then she ascended to the second floor with the Son, and now lives on the top floor with the Holy Spirit!

In the beginning this movement in Appalachia was similar to the origin of Brethren groups in Europe and in Pennsylvania. Both were born of revival among earnest laymen. Both stressed experience more than doctrine, both placed little emphasis on "book learning." Hence in both movements documentation is difficult because oral history is the main source of information.

By contrast, the leaders in the revivals or spiritual awakenings under Wycliffe, Hus, Luther, Zwingli, Grebel, Calvin, Wesley, and Finney were both devout and learned. They came to the truth through the Scriptures. It was their exposure to the Bible which led them to challenge both State and Church. Their respective movements were sustained by writing as well as by evangelism, as is evident in the ministry of Luther, Menno Simon, John Calvin and John Wesley, to name a few.

The Quakers, the Brethren, and the Pentecostals gave primacy to experience with little emphasis on doctrine. It was the Wesleyan emphasis on the witness of the Holy Spirit which was "horrible" to the Anglican Establishment. But with Wesley and the Puritans, faith was grounded in Scripture, responsibly interpreted, which kept them from going into "enthusiasm," Montanism, or what became Pentecostalism.

Meanwhile the Church of God was becoming increasingly international in scope. In March, 1951, facilitated by David J. du Plessis, the Church of God (Cleveland) effected a merger with the Full Gospel Church of South Africa with its 30,000 members and a Bible School. The merger resulted in the new name Full Gospel Church of God, with headquarters in Tennessee.[29]

Also, in South Africa, Andrew Murray (1828-1917) was urging the baptism in the Holy Spirit and holy living. His affinities were with the Keswick Movement, but he did not advocate the tongues speaking, despite this implication by Hollenweger.[30]

Since 1950 the Church of God has gradually moved from a low-income group to a middle-class Church. In the 1970's Hollenweger observed that paradoxically,

> *A remarkable change of side has taken place. The church of the poor, which protested against the way in which the New Testament [concept of the church] was overlaid by the values of church and bourgeois, is in the process itself of becoming a conservative middlle-class force, while former traditional churches suddenly appear revolutionary.*[31]

He was probably referring to several Roman Catholic, Lutheran, and Episcopal Churches which included charismatics.

2. Revival in Kansas 1900--

In 1900 a revival occurred in Topeka, Kansas, under the leadership of Charles Fox Parham. Parham, born in Iowa in 1873, was "born again" in 1886 and felt called to the ministry. After a prolonged illness he experienced a miraculous healing while a student at the Methodist College at Winfield, Kansas. He was licensed to preach in the Methodist Church and was assigned to a pastorate near Lawrence, Kansas. Here, under the influence of a "holiness Quaker," he accepted "sanctification as a second work of grace."[32]

Discouraged after this two-year pastorate, he then left the Methodist Church and entered the evangelistic field "by faith." After experiencing a sudden healing of heart trouble, he abandoned medicines and physicians. In 1898 he established Bethel Bible School and Healing Home in Topeka. Here he preached "Salvation, Healing, Sanctification, the Second Coming of Christ, and the Baptism of the Holy Spirit."[33] Rejected by the leader whom he had left in charge of the school during a trip to New England, Parham started another Bible school in 1900 with forty in attendance. During Parham's absence these students sought the "fullness" while studying the Book of Acts. When Parham returned the students told him that "other tongues" was the sign of the "baptism" according to Acts. The group fasted and prayed night and day for a second Pentecost.

One of the older students, Miss Agnes Ozman (mentioned in the Los Angeles *Apostolic Faith* report), testified in these words:

> *On this first day of January [1901] ... I asked Bro. Parham to pray and lay hands on me that I might receive theBaptism in the Holy Ghost and as he prayed and laid hands upon [sic] my head I began to speak in tongues glorifying God. Bless HIM! I talked several languages for it was manifest when a dilect [sic] was spoken.*[34]

Three days later, while Parham was preaching at a Free Methodist church at Topeka, "the fire fell on the company at Bethel." As reported by Mrs. Parham' sister,

> *Then great joy came into my soul and I began to say, "I praise Thee" .... I tried to praise Him in English but could not so I just led the praise come through in the new language given, with the floodgates of glory wide open. He had come to me, even to me, to speak not of Himself but to magnify the Christ, -- and oh, what a wonderful, wonderful Christ was revealed . . . . all around me I heard great rejoicings while others spoke in tongues and glorified God.*

Later that evening Parham rejoined the group and reported,

> *"A glory fell over me and I began to worship God in the Sweedish [sic] tongue, which later changed to other languages and continued so until morning.* "[35]

Anderson discounts these reports insisting that the "baptism" did not come as a direct result of reading Acts and prayer, but rather because of Parham's teaching. This judgment seems based on factors other than the verbatim reports of the participants.

On July 10, 1905, Parham and twenty-five workers began a revival in Houston, Texas. "A mighty revival swept the city .... scores were converted, sanctified and baptized with the Holy Spirit; many were healed" and delivered from evil spirits.[36]

In December, 1905 Parham opened a Bible School in Houston with emphasis on spiritual gifts. Among his students was a black Baptist preacher named W. J. Seymour who had been "saved and sanctified." Later he accepted an invitation to become associate pastor of a black store-front holiness congregation in Los Angeles, having been recommended by a member who had come from Texas. Parham reluctantly sent him, after the laying on of hands, thus "passing on the leadership of the movement to others" from a "small localized movement" to one of "international proportions."[37]

3. Revival in Los Angeles 1901--

Before Seymour arrived in Los Angeles a revival was in progress in several holiness and other churches. The influential Baptist evangelist, Frank Bartleman, arrived in Los Angeles in 1904 to further the work of revival. Holiness leaders there invited F. B. Meyer, who had links with the Keswick Movement, for evangelistic services in 1905. Reports of the Welch revival, fueled by reports by S. B. Shaw, G. Campbell Morgan, and Evan Roberts inspired revivals among many holiness churches and other churches as well.

But when Pastor Seymour, in Los Angeles, preached at the black Holiness Mission that the gift of tongues was essential, the congregation objected. Rejected, Seymour then led meetings in homes of black sympathizers. Help came from Parham's group in Houston, and on April 9th "the power fell." Several, including Seymour, experienced the "gift of tongues."

As noted earlier, Pentecostalism first gained world-wide notice during this revival meeting in Los Angeles in 1906, similar, in some respects to the attention given the Billy Graham revival meeting in the late nineteen-forties, also in Los Angeles. The Azusa street event was acclaimed by its participants as a second Pentecost and as evidence of the imminence of the Second Coming of Christ. In the words of an on-the-spot participant,

> *Pentecost has surely come and with it the Bible evidences are following, many being converted and sanctified, and filled with the Holy Ghost, speaking in tongues, as at Pentecost.*[38]

The movement, according to this same primary source, began at a cottage prayer meeting ("Pentecost fell there three nights") and later transferred to an abandoned Methodist Church at 312 Azusa Street, then in an urban ghetto. Gradually interest increased assisted by the earthquake in San Francisco which renewed expectation of the Second Coming. The tiny bi-racial group refused advertising and determined to wait upon the Lord for the anointing. Yet the revival increased in power and influence. The crowds increased and "multitudes" were "saved, sanctified, baptized with the Holy Ghost and healed of all manner of sicknesses." The report continued: "many are speaking in new tongues and some are on their way to the foreign fields with the gift of tongues." Obviously these "missionaries" expected to be able to communicate in the language of the peoples they had come to evangelize as soon as they arrived at their destination!

Bartleman, while promoting revivalism, took note of the Azusa Street Mission. On June 15, 1906, as he remembered it

> *At "Azusa" the Spirit dropped the "heavenly chorus" into my soul. . . It was a gift from God of high order . . . We wanted to meet God first . . . The meetings started themselves, spontaneously, in testimony, praise and worship . . . We had real testimonies from fresh heart-experience . . . A dozen might be on their feet at once, trembling under the power of God . . . All obeyed God in meekness and humility. In honor we "preferred one another." Some one would finally get up anointed for the message. All seemed to recognize this and give way . . . we rejoiced that God was working . . . The meetings were controlled by the Spirit from the Throne.*[39]

Glenn A. Cook, a holiness preacher, went to the mission to "straighten Seymour out" on doctrine, but instead was won over and became the mission's public relations man. Soon three separate Pentecostal groups were flourishing in Los Angeles.

The link between the tongues movement in Los Angeles and that in Topeka was remembered in Los Angeles. This event was recalled during the Los Angeles revival five years later:

> *After three months a sister who had been teaching sanctification for the baptism with the Holy Ghost, one who had a sweet, loving experience and all the carnality taken out of her heart, felt the Lord led her to have hands laid on her to receive the Pentecost. So when they prayed the Holy Ghost came in great power and she commenced speaking in an unknown tongue. . . . three nights later twelve [Bible School] students*

> *received the Holy Ghost and prophesied, and cloven tongues could be seen upon their heads . . . . Now after five years something like 13,000 received this gospel. It is spreading everywhere.*[40]

Reports of the Los Angeles revivals circulated among many holiness camp meetings and holiness associations throughout the country, including holiness meetings at Old Orchard, Maine, Wilmore, Ky, Nyack, N.Y., and God's Bible School in Cincinnati.

Churches, holiness associations, and camp meetings opposed the "tongues people." The Pentecostals were then on their own in promotion. Their literature was, for a while, delivered free to many holiness groups.

However, the movement continued to grow in ways which recalled the Evangelical Revival in eighteenth century England.

> *The rank and file Pentecostal preachers stumped the country, preaching wherever they could get a group together. Increasingly refused the use of holiness and other churches, they held meetings in school houses, warehouses, rented store fronts, in private homes, under brush arbors, in open fields, in forest clearings, in funeral parlors, gas stations and cafes. They preached to millhands in factories, to road gangs by the wayside, to workmen in railroad yards and iron works and to farmhands in the cotton fields. They exhorted sinners from courthouse steps and city parks, and in dance halls, gambling houses, and red light districts. They journeyed by wagon and horseback, and finally by foot, into remote and rugged mountain regions.*[41]

The Pentecostals were ostracized by the major denominations as the holiness people had been. After having been welcomed in holiness associations, they were rejected because of the emphasis on tongues.

Not surprisingly, factionalism replaced the initial unity which issued from spiritual renewal much the same as in ancient Corinth when Paul deplored factions in history's first charismatic or "Pentecostal" church (cf. I Cor. 1-3; 12-14)!

In Los Angeles Bartleman, who promoted the movement at Azusa Street from coast to coast, decided to lead a splinter group, because the original movement had become "organized." Elmer Fisher, formerly a Baptist pastor, also left to form the "Upper Room Mission" near the Azusa Street Mission.[42]

In isolation strife increased among themselves. Preachers were expected to discover new and novel insights as evidence of the intimacy with the Holy Spirit and the new truth. When the "new revelations" did not agree confusion resulted. In addition, claims of divine illumination and struggles for leadership added their toll of factions.

In 1908 W. H. Durham in *The Pentecostal Testimony* denied that "it takes two works of grace to save and cleanse a man" because of the "Finished work of Calvary." The work *for* me is done . . . the work *in* me is being done."[43]

By 1916 the movement had divided into three main streams: "Second Work Trinitarians," "Finished Work Trinitarians" and Unitarians.[44] Sub-divisions along racial lines followed.

Gradually the cleansing was minimized and progression emphasized. Thus justification became merged with sanctification (as in Lutheran and Reformed theology) and indwelling sin was assumed to remain in the believer. Pentecostals from Calvinistic and Keswick backgrounds embraced the "Finished Work" position over the "Second Work" position. In the west, the Reformed influence prevailed over the Wesleyan-Holiness position. All believers were said to have been baptized with the Spirit at conversion (cf. 1 Cor. 12:13), hence the Baptism with the Spirit was not a second work of grace.

With reference to sanctification, this majority view differed little from the Keswick view as championed by R. A. Torrey, Wilbur Chapman, A. B. Simpson, and Harry Ironside.[45] Also, since many Pentecostals had not experienced sanctification as a second work of grace, theology conformed to experience.

Those who favored the Second Work view had previously been influenced by Parham in the Mid-west, by the Holiness Movement in general, and by the Church of God movement in Appalachia. They believed, with Wesleyan-Arminians, that entire sanctification is to be distinguished from regeneration and comes, if at all, subsequent to justification-regeneration. Many of the leaders in the group had formerly been Methodist clergymen. In polity those of the "Second Work" group, reflecting their Methodist background, were more episcopal than the congregational type of the "Finished Work" group.

Although some in the Church of God Movement (Cleveland, TN) sought the "Baptism on the Spirit" as a second work of grace, they refused to call it a "third work."

However, B. H. Irwin, a preacher in the Iowa Holiness Association, began preaching the "baptism of fire" (cf. Matt. 3:ll) as a "third work" of grace. This movement spread in several mid-western states, Canada, and the Carolinas. This lead to the formation of the Fire-Baptized Holiness Association at Olmitz, Iowa, in 1895-98.[46] Later (1900) leadership was passed to J. H. King as Overseer.

The "baptism of fire" does not seem to have had a valid scriptural basis, although . . . It was an honest attempt to satisfy an unfulfilled desire . . . of the majority of those . . . sanctified.[47] A "Pentecostal baptism of the Spirit," with the gift of "tongues," was said to have replaced the "baptism of fire" and to have "saved the day."

A Methodist Pastor, A. B. Crumpler, led numerous holiness revivals in North Carolina and left the Methodists to form the Pentecostal Holiness Church in 1900. Crumpler had experienced entire sanctification and preached holiness with great effectiveness, consistently with others in the main holiness movement. However, when C. B. Cashwell came from the Azusa group for evangelistic services "many received the baptism of the Spirit and spoke in tongues." The result was a split in the group. Some with Crumpler disapproved with the "tongues" added to entire sanctification; the majority favored the "tongues" emphasis.

Crumpler and several other pastors and congregations, withdrew, but the remnant, under A. H. Butler and Cashwell, retained the name of Pentecostal Holiness Church. In 1911 The Fire-Baptized Holiness Church and the Pentecostal Holiness Church merged as the Pentecostal Holiness Church.[48]

It is quite plausible that it was during the revivals led by Crumpler that the three layman from North Carolina came preaching holiness with the resulting revival at the Shearer schoolhouse, as noted earlier.[49]

Pentecostal churches have flourished world-wide. In Brazil they constitute the largest Protestant group element in Protestantism in that country. The movement began about 1910 when two Swedish missionaries arrived in Belem, Brazil. Of these two, Gunnar Vingren experienced the "baptism of the Spirit" in Sweden in 1909. His friend, Daniel Berg, joined the Pentecostal church of W. H. Durham in Chicago. In Brazil they conducted prayer meetings in the cellar of the Baptist church in Belem. Revival followed during which many Baptists spoke in tongues. The pastor opposed this development and most of his members withdrew and followed the Swedish missionaries. The movement spread from the Amazon region south to the industrial region of Brazil. It was an indigenous movement: Brazilians witnessing to Brazilians. Fifty years later adherents numbered one million.[50] The Assemblies de Deus includes all classes of society and is sending out missionaries. In a relatively short time Brazilian Pentecostals became, and continue to be, the largest and most vigorous of vital Protestant denominations in Brazil.

Early in the movement expectation of Christ's Second Coming was prominent, even dominant. As the Parousia did not occur as expected it receded in prominence; divine healing and glossolalia came to the front in emphasis. Gradually evangelism, missionary enterprise, and health services became more prominent, especially among television evangelists, as they appealed to a larger audience. Main-line churches were also more receptive to the charismatic movement.

4. Revival with the Catholics

Charismatic renewal among Roman Catholics in the United States was experienced as a "New Pentecost" among praying students at Duquesne University at Pittsburg in February, 1967. Certain students there were concerned about critical issues in the church and world events such as civil rights and world peace. Even as earnest and alert Christians, something was lacking in their lives.

> *There was an emptiness, a lack of dynamism, a sapping of strength in their lives of prayer and action. It was as if their lives as Christians were too much of their own creation . . . as if they were moving forward under their own power . . . It seemed to them that the Christian life wasn't meant to be purely achievement.*[51]

As they fasted and prayed together that weekend, seeking the renewing and power of the Holy Spirit, their prayers were answered in a new personal Pentecost. They were transformed by what they called a "baptism in the Holy Spirit." Like the one hundred twenty in the upper room in Jerusalem, they experienced the inflowing love of God; they were empowered to bear witness of the Lord Jesus and his resurrection. They were eager to continue in prayer and in a study of the Scriptures (cf. Acts 1-4). They were eager to share what they had experienced. University students in South Bend, Ann

Arbor, New Orleans and Los Angeles also experienced a similar spiritual renewal. Spontaneous prayer groups sprang up around the world.

What proved to be the First Annual Pentecost Conference met at Notre Dame University on April 7-9, 1967, with about one hundred in attendance. In June 1973 at Notre Dame twenty-two thousand gathered from thirty-five countries. In the following year thirty thousand were in attendance, including numerous priests and bishops. It marked a Second Reformation![52]

Each recipient of the "baptism in the Holy Spirit became a witness and "missionary" to students in other campuses; numerous prayer and fellowship groups of charismatics resulted. Several monks in the Trappist Abbey near Dubuque, Iowa, were "baptized with the Spirit."

In late summer at Ann Arbor, another gathering was held of both Catholics and Protestant charismatics. Soon Ann Arbor became "something of a model and a place of pilgrimage for many Catholic Pentecostals."

In August 1967, Father Francis MacNutt attended a healing seminar sponsored by Camps Farthest Out in Maryville, Tenn. There he received "the baptism in the Spirit and spoke in tongues." Later, on numerous occasions, he addressed meetings of the Full Gospel Business Men's Fellowship International. On October 15, 1967, several Catholics met in Lansing, Michigan, for a monthly Day of Renewal. The format then adopted became a model for others: Bible vigil, a sharing session, a talk, workshops, supper and prayer meeting;[53] [reminiscent of the Ashrams sponsored by the missionary to India, E. Stanley Jones].

What are the effects of the Catholic renewal? As listed by competent critics they include (1) the preeminence given to Jesus Christ, (2) spontaneity in prayer, (3) eagerness to study the Bible, (4) social service (love of neighbor), and (5) spiritual gifts, including glossolalia. The latter is the most distinctive and problematic feature of these new Pentecostals. Unlike "classical" Pentecostals, they do not think speaking in tongues is necessary to authenticate their filling with the Spirit -- yet they welcome this gift. They do not consider "tongues" a known language, hence not miraculous.

> *Rather it is an emotional verbal release, an expression of spiritual freedom. This least of the charismata may be the opening door to the*

other gifts of the Spirit, as when one bows in humility to enter the low doorway into the Church of the Nativity in Bethlehem.[54]

How do these Catholic Pentecostals differ from the "classical" or Protestant charismatics? They (1) regard the main line Pentecostals as fundamentalists -- those who interpret the Bible literally -- and do not wish to be linked to them, (2) some are reluctant to use the biblical expression "baptism in the Holy Spirit" because of their theology which insists that the Holy Spirit is given at infant baptism and a subsequent bestowal is only more of the same; (this despite experience, logic and Scripture). This may help explain why John Wesley was loath to link the Spirit's baptism with a second work of grace. (3) Unlike the main line Pentecostals the Catholic charismatics do not consider speaking with tongues is always evidence of baptism in the Spirit. Also in their life-style Catholic Pentecostals are less likely to adopt such practices as total abstinence from alcohol and tobacco, sabbath observance, and tithing. They are also eevangeager to associate spiritual renewal with such Catholic doctrines as the mass and the veneration of Mary.[55]

Some Catholics, however, feel compelled to take a second look at infant baptism and wonder if it should be reserved for those who choose Christ and are then baptized as a public declaration of their conversion.[56]

The Catholic Pentecostals are discovering the difference between nominal Christians and evangelical, authentic believers or disciples. Many are finding a new personal relevance in the words of the litany and a new appreciation of the sacraments. They are discovering the true nature of the church as the fellowship of those who are "born again" into the body of Christ. They see a new opening in ecumenical dialogue and fellowship with believers who are not Catholic.[57] Prayer meetings tend to "obscure the issues" which divide Catholics and Protestants. They have experienced a new, authentic life in Christ made real through the baptism in the Spirit, yet they do not feel called to leave their church. The hierarchy seems disposed to accept them.

They have discovered authentic New Testament Christianity. Christ is a living Presence rather than simply a historical figure or a name in the Creed. The Holy Spirit makes it all personally present and relevant.

Many will ask, why do they not feel compelled to criticize or leave their Church as have so many Protestants? Perhaps, unlike the early reformers, such as Wycliffe, Huss, Luther and Zwingli, they were not influenced primarily by the perceived difference between the Bible and Church tradition and practice. Instead, they "hungered and thirsted for righteousness" and consequently found filling and fulfillment. Also, the hierarchy did not reject, but rather endorsed them, as it had the Friars and Brethren of the Common Life. Also, unlike "classical Pentecostals," tongues was not seen as the evidence of baptism in the Spirit. Catholic charismatics constitute a fellowship, rather than a reformation, hence are not a threat to the establishment. It is comparable to the religious societies with the Church of England in the late seventeenth and early eighteenth centuries. Their stance is *sharing* more than persuasion and restructuring. They report change they have personally experienced rather than demanding change in others.

B. CONSISTENCY WITH SCRIPTURE

In the early days of the charismatic movement they regarded the New Testament Pentecost as the "early rain" and contemporary Pentecostalism as the "latter rain" (Joel 2:23). This, they believed, heralded the approach of the end time and the Second Coming. As the imminence of this event seemed to fade, healing and glossolalia moved into prominence. Not surprisingly, the neo- Pentecostal movement, as represented by the Catholic charismatics, places little stress on eschatology and focuses instead on life in the Holy Spirit.

Divine healing represents a return to the healing ministry of Jesus. Some claim to go further than Jesus in that they not only facilitate the cure but, also identify the diseased and the disease. Hollenweger reports from personal observation that William Bransham was able "to name with astonishing accuracy the sickness . . . of people he had never seen." Hollenweger, who knew Branham and interpreted for him in Zurich, was not aware of any case in which the healer was mistaken in the often detailed statements he made. But he reports that in most instances even those who experienced healing did not remain healed. He concludes, "by contrast to what he claimed only a small percentage of those who sought healing were in fact healed."[58]

Faith healing evangelists teach that ill health is of the devil, that healing, as well as salvation, is provided in the atonement ("by his stripes we are healed" Isa. 53:5; 1 Pet. 2:24). This explains why many Pentecostals often include the exorcism of Satan in their prayers. Characteristic is the ejaculatory prayer, "in the name of Jesus -- be healed"!

Few verses of Scripture have influenced the Pentecostals as much as Mark 16:17: "They will drive out demons in my name; they will speak in strange tongues; if they pick up snakes or drink any poison, they will not be harmed; they will place their hands on sick and these will get well"(TEV). As Stanley Jones observed, "not one of [these signs has] a moral quality. If these had been 'signs' of believing Christians, then Christianity would have died out as a wonder cult. . . . Only two of these signs were found in Jesus" (exorcism and healing).[59]

Their appeal to the disputed ending of Mark reflects the eagerness of Pentecostals to rediscover the power of primitive Christianity. Unlike the Reformers, they insist that the age of miracles did not end with the apostolic age. They see themselves, as distinct from main stream denominations, proving the Reformers wrong at this point.

Like the Order of St. Luke, a group which includes several Episcopalians, they protest the use of the qualifying phrase "if be thy will." This, they say, renders the prayer of faith ineffective. A lecturer at Asbury Theological Seminary, a clergyman of the Order of St. Luke, insisted that healing will always occur if the sick is supported by a community of faith. As he spoke the wife of a faculty member in the audience was dying of cancer while surrounded by a community of faith!

Yet we learn that Jesus and the apostles saw instances of instant and permanent healing, and today numerous instances of instantaneous cures can be documented.

The Pentecostals err in two premises: (1) that remedy for physical healing is included in the atonement, on the same basis as the remedy for sin (cf. Isa. 53:5), (2) that since it is God's will that every believer enjoy good health, the devil is responsible for disease; thus divine healing involves the exorcism of demons. Based on these premises physical healing comes to have more prominence than in the New Testament Epistles or in Christian history. As in Scripture, physical healing brings a crowd today.

In Pentecostalism one sees the emphasis on spiritual gifts, especially physical healing and "tongues", as displacing the Pauline-Petron-Johannine emphasis on the fruit of the Spirit as purity and love: a case of mistaken priority. To some extent, however, the Neo-Pentecostal movement has corrected this imbalance.

The most controversial facet of Pentecostalism is the gift of tongues. That "tongues" is a genuine gift of the Spirit is clear from the Epistles of Paul (1 Cor. 12, 14). That it is linked with the Baptism in the Holy Spirit is clear from the Book of Acts (Acts 2, 10, 11, 19).

Is the modern phenomena of glossolalia, a God-given miracle, i.e., one of the family of known languages, unknown to the recipient? Among the different interpretations of this phenomena are (1) those who consider it a known language, hence miraculous; (2) those who attribute it to the devil; (3) those who consider it an emotional expression neither pathological or abnormal (Samarin and Suenens); (4) those convinced that in no instance, among modern Pentecostals is "tongues" a known language (Samarin); (5) those who consider it an emotional expression of the frustrated "disinherited" (Anderson); (6) those who distinguish between a known language (Acts 2) and an utterance unknown except to an interpreter (I Cor. 14:13-19). Which of these explanations is nearest to the truth? Consensus here is nonexistent.

Of basic concern is the question whether tongues-speaking is actually a language of which the speaker had no previous knowledge. Those who make this affirmation cite specific examples to prove their point. For example:

Rabbi Jacob Rabinowitz became a disciple of Jesus *secretly* and felt guilty. At a Pentecostal service he knelt in prayer. Several gathered around to pray with him and for him, some in English and others in "tongues." Suddenly the rabbi stood up and demanded, "Which of you is Jewish?" He identified the speaker and asked where he had learned Hebrew. The one who had spoken in "tongues" said, "I am Irish and know nothing of Hebrew," to which the rabbi said, "You said in perfect Hebrew, . . . 'you will preach of the gospel of Jesus Christ.'"[60]

How did the Irishman know the name of the Rabbi and the name of his father; how could he have spoken in Hebrew? Can such be authenticated by independent and relatively objective students of the phenomena?

Numerous other instances which seem miraculous are cited:

It is no exaggeration to say that the gift of other [known languages] have been proved thousands of times by people who have known the language spoken, and who have confirmed the interpretation as perfectly accurate.[61]

We return to the basic questions: Are the contemporary "tongues" a real language as claimed by most Pentecostals?

1) What is the biblical evidence for glossolalia?
2) Was Pentecost a miracle of speech or of hearing (Acts 2)?
3) Do Luke and Paul agree on the meaning of "tongues"?
4) Is modern glossolalia a jumble of sounds or a known language?

All of these questions are disagreed upon by those who claim to know.

Let the Pentecostals speak first. As viewed by William G. McDonald, Jesus did not speak with tongues because he did not address those outside the Jewish milieu.[62]

The apostles were regenerated when Jesus breathed on them after his resurrection (John 20:22; cf. Tit. 3:5). Later they were filled with the Holy Spirit and spoke in tongues (Acts 2:2; 4:31). In Acts "our language" (*he meterais glossais*) is synonymous with our "dialect" (*dialektoi*). In this situation Galileans spoke languages known to the pilgrims who had gathered from many ethnic groups. Upon this occasion, three objective phenomena surprised the "outsiders": wind, fire and languages. In Samaria the Spirit was given when the apostles prayed for Philip's converts in such a manner that Simon Magus "saw" and coveted the same power or authority. This implies, say the Pentecostals, that there was more than a subjective assurance of the Spirit's infilling.

Those who heard Peter's message in Caesarea received the Holy Spirit as the apostles had in Jerusalem, McDonald points out. Again there must have been some *objective* evidence of the Spirit's infilling that would convince the skeptics and be incontrovertible evidence that Gentiles were accepted by God on the same basis as Hebrews. McDonald infers that glossolalia occured in <u>all</u> instances when the Spirit was given, even in the case of Paul was "filled with the Holy Spirit in Damascus" 9:17; cf. 1 Cor. 14:33). On the basis of Acts 11:17 ("like gift") he argues unconvincingly (Acts 15:9), that the "tongues" of Acts 10 is identical with the "tongues" of Acts 2.

On the basis of the Corinthian letters he distinguishes between glossolalia which edifies the speaker (1 Cor. 14:4,5,6,9,18,23,28) and that which edifies the church (1 Cor. 12:10,28,30; 14:5,13,27,39). This is not a distinction in glossolalia itself, but a distinction only for the purpose intended (edification of self or others).

It follows, he argues, that there is no distinction between Luke and Paul in the teaching on "tongues." He asserts that since the glossolalia in Acts 8, 10, and 19 is the same as in Acts 2 it follows that the phenomenon described in 1 Cor. 12-14, are the same as reported in Acts. His conclusion is that glossolalia in Luke is identical with the glossolalia in Paul. The only distinction in both is in function or intended use. It would appear that McDonald's "exegesis" is an attempt to find a New Testament justification for his own Pentecostal experience.

A similar distortion in exegesis may be seen in Pentecostalism's most serious claim to be a responsible and unbiased exegesis: Stanley M. Horton's exposition of Galatians. In this epistle Paul demanded, "Did you receive the Spirit by the works of the law, or by hearing with faith?" (Gal. 3:2 NASB). Horton adds, "It may very well be that their response of faith came during Paul's preaching, a response not only for accepting Christ but also for receiving the baptism in the Holy Spirit."[63]

Again, ignoring the similar language in Romans 8:15, 16, linking sonship with the Spirit, Horton argues (Gal. 4:6) that since God sends his Spirit only to sons, Paul means two separate works of grace, the second being a "Pentecostal fulfillment."[64]

Horton even finds the likelihood of "tongues" in the phrase "sighs too deep for words" (Rom. 8:26). The "sealing" (Eph. 1:13) he equates with the "baptism in the Holy Spirit" on rather precarious grounds.[65] Commendably he distinguishes the Spirit's baptism into one body for unity (1 Cor. 12:13) from the baptism for purity and power (Acts 2:8 et al).

Horton's thorough and irenic biblical survey is vitiated by a tendency to draw inferences in support of his doctrine not adequately sustained by responsible exegesis. Thus he finds no difference between the "tongues" in Acts and "tongues" in Paul. As noted earlier, L. J. Cardinal Suenens of Belgium views "tongues" as neither miraculous nor pathological, not a real language. Rather, in his view, it is a genuine gift of the Spirit (1 Cor. 12:30; 14:2), like an emotional release, analogous to a release accompanied by tears, which by humble submission may lead higher gifts of the Spirit. But if it is only an emotional release why call it a gift of the Spirit? It is not, as in classical Pentecostalism, an evidence that one has been baptized in the Holy Spirit? This latter is typical of the neo-charismatics.

Catholic Pentecostals distinguish themselves from other Pentecostals in that they come from the middle class and are often collegiate types of people rather than those mostly from the poor and "disinherited." They view classical Pentecostals as derivative of the Protestant tradition of revivalism and of the Holiness Movement. As one Catholic charismatic puts it

> *Often with the revivals came a simplistic and individualistic Christian ethic. The righteous life was characterized by clean living; therefore no smoking, drinking, dancing, make-up, theater-going, or other amusements were allowed . . . The revivalistic culture continues to pervade denominational Pentecostalism.*[66]

Ranaghan concludes, "This religious style . . . is not essential or desirable for the baptism in the Holy Spirit . . ."

This last point raises serious questions. Is the "righteous life" not essential to the Spirit-filled life? Can one drink, smoke, enjoy worldly amusements and still consider his body a temple of the divine Spirit? Will the Holy Spirit baptize and fill an unclean "temple?" Can righteous living exist without self-discipline? Can "spiritual gifts" be disassociated from the Spirit of Holiness and claim to be authentic? Peter defined the *essentials* of Pentecost as "purifying their hearts by faith" (Acts 15:9). Has antinomianism invaded the modern charismatic movement? Has the life style and discipline of personal life, which usually follows revivals and personal renewals, no claim to authenticity?

At the same time who would not rejoice that thousands of Roman Catholics are experiencing a dynamic spiritual renewal, which they identify as the Baptism in the Holy Spirit, and are bearing the fruit of the Spirit in daily life and witness?

W. J. Samarin in *Tongues of Men and Angels* concludes an exhaustive "scientific" research by saying in part

> *Tape recorded examples of glossolalia . . . always turn out to be the same thing: strings of syllables, made of up of sounds taken from among all those the speaker knows, put together more or less haphazardly but*

> which nevertheless emerge as word-like and sentence-like units because of language-like rhythm and melody.... Yet, in spite of superficial similarities, glossolalia is fundamentally *not* language.... It has never been scientifically demonstrated that **xenoglossia** *[real language] occurs among Pentecostals: people just do not talk languages they are familiar with .... glossolalia is not a supernatural phenomenon .... Glossolalia is normal, not abnormal as the man in the street believes.*[67]

The same author cites examples of similar glossolalia among non-Christian groups. A former missionary told this writer that he had witnessed glossolalia among Pentecostal and voodoo worshipers in the Caribbean -- with no discernible difference in sounds. R.M. Anderson agrees with this assessment. He concludes,

> *Where it is asserted that non-Pentecostals confirmed the real linguisticality of tongue-speech, these witnesses are either unnamed, cannot be found, or are incompetent to judge. The only reliable evidence is the growing volume of recorded tongue-speech which in every single instance flatly and unambiguously contradicts Pentecostal claims to xenoglossy.*[68]

This assessment may be challenged by other data. But a similar conclusion comes from specialists in linguistics.

Dr. Eugene A. Nida, internationally known linguist of the American Bible Society, with a team of linguists representing 150 aboriginal languages from twenty five countries examined tapes of tongues speaking. Their conclusion was that these tapes showed "no resemblance to any actual language which has ever been treated by linguists," and that it is, therefore, very improbable that this is a human language of any kind what ever.[69]

Increasingly Pentecostals, both Catholic and non-Catholic, admit that their "tongues" are not a real language. But they insist that it is divinely inspired and hence a "means of grace" which leads to other higher spiritual gifts. Would Paul agree? Did it work that way in Corinth?

A helpful summary in answer to these questions is provided in G. Michael Cocoris, Pastor of the Church of the Open Door in Los Angeles. He concludes in part that

> *(1) In Acts 2 it is obvious that "tongues" were the language known to the hearers. It is likely that in other occurrences of this phenomena*

> *(Acts 8, 10, 11, 15, 19) real languages were spoken. Peter cited Acts 2 as the precedent by which to evaluate speech in Caesarea (Acts 11:17).*
>
> *(2) It is probable that Paul and Luke agree in the definition of "tongues." Furthermore, Paul cites Isaiah 28:10,11 as a precedent for "tongues" in Corinth (1Cor. 14:20). In Isaiah the "lips of foreigners" means the language of neighboring nations, hence a real language..*
>
> *(3) While Pentecostals believe "tongues" are for all or most believers, just as the baptism in the Holy Spirit is for all, Paul, by contrast, argues that "tongues" are not for all. He asks, "Are all apostles, are all prophets . . . . Do all speak in tongues?" (1 Cor. 12:29,30). Paul obviously expected a negative answer. "Tongues" is **one** of the genuine gifts of the Spirit, but not a gift for all believers, contrary to Pentecostal teaching.*
>
> *(4) Contrary to Pentecostal practice Paul says tongues are a sign for **unbelievers** (1 Cor. 14:21,22 [but see 1 Cor. 14:23-25]).*
>
> *(5) Paul insisted that not more than three speak in "tongues" and then in sequence (1Cor. 14:27). Pentecostals often speak in "tongues" simultaneously.*
>
> *(6) Those most competent to judge ["scientifically"] have concluded that "tongues" today are not a known language.*[70]

Some Pentecostals admit that "tongues" do not involve languages, yet insist on their importance, failing to recognize adequately the qualitative difference between the "gifts" and the "fruit of the Spirit" as stated in Paul's letters (1 Cor. 12;14; Gal.5). Pentecostals place prime importance on the gift of tongues: Paul, by contrast, gives tongues the lowest place in importance (1 Cor. 12:28; 14:5,19,23,39).

If contemporary tongues is not a genuine gift of a known language, as in Acts 2, why do so many find a causal relationship between "tongues," spiritual renewal, and the fruit of the Spirit? In short, why do so many witnesses report their own spiritual renewal and new dynamism as the "baptism with the Holy Spirit" accompanying with "tongues"? To this question the Bible again is the prime source of truth. Where in Scripture is there an admonition to *seek* this gift? Paul's dictum was seek not; "forbid not" (1 Cor. 14:39). In addition, for each witness of spiritual victory, freedom and effectiveness, accompanied by "tongues," one can cite *at least one* who experienced spiritual liberation, purity and power, *without* tongue-speech.

How valid is the claim of Pentecostals, whether Catholic or Protestant, that their experience of the gift of physical healing and tongue speech is nearer to the experience of the churches of the New Testament than another Christian group? On this point few would disagree. Miracles of healing, as witnessed in the Gospels and Acts, were much more prevalent in New Testament times than today. But again, the New Testament witness throughout is that the fruit of the Spirit is more essential than the Spirit's gifts, just as one's life is more *basic* than one's activities. The Corinthian Church erred in over valuing spiritual gifts and undervaluing the fruit of the Spirit such as faith, hope and love, as Paul so eloquently stated (I Cor. 13). Early in this century several in the Christian and Missionary Alliance accepted Pentecostalism. The Founder of the Alliance had to deal with the problem. The appraisal and warning of A. B. Simpson in 1903 has stood the test of time.

> *"One of these greatest errors is a disposition to make special manifestations an evidence of the Baptism of the Holy Ghost . . . as though none had received the Spirit of Pentecost but those of had the power to speak in tongues, thus leading many . . . to seek after special manifestations of other than God Himself . . . to seek rather for signs and wonders and special manifestations."*[71]

Simpson summed it up in language gleaned from Paul: "seek not; forbid not" (cf. I Cor. 14:39).

C. APPRAISAL

With reference to the question, which of these self-styled *Restoration* Movements (Anabaptists, Puritans, Pietists, Methodists, Brethren, Disciples, Pentecostals) adheres most closely to the primitive church, how do Pentecostals rate? On the plus side they (1) minister to the poor; (2) they appeal to those who lament the spiritual decline (cf. Rev. 3:16) in the major denominations; (3) they are zealous in spreading the gospel; (4) they stress the "signs and wonders" so frequently featured in the Gospels and Acts; (5) their "freedom" in worship recalls this characteristic in primitive Christian communities (Eph. 5:18-20).

On the negative side they have some characteristics of the "First Charismatic Church" (the church in Corinth), which gave Paul the most problems. They were quarrelsome (1 Cor. 1:10-13; 3:3-4; 2 Cor. 12:20-21) despite the fact that where the Spirit is in control unity prevails (Acts 2:42-47), a unity which Swete noted, was as great a miracle as those at "Pentecost itself"[72]. At Corinth some preferred Paul, some Apollos, some Cephas, and others Christ (1 Cor. 1: 12). In America alone Elmer T. Clark listed over fifty charismatic "sects."[73]

Like the Corinthians, they do not always worship "in a fitting and orderly way" (1 Cor. 14:33, 40 NIV).

As the Corinthians (like other Greeks) prided themselves on their "knowledge" (1Cor. 1:20-25; 8:1); some charismatic groups regard their glossolalia as indicative of their superior spirituality.

Also, like the Corinthians, their *priorities* are flawed; while Paul placed "tongues" as a genuine but inferior gift (I Cor. 12:28; 14:1-33, 39), they give it first place. Unlike Paul they prize the *gifts* of the Spirit (1 Cor. 12:28-31) more than the *fruit* of the Spirit (Gal. 5:22-26).

Like the Corinthians, they tend to be "childish" in that they assume "tongues" to be evidence of a higher state of grace, while Paul showed them that these are associated with immaturity (1 Cor. 13:8-13; 14:20). Instead of "majoring on minors" they should be seeking the "more excellent way" (faith, hope, and *love*.

In addition to being childish the Corinthians were also "carnal" or "fleshly" believers (even though "sanctified," or separated, 1:2), rather than being "spiritual" or mature (3:1-3; cf. Heb. 5:11-14).

Another problem with the Christians in Corinth was pride or arrogance (*hubris*). This Paul delineated in his contrast between man's assumption of knowledge (*gnosis*) and God's wisdom (1:18-31). They were "puffed up" (*phusioun*) as seen in a variety of situations (4:6, 18, 19; 5:2; 8:1 cf. 13:4). This arrogance, this assumption that they are superior to Paul, who is seen to be weak, permeates the Corinthian letters (cf. 2 Cor. 7; 9--13). In contrast to the knowing and gifted Corinthians Paul, presented himself as weak and foolish (1 Cor. 4:9-21; 2 Cor. 10:1 -- 13:10). His prayer is that they will be childlike in humility, in servitude, and in "the simplicity that is in Christ" (1 Cor. 14:20; 2 Cor. 11:2-3).

At Corinth, arrogance made *church discipline* a problem. They were tolerant of those who practiced sexual immorality, instead of exposing and excluding impenitent sinners (1 Cor. 5). Are charismatic groups, which stress emotion, signs, and gifts, more vulnerable to the "lust of the flesh" than those who focus on purity of heart and a disciplined life style? This was true of the believers in Corinth.

Gnosticism was a peril in Corinth (1 Cor. 1:18--2:l6) as elsewhere in the early churches (cf. 1 Cor. 6:13-20; Gal. 5:13, 25; 2 Pet. 2; Jude).[74] Prominent in Gnosticism is dualism (matter and spirit; body and soul cannot be joined). This can lead either to asceticism or license. The latter is akin to lawlessness or antinomianism (sins of flesh do not pollute the soul or spirit). "Holy" persons may indulge in the sins of the body without affecting the soul is the assumption. This may help explain which Paul found it difficult to enforce discipline in the church at Corinth (1 Cor. 5:l--6:20; 10:14-22; 2 Cor. 10:l- 11; 12:14-21; 13:1-10).

It can no longer be maintained that Pentecostalism is the result of being culturally deprived or "disinherited" (Anderson).[75] The rise of neo-Pentecostalism among Roman Catholics, Episcopalians and other middle income groups refutes this. Yet it cannot be denied that the charismatic message has its greatest impact on those who long for something better than present existence. But its appeal to relatively affluent Catholics and Episcopalians may be attributed to formalism in these liturgical churches in which some worshipers seek more spiritual and personal vitality; a dynamism more relevant and transforming.

Pentecostalism has least appeal to those churches and individuals who are "born again" evangelicals to whom "tongues" is diversionary, in competition with faith working by love. Also these evangelical or holiness churches feel more threatened by the tongues movement because earnest Christians are attracted to claims of being filled with the Holy Spirit. As so-called holiness churches become more ecumenical and less defensive they are likely to have fellowship with the Charismatic Movement. One clue to this change is seen in Howard Snyder, *The Divided Flame: Wesleyans and the Charismatic Renewal* (1986).

Jesus provides the final test: "by their fruits you will know them." Based on these criteria the charismatic movement, as a whole, deserves high marks, despite their problem with priorities.

Their amazing growth continues world-wide, especially in Latin America. Vinson Synan, perhaps the best informed student of Pentecostalism, has counted nearly

180,000,000 world wide![76] In overall perspective, it is important to notice that the various charismatic movements were initiated in the context of a moving of the Holy Spirit in revivals or awakenings. The same is true of many other times of revival, renewal, or "Restoration" in Christian history. The Anabaptists, Moravians, Brethren, Pietists, Methodists, and Christians (Disciples), were also born in a moving of the Spirit in renewal as at Pentecost.

Equally obvious is the tendency to gradually become "conformed to this age" (Rom. 12: 2), and lose that "first love" (Rev. 2:4). Renewal comes as a result of interaction between the seeker and the sought: "If with all your heart ye truly seek me . . . (Deut. 4:29; Jer. 29:13).

Chapter VII Endnotes

1. J. T. Nichol, *Pentecostalism*, (Harper & Row, 1966), p. xiii. See D. W. Myland,, "The Latter Rain Covenant and Pentecostal Power," in D. W. Dayton, ed., *Three Early Pentecostal Tracts*, (New York: Garland, 1985 reprint), pp. 1-122.
2. Henry P. Van Dusen, "The Third Force," *Life*, June 9, 1958, pp. 122-124.
3. Grant Wacker, "Primitivism in Early Pentecostalism," unpublished essay, University, Chapel Hill, North Carolina (1988), p. 5.
4. Vinson Synan, *The Pentecostal Movement in the United States*, (Grand Rapids: Eerdmans, 1971), p. 214.
5. T. F. Zimmerman, "Reasons for the Rise of the Pentecost Movement," in V. Synan, ed., *Aspects of Pentecostal-Charismatic Origins*, (Logos, 1975), pp. 9-11.
6. Frederick D. Bruner, *A Doctrine of the Holy Spirit*, (Eerdmans, 1970), pp. 38-39.
7. See (among others) D. W. Dayton, "Asa Mahan and the Development of American Holiness Theology," *Wesleyan Theological Journal*, 9, 1974, pp. 60-69; J. A. Knight, "John Fletcher's Influence on the Development of Wesleyan Theology in America," WTJ, 13, pp. 13-33; A. R. G. Deasley, "Entire Sanctification and the Baptism with the Holy Spirit," WTJ, 14, pp. 27-44; G. A. Turner, "The Baptism of the Holy Spirit in the Wesleyan Tradition," WTJ, 14, pp. 60-76; M. B. Wynkoop, "Theological Roots of the Wesleyan Understanding of the Holy Spirit," WTJ, 14, pp. 77-98; T. L. Smith, "How John Fletcher Became the Theologian of Wesleyan Perfectionism," WTJ, 15, pp. 68-87; D. W. Dayton, *Theological Roots of Pentecostalism*, (Zondervan, 1987).
8. H. C. Morrison, *The Baptism of the Holy Spirit*, (Louisville: Pentecostal Publishing Co., 1900).
9. A. Dallimore, *Forerunner of the Charismatic Movement, The Life of Edward Irving*, (Chicago: Moody, 1983), pp. 127- 133.
10. *The Yorkshire Post*, December 27, 1904, cited in Synan, p. 99.
11. R. M. Anderson, *Vision of the Disinherited*, (New York: Oxford, 1979), p. 4.
12. Stanley M. Horton, "The Pentecostal View," *Five Views of Sanctification*, (Grand Rapids: Zondervan, 1987), p. 105.

13. C. E. Jones, *A Guide to the Study of the Pentecostal Movement*, (Metuchen, NJ: Scarecrow Press, 1983), p. 271.
14. Elmer Clark, *Small Sects in America*, (Nashville, TN: Abingdon, 1949), pp. 100f.
15. Synan, p. 73.
16. L. H. Juillerat, ed., *Book of Minutes*, (Cleveland, TN), p. 8.
17. Charles W. Conn, *Like a Mighty Army*. (Cleveland,TN, 1955), p. 15.
18. Conn, pp. 17, 18.
19. Conn, p. 21.
20. Juillerat, p. 11.
21. Juillerat, p.11.
22. W. J. Hollenweger, *The Pentecostals*, (Minneapolis: Augsburg, 1972), p. 47.
23. Nichol, pp. 99-100.
24. Synan, p. 81.
25. Oral report of eye witnesses; Conn, p. 36.
26. Compare Rufus Jones, *The Church's Debt to Heretics*, (New York: George H. Doran, 1924), passim.
27. A. J. Tomlinson, *Diary on A. J. Tomlinson* (edited by Homer A. Tomlinson), (New York: Church of God World Headquarters, 1949), pp. 27, 28. He claims to have spoken ten languages (p. 29).
28. Conn, p. 98 (based on interviews with an eyewitness).
29. Conn, pp. 284.
30. W. J. Hollenweger, p. 114.
31. Hollenweger, p. 59.
32. Anderson, *Vision*, p. 49.
33. Sarah E. Parham, *The Life of Charles F. Parham*, (N.Y. Garland Publ. Inc., 1930, reprint 1985), p. 38.
34. Anderson, p. 53.
35. Parham, *Voice*, p. 34; cited in Anderson, p. 54.
36. S. Parham, *Life*, pp. 112, 135.
37. Anderson, p. 61.
38. *The Apostolic Faith*, Vol. 1, No. 1, (Los Angeles, Sept. 1906), p. 1.

223

39. F. Bartleman, *Another Wave Rolls In!*, J. G. Myers, Ed., (Northridge, CA: Voice Publications, 1970), pp. 57-60.
40. *Apostolic Faith*, p. 1.
41. Anderson, *Vision*, p. 77; Horton, pp. 108-109.
42. Anderson, p. 70.
43. Anderson, p. 166.
44. Anderson, p. 155.
45. Anderson, p. 173.
46. J. E. Campbell, *The Pentecostal Holiness Church*, (1951), pp. 197-198.
47. Campbell, p. 205.
48. Campbell, p. 255.
49. Synan, pp. 130-131.
50. Hollenweger, p. 78.
51. R. & D. Ranaghan, *Catholic Pentecostalism*, (New York, 1969), cited in Joseph Cardinal Suenens, *A New Pentecost*, tr. by F. Martin (Seabury Press, 1974), p. 73.
52. Suenens, *Pentecost*, p. 75.
53. James Connelly, "The Charismatic Movement 1967-1970," in Ranaghan, *As the Spirit Leads*, (Paulist Press, 1971), p. 214-220.
54. Suenens, p. 102.
55. Suenens, pp. 199-211.
56. Suenens, pp. 128-131.
57. D. L. Gelpi, *Pentecostal Piety*, (Paulist Press, 1972), p. 69.
58. Hollenweger, p. 354.
59. E. Stanley Jones, *The Holy Spirit and the Gift of Tongues*. See United Christian Ashrams, W. W. Richardson, 60 Bluff Road, Barrington, RI: nd.
60. J. L. Sherrill, *They Speak with Other Tongues*, pp. 89f., cited in Hollenweger, p. 4.
61. Howard Carter, *Gifts of the Spirit*, p. 115, cited in Bruner, *Theology of the Holy Spirit*, p 144.
62. Wm. G. McDonald, *Glossolalia in the New Testament*, (1964), p. 2.

63. Stanley M. Horton, *What the Bible Says about the Holy Spirit*, (Springfield, Mo: Gospel Publishing House, 1976), p. 171.
64. Horton, p. 173.
65. Horton, p. 239.
66. K. M. Ranaghan, "Catholics and Pentecostals Meet in the Spirit," in *As the Spirit Leads Us*, p. 129.
67. Samarin, pp. 227-229.
68. Anderson, *Vision*, p. 18.
69. E. A. Nida, *The Words and the Doctrine*, p. 341; cited in Wesley L. Duewel, *The Holy Spirit and Tongues*, (Winona Lake, IN: Light and Life Press, 1974), p. 91.
70. Cocoris, p.15.
71. A. B. Simpson, *The Gift of Tongues*, (New York: The Christian and Missionary Alliance, 260 W. 44th. St.), nd.
72. H. B. Swete, *The Holy Spirit in the New Testament*, (London: Macmillan, 1910), p. 80.
73. Clark, pp. 93-132.
74. A detailed and perceptive analysis of the church at Corinth, as a charismatic community, is presented in Bruner, pp. 285-319.
75. Anderson, passim.
76. Vinson Synan, *The Twentieth-Century Pentecostal Explosion*, (Altamonte Springs, Florida: Creation House, 1987), p. 12.

Chapter VIII
WHICH CHURCH IS CLOSEST
TO THE NEW TESTAMENT?

This search began with a question: which church today most closely resembles the church(es) as reflected in the New Testament? Now a review and assessment is called for.

In this study a distinction is recognized between a *reformation* of existing churches and a return to the church that is portrayed in the New Testament; the difference between reformation and RESTORATION. The criterion for this judgment is the New Testament, viewed with a relatively open mind, and an attempt to be objective; no easy task! This leads to a review of the earliest known data on the primitive church(es).

A. THE PRIMITIVE CHURCH IN THE NEW TESTAMENT

The earliest extant writings relevant to church planting are the letters of Paul to the believers in Thessalonica and Galatia. Which of these letters was written first is debatable, but it will be appropriate to begin with Galatians, because those to whom Paul wrote were converts from the Synagogue with Hebrew ancestry. Paul would have much in common with them.

What kind of church came into existence in Galatia? In his heated and earnest argument in his Galatian letter Paul referred to that which was most basic and indisputable in their experience. He had to begin with evidence which was incontrovertible; facts which all accepted. In Galatians 3:2 he asks whether they received the Spirit by works of the Law (the Old Covenant) or by the hearing of faith (the New Covenant). Their reception of the Spirit was the basis for determining what constitutes an authentic Christian. They had begun their new life in Christ "in the

Spirit" (Gal. 3:3). He reminds them that it is Christ who ministered to them "the Spirit" (Gal. 3:5)

Their regeneration "in the Spirit" was prompted by the preaching of Christ crucified for the salvation of sinners. This came to them as God's truth, not simply the proclamation of men. That which convinced them that the evangelist's words were true was the recital of God's wonderful works in the sending of his Son, permitting him to be crucified, then raising him from the tomb. The Holy Spirit awakened within them the conviction that this was indeed good news, and that it was for them. They were born of the Holy Spirit, and this truth was confirmed by acts which were supernatural in origin, and therefore from God: namely miracles (Gal. 3:5.).

On the basis of their spiritual conversion to Christ as Messiah, Paul went on to demonstrate that this new life in the Spirit, with truth bestowed by the risen Christ, was consistent with the Old Testament (Gal. 3:6 -- 4:31). Like the believers in Corinth, they had been baptized by one Spirit into one body and made to partake of one Spirit (1 Cor. 12:13). This "one body" was a *group of believers* who shared in common not only a new theology, but also a spiritual life of trust in God the Father, Jesus Christ as Son, and the Holy Spirit through whom the new life was bestowed. They had experienced not only a theological conversion, but a new life as well. In essence, they were changed individuals united by Christ in spiritual life and truth. Such is the nature of the church of Christ.

Paul also referred to the "church of God" in Judea which also had emerged from the synagogues in response to the "good news" (Gal. 1:13). An apt description of "church" is given by Bruce M. Metzger in a comment on this verse:

> *The **church** is the people of God, whom he has called into fellowship with himself through the redemptive work of Jesus Christ. The word may refer either to the total number of believers throughout the world, or to those in one locality, whether gathered for worship or scattered by persecution.*[1]

In Thessalonica also the "new race" (Harnack) emerged. These believers had renounced the worship of idols and embraced the good news Paul brought to them: "not in word only, but also in power, and in the Holy Spirit, and in much assurance." (1 Thess. 1:5).

From God the Father and the Lord Jesus Christ, the Thessalonians had experienced the "work of faith, labor of love, and patience of hope" (1 Thess. 1:3). They experienced a radical conversion, turning from idols to serve the living God, and waiting for the reappearance of God's Son, Jesus the Christ. Theirs was a radical separation from their contemporaries which exposed them to much persecution. Paul explained that this negative reaction to their conversion was to be expected as Jesus (Matt. 5:11-12) and Peter (1 Pet. 1:6-7; 4:1-16) explained.

The primitive church was separate and distinct from all other religious entities (a "New Race"), because they had received by faith the truth that God gave his Son for their redemption and that this had been sealed or authenticated by the Holy Spirit (cf. Eph. 1:13). In short, the Church of Christ consists only of those who are regenerated by a miracle of God's grace which transforms their mind-set, their life style, and total life.

Another picture of the primitive church is reflected in the earliest history of the church, the Book of Acts. After the resurrection and ascension of Jesus, the day of Pentecost gave confirming evidence that Jesus is alive and his mission is ongoing. Peter explained to the astonished multitude that the miracle of languages was the fulfillment of Joel's prophecy that the Spirit would be "poured out on all people" (Joel 2:21; Acts 2:17). The result was the conversion of thousands in a few days, miracles which could not be explained except as an act by the risen Christ (Acts 2:33), and a new fellowship or *koinonia* (Acts 2:42-47). The latter was as great a miracle as the phenomenon at Pentecost. The result was a new community characterized not only by fervent love, but also by courage to bear witness to its faith (Acts 4:18-31).

The church of Christ is in the tradition of the prophets rather than that of the priests (Matt. 5:11-12). The believers no longer need a priest to mediate between them and God; they are the new "holy priesthood" with direct access to the Father (1 Pet. 2:5). Indeed they have a new and great High Priest who himself provided the needed sacrifice and now leads them directly to the throne-room of the Most High (Heb. 4:14-16).

Gradually the primitive church evolved into distinctions of service and responsibilities. When complaints were voiced that Grecian widows were neglected, "the Twelve" did not make the decisions alone, as they might have done. Instead they gathered the congregation to discuss the accusations. The Apostles proposed that the congregation choose from their group a committee to supervise the distribution of resources. The qualifications of the deacons (*diakonoi*) were honesty, wisdom, and being Spirit-filled (Acts 6:1-7). The Twelve were to minister the Word; the Seven were to "serve tables" (unity and diversity), a principle which later was stressed repeatedly (1 Cor. 12:1-31; Rom. 12:4-13; Eph. 4:3-13). The Seven were also "ordained" by prayer and the laying on of hands, the latter a symbol of the bestowal of the the Holy Spirit (Acts 8:16; 2 Tim. 1:6).

At another crisis famine relief was initiated: relief came from those who had more to those who had less (Acts 11:28-30; 12:25). This initiative set a precedent which was confirmed in actions later (Gal. 2:10; 2 Cor. 8:1--9:15). Even today the church of Christ is noted for compassion for the unfortunate.

In the Synoptic Gospels the "church" is equivalent to the Kingdom of God or to the "rule of God." In Matthew's Gospel the parables of Jesus are conveniently arranged in chapter thirteen, usually introduced by the formula: "The Kingdom of God is like." These and other word-pictures display the varied facets of what we call the Christian Church.

Paul Minear has gathered thirty-two different "minor images" of the church in the New Testament such as "salt," "light," and God's "vineyard."[2] The "major images," in his analysis, are "people of God," "new creation," "fellowship in faith," and "body of Christ." The latter is the one most influential today. In the Johannine writings "fellowship of believers" is prominent; in Paul's epistles "new creation," and "body of Christ" are stressed.

From the second century a classic description of Christians by an unknown author says it well:

> *1. Christians are not distinguished from the rest of mankind by country, or by speech, or by customs. 2. For they do not dwell in cities of their*

own, or use a different language, or practice a peculiar life. . . . 5. They live in countries of their own, but simply as sojourners; they share the life of citizens; they endure the lot of foreigners; every foreign land is to them a fatherland, and every fatherland a foreign land. 6. They marry like world, they beget children, but they do not cast their offspring adrift. 7. They have a common table, but not a common bed. 8. They exist in the flesh, but they live not after the flesh. 9. They spend their existence upon earth, but their citizenship is in heaven. 10. They obey the established laws, but in their own lives they surpass the laws. 11. They love all men, and are persecuted by all.[3]

In this description addressed to non-Christians, the Christian church consists of *individuals* transformed by Christ. The seven major denominations in the Restoration movement emphasize all of the above in varying emphases.

TODAY'S SEEKERS OF THE "RESTORATION"

The Pietists

In historical sequence the Pietists claim first place in the last five hundred years of church history. Beginning with John Huss in Bohemia, the "radical reformers" or "radical pietists" were determined to go beyond the Reformation to a Restoration of the church as portrayed in the New Testament.

Pietists are not easily identified, because they are not limited to time and place like the others in this study. They place emphasis on a "religion of the heart," on spiritual rebirth, on fellowship with others who share their convictions and who stress sanctification as well as justification. They are often accused of being too introspective and individualistic. Yet their influence has permeated many denominations in the course of Christian history. Their emphasis on spiritual renewal is now shared by virtually every so-called evangelical church or denomination. The work of F. E. Stoeffler (1965, 1973, 1976) has led to a new appreciation of Pietism.

The Anabaptists

Among the first to go further than the Reformers were those "radicals" dubbed Anabaptists. With them *koinonia* (fellowship) is a major factor. The Hutterite faction went even further, stating that one cannot be a Christian unless in a community of Christians. The Anabaptists are close to New Testament Christianity when they stress obedience to Christ, a believers' church, courage in resistance to secularism, independence, the right of individual conscience, the refusal to bear arms, and the conviction that martyrdom is preferable to compromising with truth. Their love of neighbor, whether near or far, is well known.

But their defensive posture and their conviction that the state is demonic has often inhibited aggressive evangelism. Their tendency to link "the world" with contemporary lifestyles has led some to excess, such has the avoidance of motor cars, insistence on garb of the last century, the refusal to be photographed, and a tendency to view anything new as harmful. The latter is not true, of course, of most in the tradition of Menno Simon.

Paul, by contrast, took advantage of the situation by capitalizing on situations that facilitated communication. He tried to be "all things to all men," like successful politicians. In the synagogues he spoke from the Old Testament. In Athens he commended them for being "very religious." He even took his text from their monument to "the unknown god." Among the Romans he asserted his rights as a citizen, and welcomed their insistence on "law and order." Paul neatly balanced accommodation to the status quo with an announcement so radical that it "turned the world upside down" (Acts 17:6).

The Anabaptist insistence on peace is Christian; their love of fellowmen by deeds, rather than words only, is close to the Spirit of Christ. In these and other things they are a rebuke to the complacent and an example to all.

The Brethren

The Brethren, like others among the Radical Reformers or Restorationists, began as a revival among laymen in central Europe and in the Colonies of North America. They are Christians in earnest to obey God and get to heaven. They are like the primitive church with reference to fellowship, but are less evangelistic, concentratiing more on their own rectitude. The Anabaptist conservatism which they inherit has limited their evangelistic thrust. Sometimes the Brethren are not very brotherly, hence the many divisions which mark their history. Those with strong convictions find toleration more difficult than those with few convictions.

231

Some of them, the Church of the Brethren in particular, have accepted the Methodist emphasis on holiness, thus maintaining an almost unique synthesis of Anabaptism and Methodism. Their quest for the kernel of the gospel is as important as it is unique.

The Puritans

The Puritans have a strong claim to be the church of the New Testament. They and their heritage insist on adherence to the Scriptures. They take the Bible seriously with varying degrees of literalism in its interpretation and application. As people of the Book, like the Pharisees of Jesus' day, they sometimes lack love of neighbor in their quest for conformity to a written code. They are more likely to "contend for the faith" than to win converts to the Faith. While Anabaptists often stress the New Testament more than the Old, Puritans and their descendants live more in the Old Testament. As Calvinists, they stress God's sovereignty more than his love for the lost. The ecumenical movement is less important than fidelity to their convictions. Initially this movement was born as a commitment to Scripture, a new birth in the Spirit resulting in a powerful spiritual renewal or revival in individuals and in groups.

The beneficent influence of Puritanism, especially in England and New England, is incalculable. Recently the work of scholars like Perry Miller (1933, 1939, 1962) have given a new appreciation of their contribution.

The Methodists

Methodism is the most prominent expression of Pietism and is itself a confluence of many streams of Christian history. Few denominations have as much world-wide influence as the followers of John and Charles Wesley. John Wesley was a very complex person. He has been classified as (1) a low-church evangelist, (2) a theologian of experience, (3) a near-Calvinist (Cell), (4) a near-Lutheran (Hildebrand), (5) a near-pietist (Nagler), (6) a near-Roman Catholic (Piette), (7) a near-Puritan (Monk and Newton), (8) a "proto-Barthian" (Deschner), (9) a Near East Orthodox (Outler), (10) a proto-charismatic (Snyder), (11) a simple life-style Christian (Sider), and (12) an exponent of liberation theology (Runyan).[4] There is some truth in all of these. As previously mentioned his claim that Methodism is nearer to the New Testament is hard to refute. But Wesley was not an advocate of a free church until the movement that bears his name was excluded from the Anglican Church. He adhered to his Catholic-Anglican tradition of the episcopacy by forbidding his preachers to serve Communion. He insisted on the baptism of infants, jeopardizing the concept of a believers' church. But in his mature years, Wesley came to grips with the demands of the movement and reluctantly accepted a more democratic polity. Modern Methodism has rectified many of these traditions and has amplified Wesley's vision of a world-wide parish. For many Methodists today the Wesleys' insistence on entire sanctification is an embarassment. Pluralism in Methodism has eroded much of the evangelistic vigor of the founders. Those who resist this "pluralism" often separate into smaller denominations or parachurch movements. Its breadth imperils its adherence to the "first love" which brought it into existence. Fortunately, the Good News movement within Methodism and many evangelical pastors are leading in the direction of renewal in this major denomination. Methodism's major influence today is in North America, southern Africa, India, and Australia, areas where the English language is best known.

The Christians (Disciples)

The Christians (Disciples) have made a very serious attempt to *restore* or recover the primitive church by abandoning "man-made creeds" and taking the Bible, especially the New Testament, as their guide. This worthy motive is now seen in perspective as quite naive; it led to a small core of doctrine considered normative. Although their congregational polity avoided a split during the Civil War, it did not smooth over the liberal-fundamentalist tensions in the late nineteenth and twentieth centuries. Their quest for unity, as called for in the the New Testament, is yet to be realized; they have not yet agreed on a name for their movement. The Christian wing seems nearer to the primitive church, partly because it began as a revival or spiritual awakening, as did the other groups reviewed in this study. Those in the tradtion of the Campbells were more rational and less inflenced by the activity of the Holy Spirit in the church. But the quest for unity continues, as does their involvement in the ecumenical movement.

233

The Pentecostals

The Pentecostals have much to link them with the church of the first century. Their emphasis on the rule of the Spirit in public worship supports their claim. Commendably they stress what most churches neglect: the gifts of the Spirit, divine healing, prophecy, and tongues. Their insistence, despite Scripture, that "tongues" is proof of the baptism in the Spirit, has separated them from the other evangelicals and has given them the aura of a sect. They pay less attention to the *fruit* of the Spirit because of the priority of *gifts*. They reflect the primitive church in their zeal in evangelism, ministry to the poor, and dedication to what they perceive to be the truth. Too frequently enthusiam without discipline has led to disaster.

Among their weaknesses is the emphasis on spontaneity, which sometimes replaces order, and the study of "sound doctrine," as noted in the church at Corinth (1 Corinthians 12-14). Some members admit sadly that, as a whole, the movement has "lost its first love," a loss not unique to Pentecostals.

BACK TO THE NEW TESTAMENT

The Christian church, as reflected in the New Testament is a multifaceted entity. Even in the Acts and Epistles we may note its evolvement from a community of believers (Acts 2:41-47; 4:32-33) to a charismatic fellowship led by "prophets" (Acts 21:10-11; 1 Cor. 12:3-14; 2 Pet. 2:1-4; John 4:1-6; Didache Xl 7-12), to a monarchical type of leadership (1 Tim. 3:1-10; Tit. 1:5-13; Ignatius, "To the Ephesians," IV--VI. Leadership apparently passed from Apostles to elders to bishops.

Whatever else it was, it consisted of a fellowship (*koinonia*). This term has many meanings in English: partnership, communication, contribution, communion, sharing, fellowship, and participation. Of these, "fellowship" is a useful term to include all the others. Word pictures of this unique fellowship include the Vine, the Building, the Body, the Bride, the sheep, the ark, the "family of God," and, "The Way" (Acts 9:2; 19:9, 23; 22:4; 24:14, 22). Those who "walked" with Jesus were the nucleus of the church; those who did not "walk" with Jesus were not (John 6:66; 2 John 9-11).

The church consists of those who are loyal to Jesus regardless of the consequences, even if it means death. The church of Christ consists of the *hagioi*, the "holy ones" or "saints," a term which appears more than sixty times in the New Testament (I Cor. 1:2). They are "holy" as a result of the spiritual "birth" from above which separates them from "the world" and unites them to Christ and the Father. Christians are children of God; they naturally love one another (1 John 4:7-21). Paul wrote of brotherly love (1 Thess. 4:9-12) as did Plutarch. But Plutarch referred to blood relations; the Christian distinction is love for all mankind, including enemies. Each believer is a "brother" or a "sister" (Mark 3:31-35). The new relationship of children of God often strain relations with unconverted, but this is the price believers have to pay.[5]

The Brethren in Christ combine the pietism of the Methodists and the discipline of the Anabaptists, but their slow growth and influence is in contrast to the church of the New Testament.

No one denomination can claim to be nearest to the New Testament norm, but those who seek this the most earnestly and consistently should be emulated and encouraged.

A quick review may be capsulated in this matter. The Pietists are the most extensive and pervasive; they are not a denomination as such, but their influence is reflective in each of the seven. They are charactistic of a reborn, warm-hearted experience of God's gift of grace of Christ, as in Romans 5:1, I Thessanians 1:6. or Galatians 3:5.

The Anabaptists pioneered in baptism AFTER regeneration, brotherly love, and refusal to bear arms.

The Brethren were among those to stress fellowship *koinonia* so persuasive and important in the early churches.

The Puritans, merged with the Congregationalists, feature the influence of the Elders so influential in the earliest churches (Acts 14:32; 20:17).

Chapter VIII Endnotes

1. *The New Oxford Annotated Bible With Apocrypha.* (New York: Oxford, 1977), p. 1411.

2. "Epistle to Diognetus," in *Documents Illustrative of the History of the Church*, Vol. 1, B. J. Kidd, ed., (New York: Macmillan, 1938), p. 55.

3. Paul S. Minear, *Images of the Church in the New Testament*, (Philadelphia: Westminster, 1960), passim.

4. C. A. L. Villa-Vicencio, "The Origins and Witness of Methodism," in *Denominalism -- its Sources and Implications*, W. W. Vorster, ed. (Pretoria: University of South Africa, 1982), p. 65.

5. W. A. Meeks, *The Moral World of the First Christians*, (Philadelphia: Westminster Press, 1986), p. 129.

APPENDIX A

THE "WAY"

What is in the Name?

Let us examine names taken from the New Testament, then the names given by others, then the choice of each of the Denominations. We try to list in chronological sequence.

1. Names taken from the New Testament

The Pentecostals earned their name from the birth of the Church at the outpouring of the Holy Spirit during Pentecost at Jerusalem (Acts 2:2-4; 10:44-47; 11:15-16.

The first believers in Damascus were called simply Disciples (Acts:19), as also the believers which followed the missionaries in Asia (Acts 14:20, 21, 22, 28). This apt term was chosen by followers of the Campbells.

In Antioch the believers were called Christians (Acts 11:26), the term chosen by Barton Stone and his followers.

The Brethren stressed fellowship (*koinonia*) (Acts 4:32-35; I John 1:3), without overseer (bishop) or superintendent.

2. Names taken by others

Anabaptists were given that name to those believers who refused to baptize their infants until these children were enough to make it their own decision (Acts 2:38; 19:3-5). Those who were baptized in infancy, and became believers in maturity, were regenerated then baptized a second time, hence derided as the rebaptized, or anabaptists.

3. Names preferred by the believers

The Puritans, who insisted on holy living, in contrast to some nominal members in the State Church, chose a name which they considered appropriate.

The Methodist Episcopal Church, accepted the term "methodist," as they were characterized, and chose the term overseer or "bishop" (I Timothy 3:1; Titus 1:7)

The first chapter, Pietists, does not have a distinct label. But their influence permeates chapters two to seven, and it seems appropriate to make it distinct from the others. Pietism features regeneration, assurance, and love to God and neighbor.

4. Strangely, none of the denominations accepted the term ("the Way") preferred by the author of Acts (Acts 9:2; 19:9,23, 24:14, 22). Some recent parachurch groups are called "The Way." This term is appropriate since Jesus walked with his followers (cf.John 6:66). Those who followed Jesus to Jerusalem (Luke 9:51, 57, 59, 61; 13:22; 17:11; 19:28) were with him on "the way." The conduct of Jesus was as influential as his words and miracles. "The Way" was and is a pattern of new life, movement, and witness.

APPENDIX B
TO ALL NATIONS

Jesus commanded "make disciples of all nations" (Matt. 28:12). During church history, disciples were more zealous during some periods than others. In his extensive church history, Kenneth Latourette observed that at times the church was weak, but was followed by a period of renewal. However, the church always emerged stronger.

For example, the gospel was victorious during AD 30 to 100. A weaker period followed during 100-300 when ten major persecutions prevailed (EUSEBIUS). Christ was victorious over Caesar during 310-632 (DURANT). The major challenge occurred when Islam exploded from Arabia to France (632-732). Advance came by the Crusades with several victories (1095-1289), led by France and Rome. Then the Papacy was in defence between 1350-1510, (Henry VIII). But the Reformation and Protestantism prevailed with Luther (1517).

The "Great Century" (so named by Latourette) extended from 1814, with the Wesleyan revival and William Carey's pioneering missions, to 1914 with World War I. Then the church was challenged by Karl Marx ("Das Kapital") with Lenin and Communism from 1917-1990 (Gorbachev). An experienced traveller in Russia reports that atheism is not taught in the University of Moscow; Christianity is taught there now! In Russia and East Europe the Bible is being printed and Christian books are sought eagerly.

The "second Reformation," as the Pentecostal movement was called (Pres., Union Theological Seminary, N.Y.), has grown from a few hundred in 1890 to 30,000,000 by 1970. The figure now is up to 180,000,000 (Vinson Synan). Christians world-wide grew in number from 558,056,300 in 1900 to 2,130,000,000 in 1990.

Unreached peoples world: 3,500,000,000 (1900), 1,300,000,000 (1970), 450,000,000 (1990). Members, Latin America: 60,025,100 (1900), 437,449,800 (1990). Evangelicals, Latin America: 300,000 (1900), 35,000,000 (1990). House churches in China: 2,000,000 (1947), 70,000,000 (1990).

Recently Korea has become a Christian nation. In the Philippians Christians double every seventh year. In central Africa Christians multiply rapidly, especially in Ghana, once a source of slaves. Churches in South Africa support the change to democracy.

But evil also is growing. Paul reported in his world that "[a] wide door for effective work has opened to me, and there are many adversaries" (I Cor. 16:9).

Many of the "Mainline" denominations in the United States have lost membership since 1960 led by "liberal" leadership. In 1968 at Yale Divinity School, A professor, reporting his recent visit in the midwest, stated that "fundamentalism" in the midwest is finished. Since then many evangelical churches and parachurches are growing. These have experienced saving faith, the "religion of the heart" as distinct from humanism. It is noted during the examination of those who try to go beyond the Reformation in the direction of the New Testament, the movements are influenced by Pietism (response to the Word with joy and spiritual freedom). They grow despite difficulties and experience what history and Scripture witness (I John 1:1-5): love and fellowship prevail. Emerging from the struggle between the "liberals" and "fundamentalists" in the thirties, "[t]he majority of institutions that gave evangelicals a sense of identity were all created within the past fifty years" ("Christian Century," p. 1028), e.g., National Association of Evangelicals. In the thirties, the "liberal" Harry Emerson Fosdick was the major influence. Since then, revivalism was welcomed by evangelist Billy Graham and California's Crystal Cathedral with its "Positive Faith." Since 1900 the "Christian Century," the major religious magazine, was seen as liberal. "Christianity Today" began in 1956 as an evangelical magazine. While lecturing in America, Karl Barth smiled and called the magazine "Christianity Yesterday." Today, its readers far outnumber those who read "Century."

We see that those who pursue the primitive church (as in the New Testament) are growing more rapidly than those who adhere to contemporary society or tradition. The lesson today is that, as in the New Testament, the pursuit of the moving of the Spirit prevails. RESTORATION to the Word and the Spirit assures growing churches.

CHAPTER I
SELECTED BIBLIOGRAPHY

Ames, Wm. *The Marrow of Theology*, tr. from Latin by J. D. Eusen. Boston: Pilgrim Press, 1968.

Arndt, J., *True Christianity*, Eng. trans. by A.W. Boehm (1712), ed. b y C . F . Schaeffer (1917).

Bicknell, E. J. *Introduction to the Thirty-nine Articles*. New York: L o n g m a n s, 1981.

Bost, A. *History of the Moravians*. London: Religious Tract Society, nd.

Brown, Dale. *Understanding Pietism*. Grand Rapids: Eerdmans, 1978.

Cadman, S. P. *Three Religious Leaders of Oxford*. New York: Macmillan, 1916.

Davis, C. E. *Hidden Seed and Harvest*. Winston-Salem: Wachovi a Historical Society, 1973.

Fox, George, *An Epistle to all Professors in New England, Germany, and other parts of the so-called Christian World*. London, 1673.

Jones, Rufus, *Studies in Mystical Religion*. London: Macmillan, 1909.

Nickelsburg, G., & Michael Stone, *Faith and Piety in Early Judaism*. PA Trinity Press, 1993.

"Pietism." *Encyclopaedia Britannica*, 14, pp. 455-461, (excellent Biblioghaphy), University of Chicago, 1974.

Stoeffler, F. E. *German Pietism During the Nineteenth Century*. Leiden: E. J. Brill, 1973.

Schaff, D. S. *The Church*, by John Huss. New York: Scribner's Sons, 1915.

Tanis, James. "Reformed Pietism in Colonial America," in F. E. Stoffler, ed. *Continental and Early American Pietism*. Grand Rapids: Eerdmans, 1976.

Pietism and American Christianity. Grand Rapids: Eerdmans, 1976.

Smith, Robert, *John Wesley and Jonathan Edwards on Religious Experience*, Wesleyan Theological Journal, Dayton, OH, Spring 1990.

Walford, F. F. *Philip Jacob Spener.* London: S. P. C. K., 1893.

Watts, G. B. *The Waldenses in the New World.* Durham: Duke University Press, 1941.

Wells, David, *No Place for Truth*, Eerdmans, 1993.

Workman, H. B. *John Wyclif* (2 volumes). Oxford: Clarendon Press, 1926.

Ward, W. R., *The Protestant Evangelical (Pietist) Awakening.* Cambridge, University Press, 1991

CHAPTER II

SELECTED BIBLIOGRAPHY

(Anonymous). *A Short History of the Anabaptists of High and Low German.* London: Robert Austin, 1647. London, Bobert

Bender, Harold S. *Mennonite Encyclopedia.* Scottdale, PA: Herald Press, 1955.

Bender, Ross Thomas. *The People of God.* Herald Press, 1971.

Clasen, C. P. *Anabaptism: A Social History 1525-1618.* New York, Ithaca: Cornell University Press, 1972.

Catrou, P. *Histoire des Anabaptists.* Amsterdam: Jaques Desbordes, 1699.

Featley, Daniel. *Dippers -- Anabaptists Ducked and Plunged at Southwerk in 1642.* London: Richard Cotes, 1651.

Friedman, Robert. *Mennonite Piety.* Goshen, IN, 1949.

Friedman, Robert. *The Theology of Anabaptism.* Herald Press, 1973.

Hershberger, G. F., Editor. *Recovery of the Anabaptist Vision (60th Anniversary of Herald Bender).* Herald Press, 1957.

Horsh, John. "Origin and Faith of the Swiss Brethern," *Goshen College Record*, January, 1926.

Hubmaier, Balthasar, *Pastor at Waldshut*, writings collected and photographed by W. O. Lewis at William Jewell College, Liberty, MO, 1939.

Jones, Rufus. *Studies in Mystical Religions.* London: Macmillan, 1909.

Kaufman, J. H. and Leland Harden. *Anabaptists Four Centuries Later.* Herald Press, 1975.

Lewis, John. *A Brief History of the Rise and Progress of Anabaptism in England.* London: for J. Roberts in Warwick-Lane, 1738.

Littell, F. N. *The Anabaptist View of the Church.* American Society of Church History, 1952.

Noll, Mark Allen. "Melchoir Hofmann and the Lutherans," Masters Thesis, Trinity Divinity School, Deerfield, IL, 1972.

Simons, Menno. *Complete Writings.* Translated by L. Verduin, edited by J. C. Wenger. Herald Press, 1956.

Smithson, R. J. *The Anabaptists, Their Contribution to Our Protestant Heritage.* London: J. Clark & Co. LTD, 1935.

Stayer, James, M. *Anabaptists and the Sword.* Lawrence, KS: Coronado Press, 1972.

Verhoyden, A. L. E. *Anabaptism in Flanders, 1530-1650.* Herald Press, 1961.

Wenger, J. C. *Even Unto Death: The Heroic Witness of the Sixteenth Century Anabaptists.* Baltimore: John Knox Press, 1961.

Wenger, J. C. *Our Christ Centered Faith, A Brief Summary of New Testament Teaching.* Herald Press, 1973.

Westin, Gunnar. *The Free Church Through the Ages.* Translated by V. A. Olson. Nashville: Broadman Press, 1954.

Williams, G. H. *The Radical Reformation.* Westminster Press, 1962.

Williams, G. H. *Spiritual and Anabaptist Writers: Documents illustrative of the Radical Reformation and Evangelical Catholicism*; edited by A. M. Mergal. Westminster Press, 1967.

Yoder, John H. *The Legacy of Michael Sattler*, translated and edited by Yoder. Herald Press, 1973.

Zeman, J. K. *The Anabaptists and the Czech Brethren in Moravia 1526-1628*, a study of origins and contrasts. The Hague and Paris: Mouton, 1969.

CHAPTER III

SELECTED BIBLIOGRAPHY

Alderfer, O. H. "The Mind of the Brethren in Christ: a Synthesis of Revivalism and the Church Conceived as Total Community." Ph.D. Dissertation, Claremont, CA, 1963.

Boyer, J. L. "Can Forgiveness Be Revoked!" *Spire* (Grace College), Winona Lake, IN: Spring, 1985.

Brambaugh, M. G. *A History of the German Baptist Brethren*. Mt. Morris, IL: 1899.

Brethren in Christ Church. *Constitution - Doctrine, By Laws, Rituals*. Nappanee, IN: E. V. Publishing House, nd.

Church Government of the Brethren in Christ, (Compiled for the Church). Abilene, Kansas: Daily Gazette Book and Job Print, 1887.

Durnbaugh, D. F. *The Believers' Church*, Macmillan, 1908.

Durnbaugh, D. F. "Brethren Beginnings." Ph. D. Thesis, University of Pennsylvania, 1960.

Durnbaugh, D. F. *European Origins of the Brethren*. Elgin, IL: Brethren Press, 1958.

Durnbaugh, D. F. "The Brethren in Early American Church Life," in F. E. Stoeffler, *Continental Pietism and Early American Christianity*. Grand Rapids: Eerdmans, 1976.

Durnbaugh, D. F. *The Church of the Brethren, Past and Present*. Elgin, IL: Brethren Press, 1971.

Gillin, J. L. "The Dunkers, a Sociological Interpretation." Ph. D. Thesis, Columbia University. New York: A M S Press, 1974.

Holsinger, H. R. *History of the Dunkers and the Brethren Church*. Oakland, CA: Pacific Press, 1901.

Kent, Homer H. Sr. *Two Hundred Years Conquering Frontiers.* Winona Lake, IN: Brethren Missionary Herald, 1958.

Marten, Dennis. "Law and Grace, The Progressive Brethren." Master's Thesis. Wheaten College, Wheaten, IL: 1973.

Minutes, General Conference, Brethren in Christ. Air Hill, PA, 1910.

Ronk, Albert T. *History of the Brethren Church.* Ashland, OH; Brethren Publishing Co., 1968.

Schrag, M. H. "The Brethren in Christ Attitude Toward the World." Ph.D. Dissertation at Temple University. Philadelphia, PA, 1967.

Schrag, M. H. *The Ministry of Reconciliation.* Nappanee, IN: Evangel Press, 1973.

Sweet, W. W. *Religion in Colonial America.* New York: Scribners, 1943.

Whitcomb, J. C. "Could Even an Apostle be a Castaway?" *Spire* (Grace College) Winona Lake, IN: Spring, 1985.

Wittlinger, Carlton O. *Quest for Piety and Obedience.* Nappanee, IN: Evangel Press, 1978.

CHAPTER IV

SELECTED BIBLIOGRAPHY

Bailey, S. L. *Historical Sketches of Andover.* Boston: Houghton Mifflin, 1880.

Bradford, Alden. *History of Massachusetts (1620-1820).* Boston: Hilliard, Gray and Co., 1835.

Calvin, John. *Commentaries on the Epistle to the Romans*, tr. by John Owen. Eerdmans, 1948.

Conant, John. *The Woe and Weal of God's People.* London: Christopher Meridith, 1643.

Dwight, Timothy. "The Smooth Divine," in *The World's Great Religious Poetry*, C. M. Hill, Ed. New York: Macmillian, 1938.

Fagley, F. L. *The Cambridge "Platform of Church Discipline" 1648.* Boston: Commission of Congregational Christian and Unitarian Churches, 1948.

Fiske, John. *Beginnings of New England*, or Puritan Theocracy and Civil and Religious Liberty. Boston: Houghton Mifflin, 1898, 1930.

Haller, W. M. *The Rise of Puritanism.* New York: Columbia University, 1957.

Hill, Christopher. *Society and Puritanism in Pre-Revolutionary England.* New York: Schoken, 1964.

Knappen, M. M. *Tudor Puritanism*, a Chapter in the History of Idealism. Chicago: University of Chicago, 1939.

Littell, F. H. *The Free Church.* Boston: Beacon Hill, Starking Press, 1957.

Lovelace, R. F. *The American Pietism of Cotton Mather: Origins of American Evangeliscanism.* Grand Rapids: Eerdmans, 1979.

Miller, P. *Orthodoxy in Massachusetts.* Cambridge: Harvard University Press, 1933.

Miller, P. and T. H. Johnson. *The Puritans.* New York: Harpers, 1938.

Morgan, E. S. "The Half-Way Covenant Reconsidered," *Puritanism in Seventeenth-Century in Massachusetts*, D. P. Hall, Ed. New York: Holt, Rinehart, 1968.

Morrison, S. E. *Builders of the Bay Colony.* Boston: Houghton Mifflin, 1930.

Morrison, S. D. *Harvard College in the Seventeenth Century* (two volumes). Cambridge: University Press, 1936.

Morrison, S. D. *Three Centuries of Harvard.* Cambridge University Press, 1936.

Monk, R. C. *John Wesley, His Puritan Heritage.* Nashville: Abingdon, 1966.

Newton, J. A. *Methodism and the Puritans.* London: W. Williams Trust, 1964.

Nuttall, G. F. *The Holy Spirit in Puritan Faith and Practice.* Oxford: Blackwell, 1946.

Perry, R. B. *Puritan Democracy.* New York: Vanguard Press, 1944.

Porter, H. C. *Puritanism in Tudor England.* London: Macmillan, 1970.

Powell, S. D. *Puritan Village,* The Formation of a New England Town. Wesleyan University Press, 1963.

Prall, S. E. *The Puritan Revolution,* a Documentary History. Garden City, N.Y.: Anchor Books, 1968.

Pratt, J. B. *Religious Consciousness.* New York: Macmillan, 1920.

Whincop, John. *God's Call to Weeping and Mourning.* London: Robert Leyburn, 1645.

CHAPTER V
SELECTED BIBLIOGRAPHY

Baker, Frank. *John Wesley and the Church of England*. Nashville: Abingdon, 1970.

Bready, J. W. *England Before and After Wesley*. London: Hodder & Stoughton, 1938.

Borgen, O. E. *John Wesley on the Sacraments*. Francis Asbury Press, Zondervan, 1972.

Cannon, W. R. "John Wesley's Doctrine of Sanctification and Perfection," *Mennonite Quarterly Review*, April, 1961.

Fleetwood, Wm. *The Perfectionists Examined*. London: J. Roberts, 1741.

Hall, Thor. "Tradition Criticism: A New View of Wesley," The LeRoy A. Martin Lectureship, at the University of Tennessee. Chattanooga: 1987.

Heitzenrater, R. P. *Mirror and Memory*. Nashville, Abingdon, 1989.

Hudson, W. S. *Religion in America*. New York: Scribners, 1981.

Jones, C. D. *Perfectionist Persuasion*, The Holiness Movement and American Methodism, 1867-1936. Metuchen, NJ: Scarecrow Press, 1974.

Lindstrom, Harald. *Wesley and Sanctification*. Sweden, Eppsala: Nya Bokforlags Aktiebolaget, 1946.

Malone, H. T. *The Episcopal Church in Georgia*. Atlanta: The Protestant Episcopal Diocese of Atlanta, 1960.

Meeks, M. D. *The Future of Methodist Theological Traditions*. Nashville: Abingdon, 1985.

Monk, R. C. *John Wesley, His Puritan Heritage*. Abingdon, 1966.

Nagler, A. W. *Pietism and Methodism*. Nashville: Publishing House of Methodist South, 1918.

Newton, J. A. *Methodism and the Puritans*. London: D. Williams Trust, 1964.

Outler, A. C. *John Wesley*, (A Library of Protestant Thought). New York: Oxford, 1964.

Outler, A. C. "Do Methodists Have a Doctrine of the Church? in Dow Kirkpatrick, Ed., *The Doctrine of the Church*. Abingdon, 1964.

Outler, A. C. *Evangelism in the Wesleyan Spirit*. Nashville: Tidings, 1971.

Schmidt, M. *John Wesley, a Theological Biography*, Tr. by N. P. Goldhawk. London: Epworth Press, 1966, 1977.

Smith, T. L. *The Pentecostal Hymns of John and Charles Wesley*. Kansas, MO: Beacon Hill Press.

Stoeffler, F. E. "Pietism, the Wesleys, and Methodist Beginnings in America," in *Continental Pietism and Early American Christianity*, F. E. Stoeffler, Editor. Grand Rapids: Eerdmans, 1976.

Sugden, E. H. *The Standard Sermons of John Wesley*. Nashville: Lamar and Barton, nd.

Turner, G. A. *The Vision Which Transforms*, Is Christian Perfection Scriptural? Kansas: Beacon Hill, 1964.

Tyerman, Luke. *Life and Times of John Wesley*. London: James Sangster, 1976.

Villa-Vicencio, C. A. L. "The Origins and Witness of Methodism," in W. E. Vorsteried, ed. *Denominationalism -- Its Sources and Implications*. Pretoria: University of South Africa, 1982.

Wesley, John. *Works*, Third Edition (T. Jackson, 1872 edition). Grand Rapids: Baker Book House, 1978.

Wesley, John. *Explanatory Notes on the Old Testament*. Republished, Salem, OH: H. E. Schmul, 1975.

Whaling, F., ed. *John and Charles Wesley*. New York: Paulist Press, 1981.

Williams, C. W. *John Wesley's Theology Today*. Nashville: Abingdon, 1960.

CHAPTER VI

SELECTED BIBLIOGRAPHY

Bower, W. C. *Central Christian Church.* St. Louis: Bethany, 1962.

Byers, A. L. *Birth of a Reformation.* Guthrie, OK: Faith Publishing House, 1921, 1966.

Campbell, A. "Sermon on the Law," *Millennial Harbinger*, 1846.

DeGroot, A. T. *Disciple Thought: A History.* Fort Worth, TX: Texas Christian University, 1965.

Forney, C. H. *History of the Churches of God.* Harrisburg, PA: Board of Directors of the Churches of God, 1914.

Garrison, W. E. & A. T. Degroot. *The Disciples of Christ.* St. Louis: Bethany Press, 1948.

Hudson, W. S. *Religion in America.* New York: Scribner's Sons, 1981.

Kershner, F. D. *The Christian Union Overture.* St. Louis: Bethany Press, 1923.

Lair, L. E. *Christian Churches and Their Work.* St. Louis: Bethany Press, 1963.

Marty, M. E. *Righteous Empire.* New York: Dial Press, 1970.

McPherson, J. M. *The Battle Cry of Freedom.* New York: Oxford, 1988.

Murch, J. D. *Christians Only.* Cincinnati: Standard Publishing, 1962.

Smith, T. L. *Revival and Social Reform.* Nashville: Abingdon, 1957.

Stevenson, D. E. *Lexington Theological Seminary.* St. Louis: Bethany, 1964.

Stone, Barton. "Life," in J. Rogers, Ed., *The Cane Ridge Reader.* Cincinnati: J. A. & U. P. James, 1847.

Strege, M. D., Ed. *Baptism and Church, A Believer's Church Vision*. Grand Rapids: Sagamore Books, 1986.

Sweet, W. W. *The Story of Religion in America*. Grand Rapids: Baker, 1975.

Thompson, C. N., *Historical Collections of Brown County, Ohio*. Piqua, OH: Hammer Graphics, Inc., 1969.

Thompson, R. E. *A History of the Presbyterian Churches in the United States*. New York: Scribners, 1895.

Tucker, W. E. & L. G. McAllister. *Journey in Faith*, A History of the Christian Church (Disciples). St. Louis: Bethany, 1975.

Warner, D. S. *Bible Truths*. Cited in M. E. Dieter, "Holiness Revival," Ph. D. Dissertation, Temple University. Penna., 1973.

CHAPTER VII

SELECTED BIBLIOGRAPHY

Anderson, R. M. *Vision of the Disinherited.* New York: Oxford, 1979.

Bartleman, F. *Another Wave Rolls In!,* J. G. Myers, Ed. Northridge, CA: Voice Publications, 1970.

Beasley-Murray, J. F. *Baptism Today and Tomorrow.* N. Y.: Macmillan, 1966.

Bruner, F. D. *A Doctrine of the Holy Spirit.* Eerdmans, 1970.

Campbell, J. E. *The Pentecostal Holiness Church.* 1951.

Clark, Elmer. *Small Sects in America.* Nashville: Abingdon, 1949.

Conn, C. W. *Like a Mighty Army.* Cleveland, TN: Church of God Publishing House, 1955.

Davidson, C. T. *Upon This Rock.* Cleveland, TN: White Wing Publ. House, 1973.

Dallimore, A. *Forerunner of the Charismatic Movement, The Life of Edward Irving.* Chicago: Moody Press, 1983.

Dayton, D. W. *Discovering an Evangelical Heritage.* New York: Harper & Row, 1976.

Dayton, D. W. *Three Early Pentecostal Tracts.* New York: Garland, 1985.

Duewel, W. L. *The Holy Spirit and Tongues.* Winona Lake, IN: Light and Life Press, 1974.

Hollenweger, W. J. *The Pentecostals.* Minneapolis: Augsburg, 1972.

Horton, S. M. "The Pentecostal View," *Five Views of Sanctification.* Grand Rapids: Zondervan, 1987.

Horton, S. M. *What the Bible Says About the Holy Spirit.* Springfield, MO: Gospel Publishing House, 1976.

Jones, C. E. *A Guide to the Study of the Pentecostal Movement.* Metuchen, NJ: Scarecrow Press, 1983.

Jones, E. S. *The Holy Spirit and the Gift of Tongues.* Barrington, RH: United Christian Ashrams, nd.

Jones, Rufus. *The Church's Debt to Heretics.* New York: George H. Doran, 1924.

Morrison, H. C. *The Baptism of the Holy Spirit.* Louisville: Pentecostal Publ. Co., 1900.

Nichol, J. T. *Pentecostalism.* New York: Harper & Row, 1966.

Parham, S. E. *The Life of Charles F. Parham.* New York: Garland Publisher Inc., 1930, 1985.

Ranaghan, R. & D. *As the Spirit Leads.* Paulist Press, 1971.

Samarin, W. J. *Tongues of Men and Angels.* New York: Macmillan, 1972.

Simpson, A. B. *The Gift of Tongues.* New York: The Christian and Missionary Alliance, nd.

Suenens, J. C. *A New Pentecost*, tr. by F. Martin. Chicago: Seabury Press, 1974.

Swete, H. B. *The Holy Spirit in the New Testament.* London: Macmillan, 1910.

Synan, Vinson. *The Pentecostal Movement in the United States.* Grand Rapids: Eerdmans, 1971.

Tomlinson, A. J. *Diary of A. J. Tomlinson.* New York: Church of God World Quarters, 1949.

Van Dusen, H. P. "The Third Force," New York: *Life*, June 9, 1958.

ADDITIONAL SOURCES

Ahlstrom, Sidney. *A Religious History of the American People.* Yale, 1972.

Aland, Kurt. *A History of Christianity From the Reformation to the Present.* Fortress.

Arias, Mortimer and Alan Johnson. *The Great Commission*, Bible Models for Evangelism. Abingdon Press, 1991.

Beek, W.E.A., Ed., *The Quest for Purity*: Dynamics of Puritan Movements. Berlin, New York: 1988.

Benrath, Gustav Adolf. *Wyclifs Bibelkonnentar.* Berlin, New York: W.G. de Gruyter, 1956.

Berrington, David W. *William Ewart Gladstone, Faith and politics in Victorian Britain.* Eerdmans.

Borsch, Frederick Houk. *The Bible in Today's Church.* Trinity Press International, 1993.

Bradford, John. *Writings of John Bradford*: 2 vols. Banner of Truth, 1848.

Bunyan, John, *The Holy War.* Baker.

Burgess, Stanley and Gary McGee (eds.) *Dictionary of Pentecostal and Charismatic Movements.* Zondervan, 1988.

Burgess, Stanley (ed.) *Reaching Beyond*: Chapters in the History of Perfectionism, Hendrickson, 1986.

Burgess, Stanley. *The Holy Spirit*: Eastern Christian Antiquity. Hendrickson, 1989.

Dallimore, Arnold. *George Whitefield.* Crossway, 1990.

Dawson, Jan C. *The Unstable Past*: American Puritan Tradition, 1830-1930.

Dayton, Donald. *Discovering an Evangelical Heritage.* Hendrickson, 1988.

Dorsett, Lyle W. *Billy Sunday and the Redemption of Urban America.* Eerdmans.

Edwards, Jonathan. *The Works of John Edwards*, (2 volumes). Banner of Truth, 1974.

Ferguson, Everett (ed.) *Encyclopedia of Early Christianity*. Garland, 1990.

Gaustad, Edwin S. *Liberty of Conscience, Roger Williams in America*. Eerdmans, 1993.

Gonzalez, Justo L. *Out of Every Tribe and Nation, Christian Theology at the Ethnic Roundtable*. Abingdon Press, 1992.

Grant, Robert. *Augustus to Constantine*: The Rise & Triumph of Christianity in the Roman World. Harper & Row. 1990.

Greeley, Andrew. *Religious Change in America*. Harvard, 1989.

Hilderbrand, Hans J. *The Reformation*. Baker, 1989.

Hulett, Louisa. *Christianity and Modern Politics*, Ed. Berlin, New York. W.G. de Gruyterm, 1993.

Josephus, Flavius. *Works of Josephus* (4 volumes). Hendrickson, 1987.

Keck, Leander E. *The Church Confident*, Renewal for Mainline Churches. Abingdon Press, 1993.

Latourette, Kenneth Scott. *Christianity Through the Ages*. Harper & Row, 1965.

Lee, Sang Hyun. *The Philosophical Theology of Jonathan Edwards*. Princeton, 1988.

Lincoln, C. Eric and Lawrence H. Maniya. *The Black Church in the African American Experience*. The Alban Institute, Washington, D.C., 1993.

Lloyd-Jones, D. Martin. *Puritans*: Origins and Succesions. Banner of Truth. 1987.

MacArthur, Jr. *Rediscovering Expository Preaching*. Word Publishing, 1992.

Marquardt, Manfred. *John Wesley's Social Ethics, Praxis and Principles*. Abingdon Press, (German 1976, English, 1992).

Marsden, George (ed.). *Understanding Fundamentalism and Evangelicalsim*. Eerdmans, 1991.

Marty, Martin E. *Modern American Religions*. University of Chicago, 1986.

Moravian Daily Texts, *Bible texts with hymn verses.* The Moravian Church, Bethlehem, PA., 1978.

Newton, John. *Works of John Newton* (6 vols.). Banner of Truth, 1850.

Noll, Mark A. *A History of Christianity in the U.S. and Canada.* Eerdmans, 1992.

Ozment, Steven. *The Age of Reform. 1250-1550: An Intellectual and Religious History of Late Medieval and Reformation Europe.* Yale, 1981.

Ozment, Steven. *Protestants: The Birth of a Revolution.* Doubleday, 1992.

Rupp, George: *Christologies and Cultures.* Toward a Topology of Relgious Worldviews. Berlin, New York, 1974.

Stange, Carl. *Luther und das Evangelium.* Berlin, New York: W.G. de Gruyterm, 1966.

Stout, Harry S. *The Divine Dramatist,* George Whitefield and the Rise of Modern Evangelism. Eerdmans, 1992.

Toulouse, Mark G. *Joined in Discipleship,* the Maturing of an American Religious Movement. Chalice Press, 1992.

Turner, Harold W. *From Temple to Meeting House.* The Phenominology and Theology of Places of Worship. Berlin, New York, 1979.

Waldrop, Charles T. *Karl Barth's Christology.* Berlin, New York. W.G. de Gruyterm, 1984.

Ward, W. Reginald & Richard Heitzenrather (eds.) *The Works of John Wesley,* Journal and Diaries IV. Abingdon Press, 1992.

Watkins, Keith. *Baptism and Belonging,* A Resource for Christian Worship. St. Louis, MO, Chalice Press, 1991.

Whitefield, George. *Whitefield's Journals.* Banner of Truth, 1960.

Williams, D. Newell (ed.). *A Case Study of Mainstream Protestantism,* The Disciples' Relation to American Culture, 1880-1989. Eerdmans, 1992.

Wolfson, H.A. *The Philosophy of the Church Fathers.* Harvard, 1970.

Woodbridge, John. *Great Leaders of the Christian Church.* Moody, 1988.

INDEX

1536 .... 52, 58, 59, 102
A. W. Nagler 155
Aldersgate 133, 134
Alexander Campbell 166, 171, 172, 175 .... 176, 188
Ambrose 18, 116
America 53, 61, 73, 74, 76, 84, 92, 97, 98, 115, 117, 118, 120, 121, 128-130, 133, 137, 147, 154, 157, 161, 165, 167-170, 179, 187, 192, 218 220-222, 230, 232, 239-241, 246, 249-253, 255, 256
Ames . 37-38, 43, 109, 116, 124, 241
Amish 4, 61-63
Anabaptists ... 30, 34, 36, 39, 45-52, 54-61, 65, 66, 72, 73, 88, 90, 101, 109, 112, 113, 118, 120, 130, 136, 139, 142, 150, 153, 165, 175, 183, 217, 220, 229, 230, 233, 234, 237, 243, 244
Anderson .. 183, 201, 211, 215, 219 221-224, 253
Andrew Murray 199
Anglicanism 16, 116, 153
Ann Arbor 207
Anselm 18
Anspach 81
Anthony 33, 85
Arminian .. 115, 118, 119, 124, 154 195, 198
Arminian Magazine .. 115, 124, 154
Arminian-Pietist-Methodist 118
Arndt 35, 69, 156, 241
Arnold 69, 255
Asa Mahan 92, 193, 221
Ashland 80-83, 97, 157, 246
Assoc of Evangelicals 94, 240
Atonement 109, 118, 140, 144, 146, 163, 166, 192, 198, 210
Augustine 18-20, 24-26, 51, 105

Austria 49
Bailey 101, 125, 247
Baptism of Infants ... 139, 140, 144, 145, 231
Baptists ... 34, 72, 76, 78, 109, 118 120, 160, 162, 163, 165, 171, 172, 174-176, 179, 194, 206
Bartleman 201-203, 223, 253
Bay Colony 105, 108, 121, 248
Beaver Association of Baptists .. 175
Believers 20, 26, 30, 31, 34, 37 38, 43, 46, 47, 49, 52, 53, 55, 57-59, 64, 91, 93, 96, 99, 102, 103, 105, 107, 109, 112, 120, 128, 132, 136, 144-146, 166, 176, 181, 185, 188, 191, 195, 196, 204, 208, 216, 218, 219, 225-229, 231, 233, 237, 245
Bender 50, 65-67, 243
Berea College 177
Bethany College 177
Biederwolf 82
Bishop Taylor 131
Blanke 49, 65
Boehm 84, 86, 241
Bohemia . 23, 27-31, 45, 48, 84, 229
Bohemian Bible 30
Bohemian Brethren 4, 27
Book of Common Prayer .. 140, 156
Brethren 27, 29-32, 34, 36, 39 46-50, 54, 65, 69, 71-100, 114, 128, 130, 137, 142, 164, 165, 167, 198, 199, 209, 217, 220, 230, 233, 234, 237, 244-246
Brethren in Christ 84-86, 92-95, 100, 233, 245, 246
Brownists 103, 104
Bruderhof 53
Bruner 192, 221, 223, 224, 253
Brush Run Church 170, 171

C. Wesley King 143, 156
Cadman 15, 41, 129, 154, 241
Calvin ... 18, 20, 24, 37, 38, 46, 51, 58, 104, 105, 109, 110, 138, 198, 199, 247
Cambridge ... 37, 43, 67, 103, 104, 107-109, 123, 124, 129, 156, 242, 247, 248
Camp meetings 161
Canada 53, 94, 120, 205, 257
Cane Ridge 159-162, 166, 177, 187, 251
Cartwright 103, 121
Cashwell 197, 205
Catechism 29, 66
Catholic Pentecostals . 207, 208, 214
Chalcedon (451) 15
Chalice 28, 257
Chelchicky 28, 35
Christ .. 15-18, 20, 24-26, 28, 31-33, 36-39, 46, 47, 49-51, 53, 54, 56-60, 62, 64, 69, 71, 75, 76, 84-86, 88, 91-96, 99-101, 106-108, 110, 111, 117, 119, 130, 131, 133, 135, 136, 138, 140-142, 144, 146, 147, 150, 152, 163, 164, 166, 169, 172-176, 178, 180, 183, 184-188, 194, 200, 202, 206-209, 211, 213, 218, 225-230, 233, 234, 239, 244, 245, 246, 251
Christ Church College, Oxford .. 130
Christ-likeness 88
Christian Baptist 175
Christian Century 177, 189, 240
Christian David 31
Christian perfect 39, 50, 71, 90 116, 130, 131, 152, 194, 250
Christian Standard 177
Christians ... 35, 47, 48, 50, 51, 56, 62, 75, 76, 80, 87, 92, 107, 109, 112, 114, 119, 132, 141, 142, 145, 148, 159, 160, 163-165, 167-169, 171, 172, 176, 178, 179, 181, 182-187, 194, 206, 208, 210, 218-220, 228-230, 232, 233, 235, 237, 239, 240, 251

Church of Christ ... 20, 26, 47, 60, 169, 176, 183, 184, 186, 226-228, 233
Church of England 16, 17, 101, 103, 105, 107, 108, 115, 120, 130, 133, 138, 149, 156, 209, 249
Church of God 180-183, 186, 196-199, 204, 205, 222, 226, 253, 254
Circumcision of Heart . 66, 131, 154
Cleveland ... 196-199, 205, 222, 253
Cocoris 215, 224
Colet 102
College of the Bible 177
Commenius 30, 32
Commonwealth .. 110, 112, 122, 124
Compacta of Basel 28
Congregation ... 25, 26, 32, 35, 53, 54, 65, 70, 75, 85, 90, 107, 109, 115, 118, 164, 168, 175, 176, 201, 227
Congregationalists ... 103, 106-108, 118, 121, 128, 162, 234
Conn 195, 222, 253
Conservatives ... 79-81, 84, 176-178
Consistency with Scripture ... 6, 209
Corinthian Church 217
Cotton Mather ... 118, 119, 125, 247
Covenant of Baptism 144
Covenant Service 116
Covenant Theology 102, 110, 113, 114, 116, 120
Cromwell 57, 103, 111
Crumpler 205
Cumberland 163
Dallas 83, 86
Darby 85, 86
Dacons 53, 107, 227
Declaration of Independence . 48, 108
Dedication of infant 144
Desired Piety 35
Diet 27, 49
Diognetus 235
Disciples .. 16, 37, 39, 51, 63, 71, 76, 85, 87, 96, 109, 130, 148, 159, 160, 167, 168, 169, 171-180, 183,

184, 186-190, 208, 217, 220, 232, 237, 239, 251, 252, 257
Disciples of Christ ... 37, 39, 71, 85, 172, 176, 178, 180, 187, 188, 251
Discipline ... 16, 32, 36, 51, 52, 54, 60-62, 64, 74, 79, 88, 96, 102, 103, 106, 107, 113, 117, 123, 145, 152, 153, 170, 184, 214, 219, 232, 233, 247
Divine healing .. 197, 198, 206, 209, 210, 232
Divine right of kings 104
Doctrine 16, 18, 20, 22, 23, 31, 36-38, 40, 41, 43, 50, 51, 54, 59, 71, 77, 80, 85, 90, 92, 93, 96, 102, 105, 114, 118-120, 132-134, 138, 143, 148, 149, 152, 156, 157, 163, 166, 168, 169-172, 177, 179, 182, 183, 185, 186, 193, 195, 197-199, 202, 213, 221, 224, 232, 245, 249, 250, 253
Double predestination 26, 118
Dunkers 72-75, 87, 97, 245
Duns Scotus 20
Durant 41, 239
Durham 204, 206, 242
Dyke 66
E. H. Sugden 154
Eck 49, 50
Ecumenical 15, 16, 34, 62, 83, 94, 96, 119, 148, 157, 177, 180, 192, 208, 219, 231, 232
Edward VI 102
Ejaculatory prayer 210
Elizabeth 102, 103
English Colonies 34
Enthusiasm ... 35, 51, 74, 133, 162, 175, 199
Ephesus (431) 15
Ephrata 74-76
Establishment 29, 48, 107, 115, 143, 199, 209
Evangelical Revival 5, 127, 132, 147, 203
Existentialist 50, 51
Externals 88, 94, 96
Factionalism 96, 203

Faith 24, 28, 29, 31-38, 45, 46, 48, 49, 51, 53, 56, 59, 62, 67, 71, 72, 74, 76, 85, 87, 90, 93, 94, 99, 108-110, 113, 114, 116, 119, 123, 124, 128, 132-134, 137, 138, 140, 141, 143, 145-147, 151, 152, 156, 159, 160, 164, 169-171, 175, 180-182, 186, 187, 189, 192-194, 196, 197, 199, 200, 210, 213, 214, 217-219, 222, 223, 225, 227, 228, 230, 240, 241, 243, 244, 248, 251, 252, 255
Felix Manz 47
Ferdinand 29, 52
Finney .. 79, 162, 178, 185, 193, 198
Fletcher 32, 92, 193, 221
Foot washing . 73, 76, 77, 80, 93-96, 172, 196, 198
Francis Asbury 84, 249
Frank Baker 143, 156
Free church 30-32, 42, 47, 48, 66, 70, 84, 101, 108, 121, 122, 147, 172, 231, 244, 247
Free Methodist ... 82, 93, 143, 157, 192, 200
Frelinghuysen 73, 128
Friedman 50, 65, 243
Garrison 178, 187, 251
Geneva 46, 101, 102, 104
Gillin 81, 97, 245
Good News .. 84, 152, 161, 226, 231
Gospel 19, 23, 33, 50, 52, 56, 60, 78, 105, 116, 141, 143, 148, 152, 153, 161, 163, 164, 170, 172, 173-175, 178, 180, 183, 184, 199, 203, 207, 211, 217, 224, 228, 230, 239, 253
Gospel Trumpet 183
Grace Brethren 82, 83
Great Awakening .. 73, 74, 117, 121, 128, 134, 160-162, 165, 173, 178
Greenham 104
Haggard 165
Half-Way Covenant .. 109, 124, 248
Halle 31, 36, 70
Harvard ... 37, 38, 43, 67, 105, 106, 121, 123, 148, 156, 248, 256, 257

Henry Sloan Coffin 192
Herrnhut 31-34, 128, 134
Hidden seed 30, 31, 42, 241
Hierarchy 15, 20, 105, 117, 136, 208, 209
High Priest 227
Hockman 71
Holiness Movement 88, 90-92, 162, 182, 193, 204, 205, 214, 249
Hollenweger 199, 209, 222, 223, 253
Holsinger 78-80, 97, 98, 245
Holy Club 129, 130
Horton 43, 124, 213, 221, 223, 224, 253
Hostetter 94
House of Commons 110, 111, 124, 137
Howel Harris 128
Hubmaier 49, 50, 243
Huss 17, 21, 23-28, 30, 35, 41, 42, 45, 209, 229, 241
Hussite Movement 27, 28, 48
Hutter 52, 65
Hypocrisy 16, 50
Independents .. 54, 57, 103, 105, 120, 139, 148
Indulgences 20, 23, 24
Inner testimony of the Spirit 115
Irwin 157, 205
James McGready 162
James O'Kelley 164
Jefferson 48, 114
Jerome 25
John Owen 114
John Robinson 107
John Whincop 111, 124
Journal 69, 105, 116, 123, 125, 154, 55, 157, 166, 189, 221, 242, 257
Keeney 66
Keswick Movement .. 133, 199, 201
Kralitz Bible 29
L. R. Marston ... 134, 144, 154, 157
Last Supper 18
Latin ... 19, 114, 172, 220, 239, 241
Latter Rain 191, 209
Lexington .. 162, 163, 165, 172, 177, 178, 187, 189, 251
Lexington Herald-Leader 177
Lexington Theological Seminary 177, 178, 189, 251
Lititz 29, 31
Logan County 160, 162
Lollards .. 22, 41, 71, 101, 152, 167
Lord's Prayer 55, 116
Lord's Supper 5, 26, 53, 59, 63, 71, 72, 76, 77, 85, 86, 109, 138, 145, 146, 168, 170, 175, 184
Love feast 34, 73, 74, 89
Love for God 16, 135, 136
Love for neighbor 135
Love of neighbor 5, 17, 39, 64, 135, 207, 229, 230
Lucile 62
Luke ... 26, 29, 140, 143, 146, 154, 174, 79, 193, 210, 212, 213, 216, 238, 250
Luke Tyerman 154
Lutheranism 16, 31
Lutterworth 17, 18, 21
Luxury 37, 62, 89
Mack 70-73, 76, 77, 87
Magistrate(s) 30, 46, 47, 54, 55, 60, 62, 70
Martyr complex 64, 76
Mary 26, 58, 103, 208
Mayflower Compact 110
McClain 81, 83
McDonald 212, 213, 223
Means of grace 215
Mennonites 4, 46, 53, 58, 60-63, 66, 67, 72, 75-77, 87, 135
Merger Christians/Disciples 171
Methodists .. 16, 21, 22, 32, 34, 36, 48, 51, 63, 71, 74, 76, 78, 84, 85, 87, 90, 93, 105, 106, 114, 115, 117, 118, 127, 130, 133, 136, 137, 143, 147, 152, 153, 160, 162, 163-166, 168, 179, 182, 183, 205, 217, 220, 231, 233, 250
Middle Ages 15
Millennial Harbinger 176, 188, 189, 251
Minear 228, 235

Montanism 191, 199
Moore 67, 80, 156
Morrison . . . 123, 193, 221, 248, 254
Mt. Tabor 28
Muhlenberg 75
Muller 85
Muntzer 49, 56, 57
Murch 183, 187, 188, 190, 251
Nazarene 93, 193
New birth . . . 31, 48, 51, 59, 84, 86, 87, 90, 107, 109, 119, 121, 133, 139, 140, 155, 161, 185, 194, 197, 198, 231
New Testament 16, 17, 19, 20, 22, 26, 27, 30-33, 39, 40, 47, 48, 50, 53, 57, 58, 59, 60, 71, 75-78, 80, 83, 85, 87-89, 95, 96, 101-103, 107-109, 112, 113, 118, 119, 120, 127, 130, 132, 136, 140, 143, 145, 146, 150, 152, 153, 156, 159, 167, 169, 172, 173, 175, 176, 180, 183-185, 191, 194, 209, 211, 213, 217, 223-225, 228-233, 235, 237, 240, 244, 254
New race (Harnack) 226
New Testament is convincing. . . . 153
New World . 34, 47, 62, 79, 159, 242
Nida 215, 224
Non-resistance 53, 64, 94
Notre Dame 207
Oberlin 92
Office for Baptism 138
Old Order 79, 80
Oral history 198
Order of St. Luke 210
Orthodox churches 15, 27
Otterbein 84, 87
Ozman 200
Paradise Lost 104
Parham 199-201, 204, 222, 254
Pastor Barton Stone 160
Peasants' Revolt 55, 56
Penitential struggle 32, 36, 179
Pentecostals 16, 130, 133, 165, 191-193, 199, 203, 204, 206-212, 214-217, 222, 224, 232, 237, 253
Perkins 37, 105, 109

Perry Miller 124, 125, 231
Pharisees 51, 63, 96, 230
Pietists 15-17, 33, 37, 39, 40, 46, 51, 69-71, 84, 87, 118, 119, 130, 137, 153, 217, 220, 229, 234, 238
Pilgrim's Progress 104
Plymouth 85, 86, 104, 105, 108, 112, 120
Pontiff 15, 25
Prague 23, 24, 27-29, 52
Prayer veiling 89, 94
Predestinate 20, 25, 26
Presbyterian 103, 114, 117, 118, 125, 160, 162-166, 168, 170, 178, 187, 193, 252
Presbyterians in Parliament 108
Primitive church 27, 45, 77, 93, 130, 164, 165, 185, 186, 217, 225, 227, 230, 232, 240
Progressives 79-81, 84, 177
Proselytes 142, 156
Protestant 29, 30, 33, 40, 45-48, 94, 162, 178, 180, 205-208, 214, 217, 242, 244, 249, 250
Protracted meetings . . 76, 79, 80, 93
Puritan Perfectionism 114
Puritans 16, 21, 32, 39, 57, 101, 103-111, 113-121, 124, 125, 128, 130, 136, 137, 147, 165, 168, 199, 217, 230, 234, 237, 248, 249, 256
Quakers . . . 22, 75-78, 86, 114, 115, 120, 135, 136, 142, 150, 153, 191, 199
Quest for holiness 74, 130, 192
Quest for unity 169, 175, 185, 186, 232
Rabinowitz 211
Radical Reformation 21, 39, 42, 65, 69, 244
Radical Reformers 16, 27, 71, 229, 230
Ranaghan 214, 223, 224, 254
Rebirth . . . 32, 38, 53, 73-75, 77, 87, 106, 128, 229
Regeneration 38-40, 59, 62, 69, 72, 74, 87, 90, 92, 93, 109, 114, 119, 135, 138, 139, 143, 153, 155,

156, 173, 174, 179, 197, 198, 204, 226, 234, 238
Renewal 15, 16, 39, 51, 73, 74, 94, 114, 129, 130, 137, 141, 146, 161, 186, 203, 206, 207, 208, 214, 216, 219, 220, 229, 231, 239, 256
Reprobate 20, 25, 26
Restoration .. 16, 17, 21, 27, 30, 31, 45, 69, 71, 101, 120, 127, 136, 165, 172, 173, 174, 183, 192, 217, 220, 225, 228, 229, 240
Revival in Appalachia 5, 193
Rhine 21, 27, 70
Richard Baxter 103, 114, 115
Richard Hooker 103, 138, 155
River Brethren 4, 86, 87, 90
Robert Hughes 155
Roman Catholic .. 15, 27, 32, 40, 41, 45, 129, 131, 145, 199, 231
Roman pontiff 15
Roxbury 92
Ruskin 110
Sabbatarians 74, 75
Sacramental .. 18, 77, 143, 146, 147
Samarin 211, 214, 224, 254
Sanctification . 35, 36, 38-40, 53, 56, 57, 69, 74, 90-93, 105, 119, 131, 132, 134, 135, 153, 181, 192, 193-195, 197-200, 203-205, 221, 229, 231, 249, 253
Sattler 49, 244
Sauer 76
Saxony 30, 31, 128
Schaff 41, 42, 241
Schattschneider 42
Scriptures 19, 20, 22, 24, 47, 56, 60, 72, 85, 106, 108, 117, 129, 131, 133, 137, 168, 169, 171, 175, 184, 186, 194, 198, 207, 230
Second Great Awakening .. 121, 160, 173, 178
Second work 90, 92, 93, 135, 181, 194, 199, 204, 205, 208
Secret societies 89, 198
Separtists 107
Sewall's diary 106

Seymour 201, 202
Shakers 165
Sigismund 27, 28
Simony 23, 24, 41, 45
Simplicity ... 17, 20, 77, 83, 85, 86, 88, 93, 96, 118, 149, 173, 218
Simpson ... 191, 204, 217, 224, 254
Spangenberg 33, 35, 36, 43, 74, 75, 98, 133
Spener 35, 39, 42, 69, 161, 242
Spurling 193-196
Stadler 53
State 17, 19, 30, 31, 45-48, 50, 51, 57, 61, 63, 64, 103, 104, 106, 108-110, 112, 118, 120, 121, 129, 147, 152, 161, 168, 198, 218, 229, 237
Stoeffler 39, 41-43, 97, 98, 155, 157, 229, 241, 245, 250
Strassburg 56
Susanna 116, 154
Swiss Brethren 46
Synagogues 226, 230
Synan 220-224, 239, 254
Synod of Dort 40, 61
Tasmania 137
Teellinck 37
Temperance 88, 90, 135, 162
The baptized 26
The Christian ... 16, 51, 53, 78, 87, 90, 94, 96, 112, 119, 132, 142, 144, 164-168, 170, 172, 173, 175, 177, 178, 180, 184, 187-189, 192-194, 196, 206, 217, 224, 228, 232, 233, 251, 252, 254, 257
The Evangelist 174, 226
Thomas Campbell ... 168, 173, 174, 176, 183, 186
Thomas Case 110, 124
Thomas Kempis 131
Thor Hall 148, 157
Three schisms 90
Timothy Dwight, Pres. of Yale .. 106
Tomlinson 196, 197, 222, 254
Tongues 69, 191, 193, 195-203, 205-219, 223, 224, 232, 253, 254
Trans-substantiation 18

Transylvania University 177
Tunkers 72, 77, 78, 97
Twelve Conclusions 22
Tyndale 102, 110, 113
Unitas Fratrum . . . 29-31, 33, 35, 36,
　　48, 69, 74, 84, 118, 128
Utraquists 28
Visitor 78, 90, 92
Wales 128, 129, 192
Walter Scott 172, 176, 188
Warner 181-183, 185, 189, 252
Warner's wife Sarah 181
Weill 66
Welsh revival 193
Wesley 34, 35, 37, 38, 43,
　　59, 66, 69, 74, 75, 90-92, 105, 106,
　　108, 112, 114-118, 122-125, 127,
　　129-143, 145-152, 154-158, 167,
　　179, 185, 193, 194, 198, 199, 208,
　　224, 231, 242, 248-250, 256, 257
Wesleyan 90, 91, 93, 117, 118,
　　132-134, 148, 150, 151, 156, 178,
　　183, 192-195, 198, 199, 204, 221,
　　239, 242, 248, 250
Wesleyan-Arminian 195, 198
Westminister 103, 108
Westminster Confession 163
Whitefield 21, 73, 108, 115, 128,
　　129, 134, 135, 161, 185, 193, 255,
　　257
Whitfield 115
Wigram 85
Wilderness Revival 161, 162
William Law 131
William of Orange 60
Winebrinner 180, 183
Winthrop 105, 110, 154
Word of God 16, 47, 50, 56, 59, 105,
　　132, 179, 181
Workman 21, 41, 242
Wycliffe . . 15, 17-25, 27, 34, 38, 45,
　　101, 129, 130, 152, 167, 198, 209
Zinzendorf . . 31-34, 36, 71, 128, 169
Ziska 28, 30